North American Repeater Atlas

1998/99 Edition

By
Bob Martin, N7JXN

Published By:

American Radio Relay League
225 Main St.
Newington, CT 06111

TABLE OF CONTENTS

PREFACE

The second edition of the North American Repeater Atlas is here! It's been a few years since the first edition, but I believe that the long wait for this edition will prove to be very much worthwhile. We have incorporated a lot of additional information into this new edition, and I'm sure that you will find this edition to be informative and easy to use. I believe that having a listing of repeaters in this format will make your travel more pleasurable and help you make more contacts along the highway.

Ham Radio is really a great hobby, and I have to say that repeater use is probably the most widely popular aspect of the hobby. There are people interested in many "sub-hobbies" within ham radio, like ATV, DXing, or many others, but almost every ham has a 2 meter rig! So, keep using those repeaters!

Remember, fun is what a hobby is supposed to be all about. If you hear somebody new on the local repeater be sure to welcome them, and get to know them, it may make the hobby more fun for you. Remember, when you are travelling, and using repeaters around the country, please drive safely! Above all, enjoy yourself on the road and on the air!

73,

Bob

Bob Martin, N7JXN

This work is dedicated to my youngest son, Aaron Joseph Martin. Although he's only 18 months old, he tried to help out a lot while I was working on this book! Thanks for the help, AJ, I love you.

CTCSS TONES

A=67.0	Q=107.2	E=173.8
B=69.3	R=110.9	F=179.9
C=71.9	S=114.8	G=186.2
D=74.4	T=118.8	H=192.8
E=77.0	U=123.0	J=203.5
F=79.7	V=127.3	K=206.5
G=82.5	W=131.8	L=210.7
H=85.4	X=136.5	M=218.1
J=88.5	Y=141.3	N=225.7
K=91.5	Z=146.2	P=229.1
L=94.8	A=151.4	Q=233.6
M=97.4	B=156.7	R=241.8
N=100.0	C=162.2	S=250.3
P=103.5	D=167.9	T=254.1

ME

Augusta●
53.29-X

Washington●
53.55-K

Winthrop●
53.15-

Gray●
53.57-X

VT

NH

Concord●
53.59-N

Deerfield●
53.04-N

Goffstown●
53.42-N

Haverhill●
29.66-W

Peterborough
● 53.19-

Danvers
52.42-N

Billerica●
Fitchburg   53.07-N
● 53.83-C

Winchester●
53.25-

North Adams●
53.23-C

Princeton●
53.31-

Maynard●
● 53.61-

Boston
29.68-W

● Windsor
53.19-

MA

Bolton●
29.62-W
53.01-

Marlborough●
53.47-N

Amherst●
53.35-C

Oakham●   Paxton●
53.67-N   53.33-

53.81-C

Fall River
● 53.91-

E. Hartland
53.19-

Tolland●
53.15-N

RI

Hartford●
29.68-
53.01-   Rocky Hill●
53.05-   53.39-C
53.19-C   ●Bristol

Columbia●
29.65-

CT

W. Greenwich
29.68-

Bethany
53.19-

Old Saybrook●
52.29-C

N. Coventry
29.64-

New London
29.67-

Bridgeport●
53.59-N

Notes:
+ indicates + offset
- indicates - offset
@ indicates Autopatch
for information on use of Autopatch
be sure to check with repeater owner.

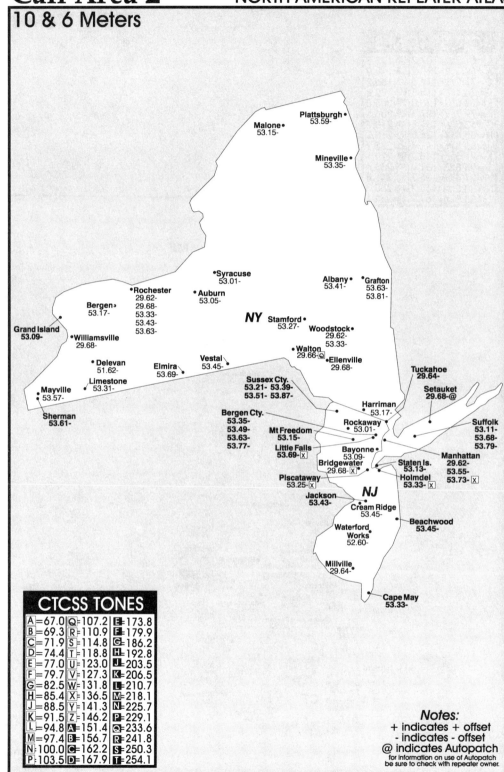

Plattsburgh •
53.59-

Malone •
53.15-

Mineville •
53.35-

•Syracuse
53.01-

Albany •   •Grafton
53.41-   53.63-
            53.81-

•Rochester   • Auburn
29.62-   53.05-
29.68-
53.33-
53.43-
53.63-

Bergen >
53.17-

NY   Stamford •
       53.27-   Woodstock •
                  29.62-
                  53.33-

Grand Island
53.09-

•Williamsville
29.68-

• Walton
29.66-@   •Ellenville
         29.68-

Tuckahoe
29.64-

• Delevan
51.62-

Elmira   Vestal ᐳ
53.69-   53.45-

Setauket
29.68-@

Limestone
53.31-

Harriman
• 53.17-

Mayville
• 53.57-

Sussex Cty.
53.21- 53.39-
53.51- 53.87-

Rockaway
• 53.01-

Suffolk
53.11-
53.68-
53.79-

Sherman
53.61-

Bergen Cty.
53.35-
53.49-
53.63-
53.77-

Mt Freedom
53.15-

Little Falls
53.69-[X]

Bayonne
53.09-

Manhattan
29.62-
53.55-
53.73-[X]

Bridgewater
29.68-[X]

Staten Is.
53.13-

Piscataway
53.25-[X]

Holmdel
53.33-[X]

NJ

Jackson
53.43-

Cream Ridge
53.45-

Beachwood
53.45-

Waterford
Works
52.60-

Millville
29.64-•

Cape May
53.33-

Notes:
+ indicates + offset
- indicates - offset
@ indicates Autopatch
for information on use of Autopatch
be sure to check with repeater owner.

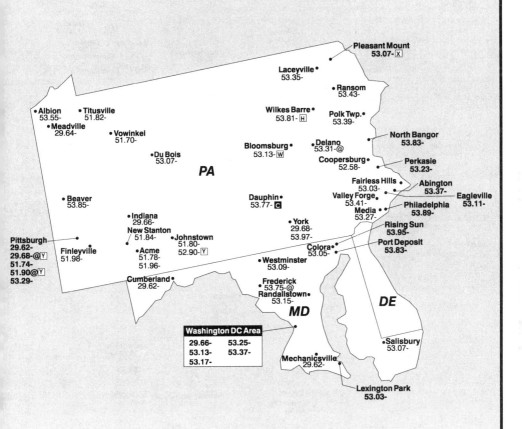

PA

MD

DE

Pleasant Mount
53.07- X

Laceyville •
53.35-

• Ransom
53.43-

Wilkes Barre •
53.81- H

Polk Twp.•
53.39-

North Bangor
53.83-

• Albion
53.55-

• Titusville
51.82-

• Meadville
29.64-

• Vowinkel
51.70-

• Du Bois
53.07-

Bloomsburg •
53.13- W

• Delano
53.31-@

Coopersburg•
52.58-

• Perkasie
53.23-

Fairless Hills •
53.03-

Abington
53.37-

Eagleville
53.11-

Valley Forge•
53.41-

Media • •
53.27-

• Philadelphia
53.89-

• Beaver
53.85-

Dauphin•
53.77- C

• York
29.68-
53.97-

Rising Sun
53.95-

• Indiana
29.66-

New Stanton
• 51.84-

• Johnstown
51.80-
52.90- Y

Colora •
53.05-

Port Deposit
53.83-

Pittsburgh
29.62-
29.68-@ Y
51.74-
51.90@ Y
53.29-

Finleyville
51.98-

•Acme
51.78-
51.96-

• Westminster
53.09-

Cumberland •
29.62-

Frederick
• 53.75-@
Randallstown•
53.15-

Salisbury
53.07-

Washington DC Area

29.66-	53.25-
53.13-	53.37-
53.17-	

Mechanicsville•
29.62-

Lexington Park
53.03-

CTCSS TONES

A=67.0	Q=107.2	E=173.8
B=69.3	R=110.9	F=179.9
C=71.9	S=114.8	G=186.2
D=74.4	T=118.8	H=192.8
E=77.0	U=123.0	J=203.5
F=79.7	V=127.3	K=206.5
G=82.5	W=131.8	L=210.7
H=85.4	X=136.5	M=218.1
J=88.5	Y=141.3	N=225.7
K=91.5	Z=146.2	P=229.1
L=94.8	A=151.4	Q=233.6
M=97.4	B=156.7	R=241.8
N=100.0	C=162.2	S=250.3
P=103.5	D=167.9	T=254.1

Notes:
+ indicates + offset
- indicates - offset
@ indicates Autopatch
for information on use of Autopatch
be sure to check with repeater owner.

Call Area 4

10 & 6 Meters

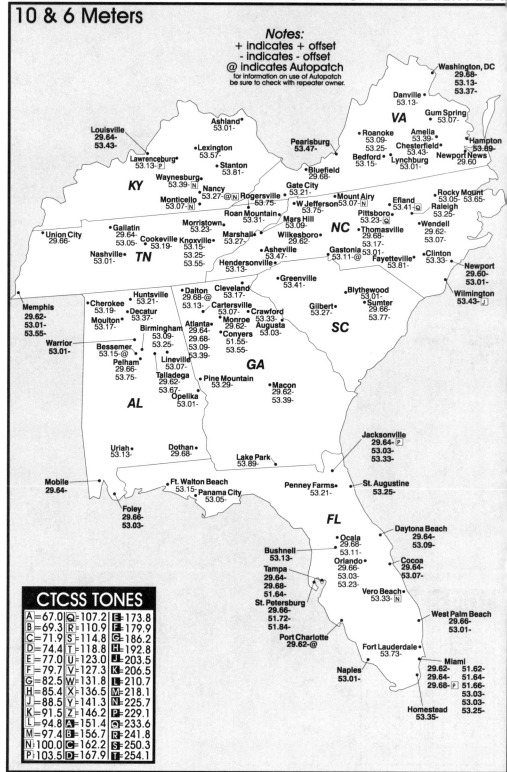

Notes:
+ indicates + offset
- indicates - offset
@ indicates Autopatch
for information on use of Autopatch
be sure to check with repeater owner.

Washington, DC
29.68-
53.13-
53.37-

Danville •
53.13-

Gum Spring •
53.07-

VA

Ashland •
53.01-

Roanoke
53.09-
53.25-

Amelia
53.39-

Louisville
29.64-
53.43-

Lexington
53.57-

Pearlsburg •
53.47-

Chesterfield
53.43-

Hampton
53.69-

Bedford •
53.15-

Lynchburg
53.01-

Newport News
29.60

Stanton
53.81-

Lawrenceburg• P
53.13-

Waynesburg•
53.39- N

Bluefield
29.68-

KY

Nancy
53.27-@ N

Rogersville
53.75-

Gate City
53.21-

Rocky Mount
53.05- 53.65-

Monticello
53.07- N

W Jefferson 53.07- N
53.75-

Mount Airy

Efland
53.41- Q

Raleigh
53.25-

Roan Mountain•
53.31-

Mars Hill
53.09-

Pittsboro•
53.23- Q

Wendell
29.62-
53.07-

Union City •
29.66-

Gallatin
29.64-
53.05-

Morristown•
53.23-

Marshall
53.27-

Wilkesboro
29.62-

NC

Thomasville
29.68-
53.17-

Cookeville Knoxville
53.19- 53.15-

Asheville
53.47-

Gastonia 53.01-
53.11-@

Clinton
53.33-

Nashville•
53.01-

TN

53.25-
53.55-

Hendersonville•
53.13-

Fayetteville
53.81-

Newport
29.60-
53.01-

Greenville •
53.41-

Blythewood
53.01-

Wilmington
53.43- J

Memphis
29.62-
53.01-
53.55-

Huntsville
53.21-

Dalton
29.68-@
53.13-

Cleveland
53.17-

Cherokee
53.19-

Decatur
53.37-

Cartersville
53.07-

Crawford
53.33-

Gilbert•
53.27-

Sumter
29.66-
53.77-

Warrior
53.01-

Moulton•
53.17-

Birmingham
53.09-

Atlanta
29.64-
29.68-
53.09-
53.39-

Monroe
29.62-

Augusta
53.03-

SC

Conyers
51.55-
53.55-

Bessemer
53.15-@

Lineville
53.07-

Pelham
29.66-
53.75-

Talladega
29.62-
53.67-

Pine Mountain
53.29-

GA

Macon
29.62-
53.39-

Opelika
53.01-

AL

Jacksonville
29.64- P
53.03-
53.33-

Uriah•
53.13-

Dothan
29.68-

Lake Park
53.89-

Penney Farms•
53.21-

St. Augustine
53.25-

Mobile
29.64-

Ft. Walton Beach
53.15- Panama City
53.05-

FL

Foley
29.66-
53.03-

Daytona Beach
29.64-
53.09-

Ocala
29.68-
53.11-

Bushnell
53.13-

Orlando•
29.66-
53.03-
53.23-

Cocoa
29.64-
53.07-

Tampa
29.64-
29.68-
51.64-

Vero Beach•
53.33- N

St. Petersburg
29.66-
51.72-
51.84-

West Palm Beach
29.66-
53.01-

Port Charlotte
29.62-@

Fort Lauderdale
53.73-

Miami
29.62- 51.62-
29.64- 51.64-
29.68- P 51.66-
53.03-
Naples   53.03-
53.01-   53.25-

Homestead
53.35-

CTCSS TONES

A=67.0	Q=107.2	E=173.8	
B=69.3	R=110.9	F=179.9	
C=71.9	S=114.8	G=186.2	
D=74.4	T=118.8	H=192.8	
E=77.0	U=123.0	J=203.5	
F=79.7	V=127.3	K=206.5	
G=82.5	W=131.8	L=210.7	
H=85.4	X=136.5	M=218.1	
J=88.5	Y=141.3	N=225.7	
K=91.5	Z=146.2	P=229.1	
L=94.8	A=151.4	Q=233.6	
M=97.4	B=156.7	R=241.8	
N=100.0	C=162.2	S=250.3	
P=103.5	D=167.9	T=254.1	

Call Area 5
10 & 6 Meters

Notes:
+ indicates + offset
- indicates - offset
@ indicates Autopatch
for information on use of Autopatch
be sure to check with repeater owner.

MS

Poplarville
29.62-

Byhalla
53.27-

Ellisville
53.01-

Hammond
53.09-
Covington
53.13-
New Orleans
29.62-
29.68-
53.21-

Jonesboro•
53.125-

AR

Clinton
29.68-Ⓓ
53.07+@

Lonoke
52.89-

Fayetteville
• 52.77+

Mt Ida
52.91-
Little Rock
52.81-
53.31-

Rudy
29.62-
53.11-

Russellville
51.31+

Benton
52.23-

W Monroe•
53.61-

LA

Rogers
29.64-
53.47-

Decatur•
51.925+

Hot Springs•
52.50-
53.25-

Crosby•
52.01-

Tulsa•
29.64-
53.65-

OK

Longview•
52.41 +

Houston•
52.65-Ⓗ

Oklahoma City•
52.81-@
53.01-
53.05-Ⓨ
53.09-
53.17-
53.23-@
53.33-@

Dallas/Ft. Worth•
29.86-Ⓗ
53.93-

Glen Rose•
53.69-

Georgetown•
53.05-

Bastrop•
29.64-

Weatherford•
53.15-

TX

Austin•
52.65-Ⓢ
53.67-

San Antonio•
53.03-Ⓨ
53.13-
53.17-

Victoria•
53.07-

Edinburg•
29.68-Ⓢ
53.37-Ⓢ

Amarillo•
52.65-Ⓣ

Midland•
53.11-

Andrews•
53.25-Ⓓ

Odessa•
29.64-Ⓓ
Barstow•
53.05-

NM

El Paso•
53.55-

CTCSS TONES

A=67.0	Q=107.2	E=173.8	
B=69.3	R=110.9	F=179.9	
C=71.9	S=114.8	G=186.2	
D=74.4	T=118.8	H=192.8	
E=77.0	U=123.0	J=203.5	
F=79.7	V=127.3	K=206.5	
G=82.5	W=131.8	L=210.7	
H=85.4	X=136.5	M=218.1	
J=88.5	Y=141.3	N=225.7	
K=91.5	Z=146.2	P=229.1	
L=94.8	A=151.4	Q=233.6	
M=100.0	B=156.7	R=241.8	
N=100.0	C=162.2	S=250.3	
P=103.5	D=167.9	T=254.1	

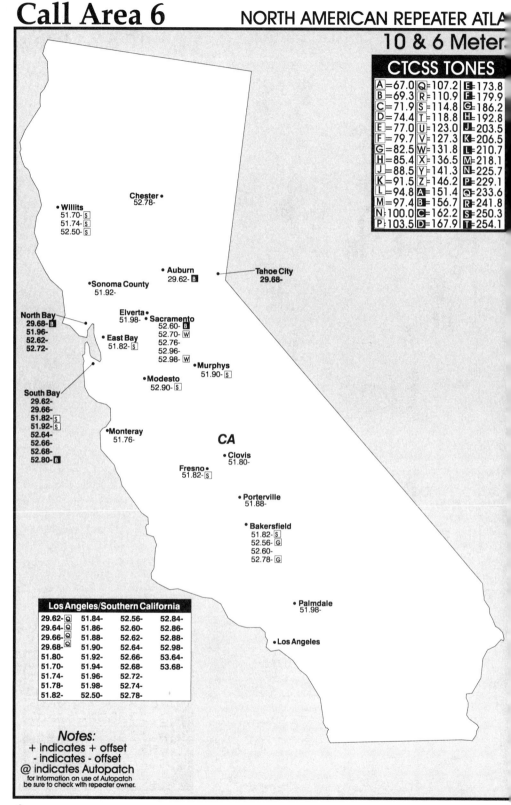

CTCSS TONES

A=67.0	Q=107.2	E=173.8	
B=69.3	R=110.9	F=179.9	
C=71.9	S=114.8	G=186.2	
D=74.4	T=118.8	H=192.8	
E=77.0	U=123.0	J=203.5	
F=79.7	V=127.3	K=206.5	
G=82.5	W=131.8	L=210.7	
H=85.4	X=136.5	M=218.1	
J=88.5	Y=141.3	N=225.7	
K=91.5	Z=146.2	P=229.1	
L=94.8	A=151.4	Q=233.6	
M=97.4	B=156.7	R=241.8	
N=100.0	C=162.2	S=250.3	
P=103.5	D=167.9	T=254.1	

Chester •
52.78-

• Willits
51.70- S
51.74- S
52.50- S

• Auburn
29.62- B

Tahoe City
29.68-

•Sonoma County
51.92-

Elverta •
51.98-

North Bay
29.68- B
51.96-
52.62-
52.72-

• East Bay
51.82- S

• Sacramento
52.60- B
52.70- W
52.76-
52.96-
52.98- W

•Murphys
51.90- S

South Bay
29.62-
29.66-
51.82- S
51.92- S
52.64-
52.66-
52.68-
52.80- B

• Modesto
52.90- S

•Monteray
51.76-

CA

• Clovis
51.80-

Fresno •
51.82- S

• Porterville
51.88-

• Bakersfield
51.82- S
52.56- G
52.60-
52.78- G

• Palmdale
51.98-

•Los Angeles

Los Angeles/Southern California

29.62- Q	51.84-	52.56-	52.84-
29.64- Q	51.86-	52.60-	52.86-
29.66- Q	51.88-	52.62-	52.88-
29.68- Q	51.90-	52.64-	52.98-
51.80-	51.92-	52.66-	53.64-
51.70-	51.94-	52.68-	53.68-
51.74-	51.96-	52.72-	
51.78-	51.98-	52.74-	
51.82-	52.50-	52.78-	

Notes:
+ indicates + offset
- indicates - offset
@ indicates Autopatch
for information on use of Autopatch
be sure to check with repeater owner.

Call Area KH6/KL7

10 & 6 Meters

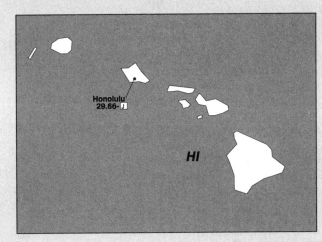

Honolulu
29.66- J

CTCSS TONES

A=67.0	Q=107.2	E=173.8
B=69.3	R=110.9	F=179.9
C=71.9	S=114.8	G=186.2
D=74.4	T=118.8	H=192.8
E=77.0	U=123.0	J=203.5
F=79.7	V=127.3	K=206.5
G=82.5	W=131.8	L=210.7
H=85.4	X=136.5	M=218.1
J=88.5	Y=141.3	N=225.7
K=91.5	Z=146.2	P=229.1
L=94.8	A=151.4	Q=233.6
M=97.4	B=156.7	R=241.8
N=100.0	C=162.2	S=250.3
P=103.5	D=167.9	T=254.1

Notes:
+ indicates + offset
- indicates - offset
@ indicates Autopatch

for information on use of Autopatch
be sure to check with repeater owner.

7

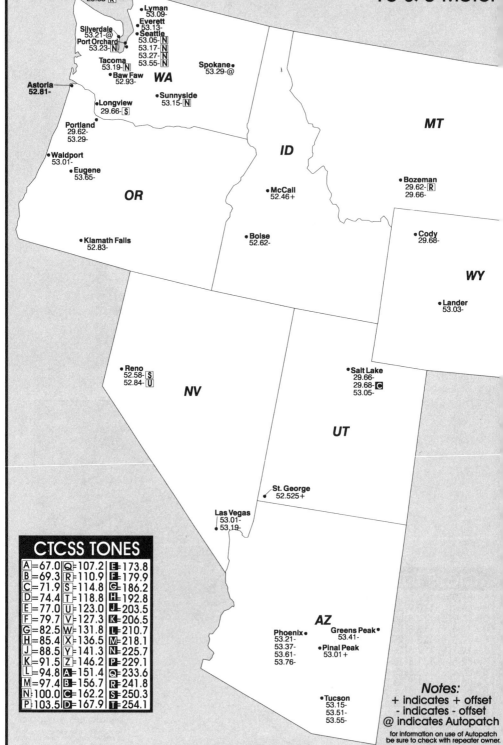

Call Area 7

Mt Constitution
29.68-[R]

Lyman
53.09-

Everett
53.13-

Silverdale
53.21-@

Seattle
53.05-[N]
53.17-[N]
53.27-[N]
53.55-[N]

Port Orchard
53.23-[N]

Tacoma
53.19-[N]

Spokane
53.29-@

Baw Faw
52.93-

WA

Astoria
52.81-

Longview
29.66-[S]

Sunnyside
53.15-[N]

Portland
29.62-
53.29-

MT

Waldport
53.01-

Eugene
53.65-

OR

ID

Bozeman
29.62-[R]
29.66-

McCall
52.46+

Cody
29.68-

WY

Klamath Falls
52.83-

Boise
52.62-

Lander
53.03-

Reno
52.58-[S]
52.84-[U]

NV

Salt Lake
29.66-
29.68-[C]
53.05-

UT

St. George
52.525+

Las Vegas
53.01-
53.19-

CTCSS TONES

A=67.0	Q=107.2	E=173.8
B=69.3	R=110.9	F=179.9
C=71.9	S=114.8	G=186.2
D=74.4	T=118.8	H=192.8
E=77.0	U=123.0	J=203.5
F=79.7	V=127.3	K=206.5
G=82.5	W=131.8	L=210.7
H=85.4	X=136.5	M=218.1
J=88.5	Y=141.3	N=225.7
K=91.5	Z=146.2	P=229.1
L=94.8	A=151.4	Q=233.6
M=97.4	B=156.7	R=241.8
N=100.0	C=162.2	S=250.3
P=103.5	D=167.9	T=254.1

AZ

Phoenix
53.21-
53.37-
53.61-
53.76-

Greens Peak
53.41-

Pinal Peak
53.01+

Tucson
53.15-
53.51-
53.55-

Notes:
+ indicates + offset
- indicates - offset
@ indicates Autopatch

for information on use of Autopatch
be sure to check with repeater owner.

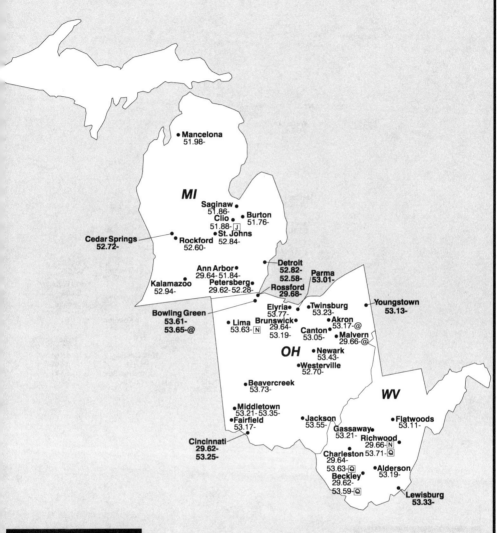

MI

Mancelona
51.98-

Saginaw
51.86-
Clio
51.88- J
Burton
51.76-

Cedar Springs
52.72-

Rockford
52.60-

St. Johns
52.84-

Ann Arbor
29.64-51.84-
Petersberg
29.62-52.28-

Kalamazoo
52.94-

Detroit
52.82-
52.58-

Parma
53.01-

Rossford
29.68-

Bowling Green
53.61-
53.65-@

Elyria
53.77-

Lima
53.63- N

Brunswick
29.64-
53.19-

Twinsburg
53.23-

Youngstown
53.13-

Akron
53.17-@

Canton
53.05-

Malvern
29.66-@

OH

Newark
53.43-

Westerville
52.70-

Beavercreek
53.73-

WV

Middletown
53.21-53.35-
Fairfield
53.17-

Jackson
53.55-

Flatwoods
53.11-

Gassaway
53.21-
Richwood
29.66- N

Cincinnati
29.62-
53.25-

Charleston
29.64-
53.63- Q
Beckley
29.62-
53.59- Q

53.71- Q

Alderson
53.19-

Lewisburg
53.33-

CTCSS TONES

A = 67.0	Q = 107.2	E = 173.8
B = 69.3	R = 110.9	F = 179.9
C = 71.9	S = 114.8	G = 186.2
D = 74.4	T = 118.8	H = 192.8
E = 77.0	U = 123.0	J = 203.5
F = 79.7	V = 127.3	K = 206.5
G = 82.5	W = 131.8	L = 210.7
H = 85.4	X = 136.5	M = 218.1
J = 88.5	Y = 141.3	N = 225.7
K = 91.5	Z = 146.2	P = 229.1
L = 94.8	A = 151.4	Q = 233.6
M = 97.4	B = 156.7	R = 241.8
N = 100.0	C = 162.2	S = 250.3
P = 103.5	D = 167.9	T = 254.1

Notes:
+ indicates + offset
- indicates - offset
@ indicates Autopatch

for information on use of Autopatch
be sure to check with repeater owner.

9

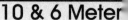

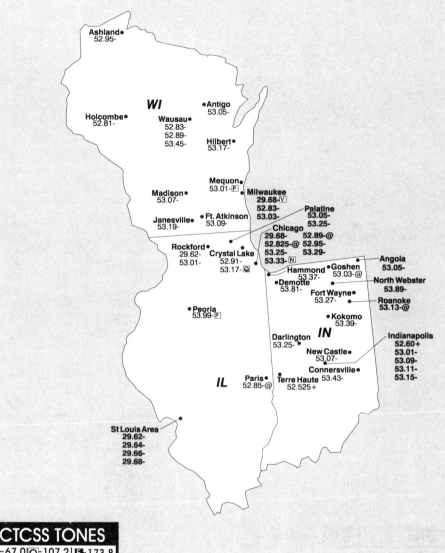

Ashland●
52.95-

WI

●Antigo
53.05-

Holcombe●
52.81-

Wausau●
52.83-
52.89-
53.45-

Hilbert●
53.17-

Mequon●
53.01-P

Milwaukee
29.68-V
52.83-
53.03-

Madison●
53.07-

Janesville●
53.19-

●Ft. Atkinson
53.09-

Palatine
53.05-
53.25-

Chicago
29.68-   52.89-@
52.825-@   52.95-
53.25-   53.29-
53.33-N

Rockford●
29.62-
53.01-

Crystal Lake
52.91-
53.17-Q

Hammond●
53.37-

●Goshen
53.03-@

Angola
53.05-

North Webster
53.89-

●Demotte
53.81-

Fort Wayne●
53.27-

Roanoke
53.13-@

Peoria●
53.99-P

●Kokomo
53.39-

IN

Darlington●
53.25-

New Castle●
53.07-

Indianapolis
52.60+
53.01-
53.09-
53.11-
53.15-

Connersville●

IL

Paris●
52.85-@

●Terre Haute
52.525+

53.43-

St Louis Area
29.62-
29.64-
29.66-
29.68-

CTCSS TONES

A=67.0	Q=107.2	E=173.8
B=69.3	R=110.9	F=179.9
C=71.9	S=114.8	G=186.2
D=74.4	T=118.8	H=192.8
E=77.0	U=123.0	J=203.5
F=79.7	V=127.3	K=206.5
G=82.5	W=131.8	L=210.7
H=85.4	X=136.5	M=218.1
J=88.5	Y=141.3	N=225.7
K=91.5	Z=146.2	P=229.1
L=94.8	A=151.4	Q=233.6
M=97.4	B=156.7	R=241.8
N=100.0	C=162.2	S=250.3
P=103.5	D=167.9	T=254.1

Notes:
+ indicates + offset
- indicates - offset
@ indicates Autopatch
for information on use of Autopatch
be sure to check with repeater owner

Call Area 0
10 & 6 Meters

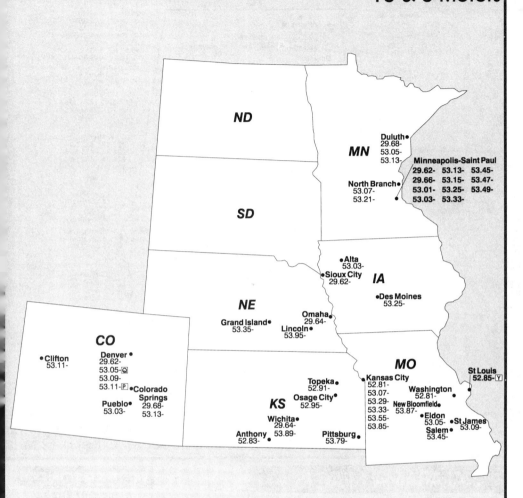

ND

MN

Duluth •
29.68-
53.05-
53.13-

Minneapolis-Saint Paul
29.62- 53.13- 53.45-
29.66- 53.15- 53.47-
53.01- 53.25- 53.49-
53.03- 53.33-

North Branch •
53.07-
53.21-

SD

• Alta
53.03-
• Sioux City
29.62-

IA

• Des Moines
53.25-

NE

Omaha •
29.64-
Grand Island •
53.35-
Lincoln •
53.95-

CO

• Clifton
53.11-

Denver •
29.62-
53.05-Q
53.09-
53.11-P •Colorado
Springs
Pueblo • 29.68-
53.03-   53.13-

KS

Topeka •
52.91-
Osage City •
52.95-

Wichita •
29.64-
53.89-
Anthony •
52.83-

Pittsburg •
53.79-

MO

Kansas City •
52.81-
53.07-
53.29-
53.33- New Bloomfield •
53.55- 53.87-
53.85-

Washington •
52.81-

• Eldon
53.05-
Salem •
53.45-

St James •
53.09-

St Louis
52.85-Y

CTCSS TONES

A=67.0	Q=107.2	E=173.8
B=69.3	R=110.9	F=179.9
C=71.9	S=114.8	G=186.2
D=74.4	T=118.8	H=192.8
E=77.0	U=123.0	J=203.5
F=79.7	V=127.3	K=206.5
G=82.5	W=131.8	L=210.7
H=85.4	X=136.5	M=218.1
J=88.5	Y=141.3	N=225.7
K=91.5	Z=146.2	P=229.1
L=94.8	A=151.4	Q=233.6
M=97.4	B=156.7	R=241.8
N=100.0	C=162.2	S=250.3
P=103.5	D=167.9	T=254.1

Notes:
+ indicates + offset
- indicates - offset
@ indicates Autopatch
for information on use of Autopatch
be sure to check with repeater owner.

11

Alabama

222 & UP

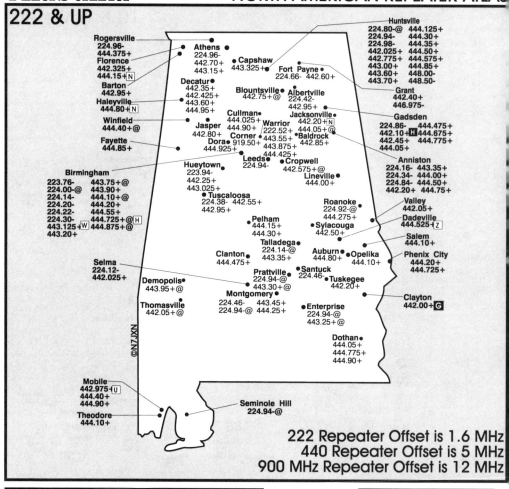

Rogersville
224.96-
444.375+

Athens
224.96-
442.70+
443.15+

Capshaw
443.325+

Huntsville
224.80-@   444.125+
224.94-   444.30+
224.98-   444.35+
442.025+   444.50+
442.775+   444.575+
443.00+   444.85+
443.60+   448.00-
443.70+   448.50-

Fort Payne
224.66- 442.60+

Florence
442.325+
444.15+

Barton
442.95+

Decatur
442.35+
442.425+
443.60+
444.95+

Blountsville
442.75+@

Albertville
224.42-
442.95+

Grant
442.40+
446.975-

Haleyville
444.80+

Winfield
444.40+@

Cullman
444.025+
444.90+

Jacksonville
442.20+

Gadsden
224.86-   444.475+
442.10+444.675+
442.45+   444.775+
444.05+

Jasper
442.80+

Warrior
222.52+

Baldrock
442.85+

Fayette
444.85+

Corner
443.55+

Dora
444.925+

Leeds
224.94-

Cropwell
442.575+@

Anniston
224.16- 443.35+
224.34- 444.00+
224.84- 444.50+
442.20+ 444.75+

Hueytown
223.94-
442.25+
443.025+

Lineville
444.00+

Birmingham
223.76-   443.75+@
224.00-@ 443.90+
224.14-   444.10+@
224.20-   444.20+
224.22-   444.55+
224.30-   444.725+@
443.125+ 444.875+@
443.20+

Tuscaloosa
224.38- 442.55+
442.95+

Roanoke
224.92-@
444.275+

Valley
442.05+

Dadeville
444.525+

Pelham
444.15+
444.30+

Sylacouga
442.50+

Salem
444.10+

Talladega
224.14-@
443.35+

Auburn
444.80+

Opelika
444.10+

Phenix City
444.20+
444.725+

Clanton
444.475+

Selma
224.12-
442.025+

Prattville
224.94-@
443.30+@

Santuck
224.46-

Demopolis
443.95+

Montgomery
224.46-   443.45+
224.94-@ 444.25+

Tuskegee
442.20+

Clayton
442.00+

Thomasville
442.05+@

Enterprise
224.94-@
443.25+@

Dothan
444.05+
444.775+
444.90+

Mobile
442.975-
444.40+
444.90+

Seminole Hill
224.94-@

Theodore
444.10+

©N7IXN

222 Repeater Offset is 1.6 MHz
440 Repeater Offset is 5 MHz
900 MHz Repeater Offset is 12 MHz

ALABAMA FACTS

NUMBER OF HAMS: 9,467

CALL AREA: 4

STATE NICKNAME: HEART OF DIXIE

HIGHEST POINT:

CHEAHA MOUNTAIN (2,407 FT.)

STATE CAPITAL: MONTGOMERY

NUMBER OF COUNTIES: 67

NUMBER OF 2M REPEATERS: 172

222 REPEATERS: 29

440 REPEATERS: 95

900 MHz REPEATERS: 0

1.2 GHz REPEATERS: 0

CTCSS TONES

A=67.0	Q=107.2	E=173.8	
B=69.3	R=110.9	F=179.9	
C=71.9	S=114.8	G=186.2	
D=74.4	T=118.8	H=192.8	
E=77.0	U=123.0	J=203.5	
F=79.7	V=127.3	K=206.5	
G=82.5	W=131.8	L=210.7	
H=85.4	X=136.5	M=218.1	
J=88.5	X=141.3	M=225.7	
K=91.5	Y=146.2	N=229.1	
K=94.8	Z=151.4	P=233.6	
L=97.4	A=156.7	Q=241.8	
M=100.0	B=162.2	R=250.3	
N=103.5	C=167.9	S=254.1	
P	D	T	

Alabama
2 METERS

Huntsville Metro Area	
145.23-	146.94-
145.29-	147.10+
145.33-	147.14+
145.39-	147.18+@
145.43-	147.22+
145.47-	147.24+@
146.74-	147.30+
146.86-	147.46-

Birmingham Metro Area	
145.19-	146.88-@
145.23-	147.14+
145.41-	147.28+@
146.62-	147.34+
146.76-@	

Mobile Metro Area	
146.82-	147.12+
146.895- [U]	147.15+
146.94-	

Montgomery Metro Area	
146.64-@	146.92-@
146.84-	147.00-
146.86-[J]	147.18+

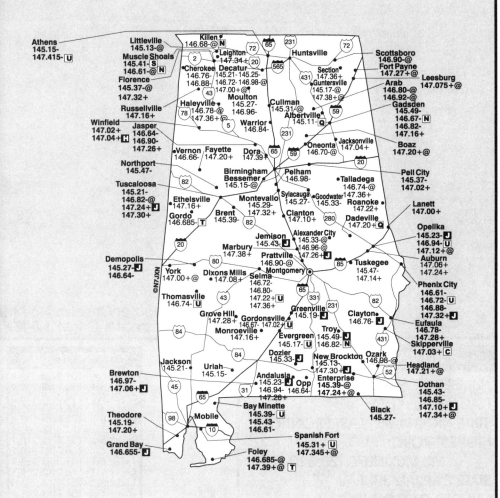

Notes:
+ indicates + offset
- indicates - offset
@ indicates Autopatch

for information on use of Autopatch
be sure to check with repeater owner.

See UHF Map page
for CTCSS tone chart.

2 Meter Repeater Offset is 600 KHz

Alaska

222 & UP

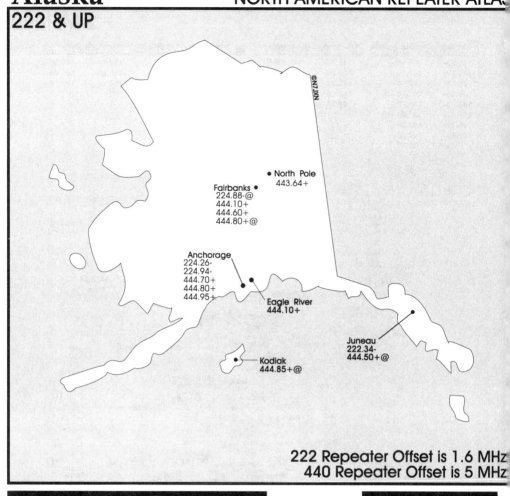

©N7JXN

North Pole
443.64+

Fairbanks •
224.88-@
444.10+
444.60+
444.80+@

Anchorage
224.26-
224.94-
444.70+
444.80+
444.95+

Eagle River
444.10+

Juneau
222.34-
444.50+@

Kodiak
444.85+@

222 Repeater Offset is 1.6 MHz
440 Repeater Offset is 5 MHz

ALASKA FACTS

NUMBER OF HAMS: 2,895

CALL AREA: KL7

STATE NICKNAME: LAST FRONTIER

HIGHEST POINT:
  MT. McKINLEY (20,320 FT.)

STATE CAPITAL: JUNEAU

NUMBER OF COUNTIES: 4

NUMBER OF 2M REPEATERS: 51
  222 REPEATERS: 4
  440 REPEATERS: 10
  900 MHz REPEATERS: 0
  1.2 GHz REPEATERS: 0

CTCSS TONES

A=67.0	Q=107.2	E=173.8
B=69.3	R=110.9	F=179.9
C=71.9	S=114.8	G=186.2
D=74.4	T=118.8	H=192.8
E=77.0	U=123.0	J=203.5
F=79.7	V=127.3	K=206.5
G=82.5	W=131.8	L=210.7
H=85.4	X=136.5	M=218.1
J=88.5	Y=141.3	N=225.7
K=91.5	Z=146.2	P=229.1
L=94.8	A=151.4	Q=233.6
M=97.4	B=156.7	R=241.8
N=100.0	C=162.2	S=250.3
P=103.5	D=167.9	T=254.1

Alaska
2 METERS

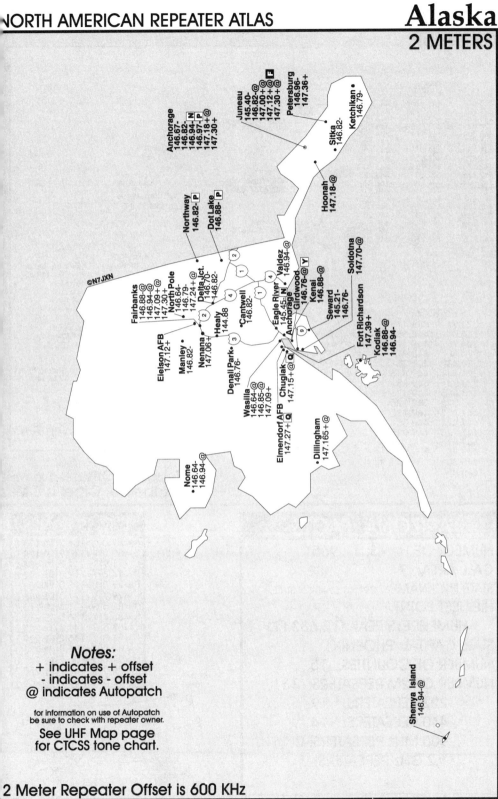

©N7JXN

Juneau
145.40-
146.82-@
147.00+@
147.12+@
147.30+@ **F**

Petersburg
146.96-
147.36+

Ketchikan •
146.79-

Sitka •
146.82-

Hoonah
147.18-@

Anchorage
146.67-
146.82-
146.94- **N**
146.97-@ **P**
147.18+@
147.30+

Northway
146.82- **P**

Dot Lake
146.88- **P**

Fairbanks
146.88-@
146.94-@
147.09+@
147.30+
North Pole
146.64-
146.79-
147.24+ @
Delta Jct.
146.70-
146.82-

②

①

④

Cantwell
146.82-

Healy
144.88

Eielson AFB
147.12+

Manley •
146.82-

Nenana
147.06+

②

③

Denali Park •
146.76-

Eagle River
145.45- **N**
Girdwood
146.76-@ **Y**
Valdez
146.94-@

Kenai
146.88-@

Seward
145.21-
146.76-

Soldotna
147.70-@

④

①

①

Anchorage
147.15+ @ **Q**

⑨

Fort Richardson
147.39+

Kodiak
146.88-@
146.94-

Wasilla
146.64-@
146.85-@
147.09+

Chugiak
147.15+ @ **Q**

Elmendorf AFB
147.27+ **Q**

Dillingham
147.165+ @

Nome
• 146.64-
146.94-@

Shemya Island
146.94-@

2 Meter Repeater Offset is 600 KHz

15

222 & UP

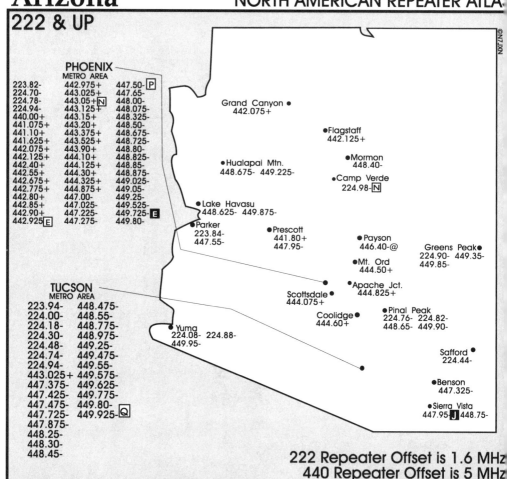

PHOENIX METRO AREA

223.82-	442.975+	447.50- P
224.70-	443.025+	447.65-
224.78-	443.05+ N	448.00-
224.94-	443.125+	448.075-
440.00+	443.15+	448.325-
441.075+	443.20+	448.50-
441.10+	443.375+	448.675-
441.625+	443.525+	448.725-
442.075+	443.90+	448.80-
442.125+	444.10+	448.825-
442.40+	444.125+	448.85-
442.55+	444.30+	448.875-
442.675+	444.325+	449.025-
442.775+	444.875+	449.05-
442.80+	447.00-	449.25-
442.85+	447.025-	449.525-
442.90+	447.225-	449.725- E
442.925 E	447.275-	449.80-

Grand Canyon ●
442.075+

●Flagstaff
442.125+

●Hualapai Mtn.
448.675- 449.225-

●Mormon
448.40-

●Camp Verde
224.98- N

●Lake Havasu
448.625- 449.875-

●Parker
223.84-
447.55-

●Prescott
441.80+
447.95-

●Payson
446.40-@

Greens Peak●
224.90- 449.35-
449.85-

●Mt. Ord
444.50+

●Apache Jct.
444.825+

TUCSON METRO AREA

223.94-	448.475-
224.00-	448.55-
224.18-	448.775-
224.30-	448.975-
224.48-	449.25-
224.74-	449.475-
224.94-	449.55-
443.025+	449.575-
447.375-	449.625-
447.425-	449.775-
447.475-	449.80-
447.725-	449.925- Q
447.875-	
448.25-	
448.30-	
448.45-	

Scottsdale ●
444.075+

Coolidge ●
444.60+

●Pinal Peak
224.76- 224.82-
448.65- 449.90-

●Yuma
224.08- 224.88-
449.95-

Safford ●
224.44-

●Benson
447.325-

●Sierra Vista
447.95- J 448.75-

222 Repeater Offset is 1.6 MHz
440 Repeater Offset is 5 MHz

©N7JXN

ARIZONA FACTS

NUMBER OF HAMS: 12,965

CALL AREA: 7

STATE NICKNAME: GRAND CANYON STATE

HIGHEST POINT:
   HUMPHREYS PEAK (12,633 FT.)

STATE CAPITAL: PHOENIX

NUMBER OF COUNTIES: 15

NUMBER OF 2M REPEATERS: 131

   222 REPEATERS: 19

   440 REPEATERS: 94

   900 MHz REPEATERS: 0

   1.2 GHz REPEATERS: 0

CTCSS TONES

A=67.0	Q=107.2	E=173.8
B=69.3	R=110.9	F=179.9
C=71.9	S=114.8	G=186.2
D=74.4	T=118.8	H=192.8
E=77.0	U=123.0	J=203.5
F=79.7	V=127.3	K=206.5
G=82.5	W=131.8	L=210.7
H=85.4	X=136.5	M=218.1
J=88.5	Y=141.3	N=225.7
K=91.5	Z=146.2	P=229.1
L=94.8	A=151.4	Q=233.6
M=97.4	B=156.7	R=241.8
N=100.0	C=162.2	S=250.3
P=103.5	D=167.9	T=254.1

Arizona
2 METERS

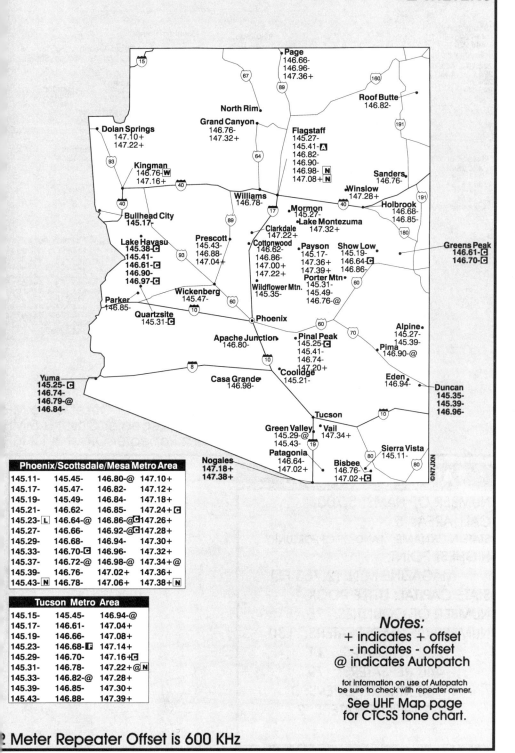

Page
146.66-
146.96-
147.36+

Roof Butte
146.82-

North Rim

Grand Canyon
146.76-
147.32+

Flagstaff
145.27-
145.41-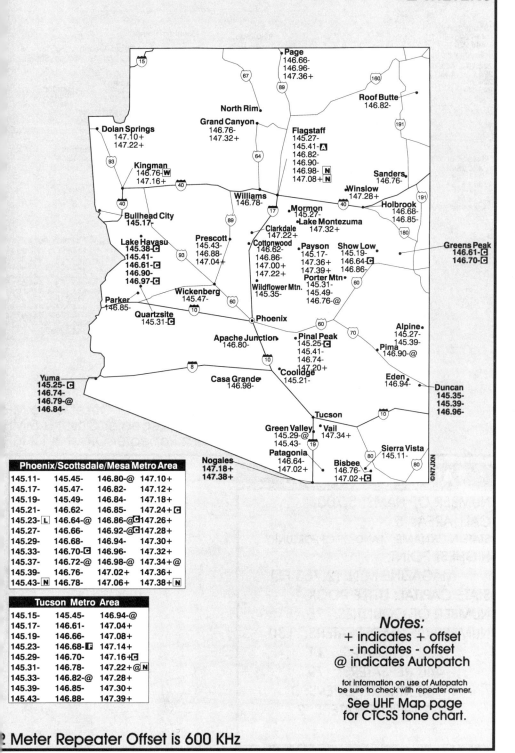
146.82-
146.90-
146.98-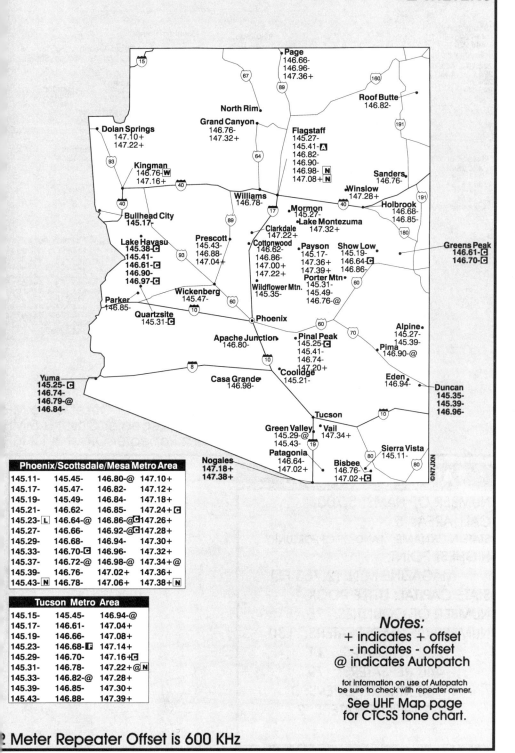
147.08+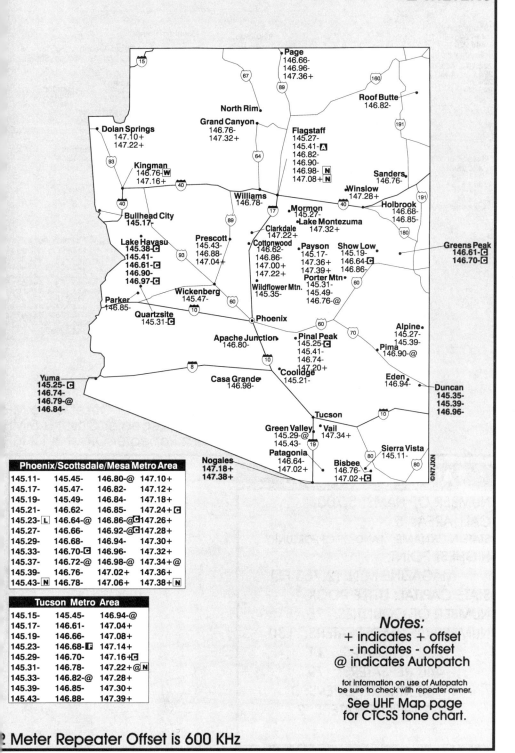

Sanders
146.76-

Winslow
147.28+

Dolan Springs
147.10+
147.22+

Kingman
146.76-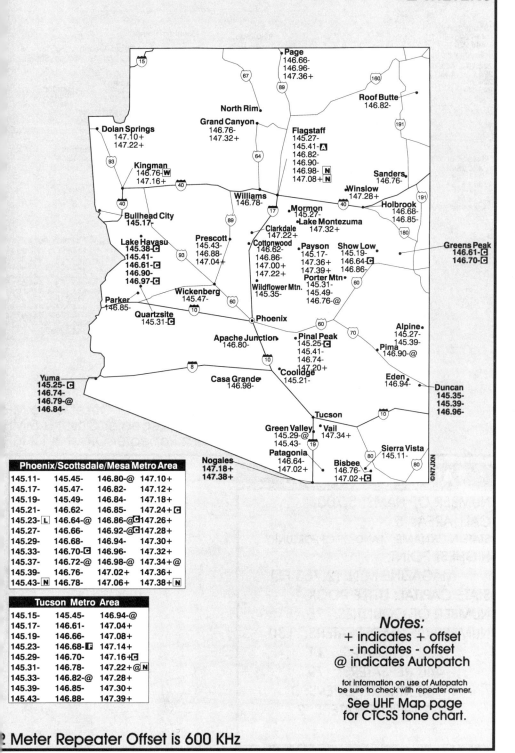
147.16+

Williams
146.78-

Mormon
145.27-

Lake Montezuma
147.32+

Holbrook
146.68-
146.85-

Bullhead City
145.17-

Clarkdale
147.22+

Cottonwood
146.62-
146.86-
147.00+
147.22+

Payson
145.17-
147.36+
147.39+

Show Low
145.19-
146.64-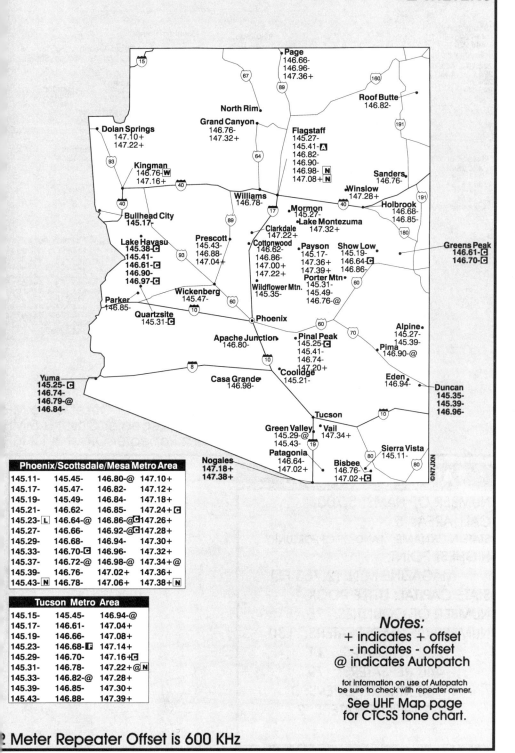
146.86-

Greens Peak
146.61-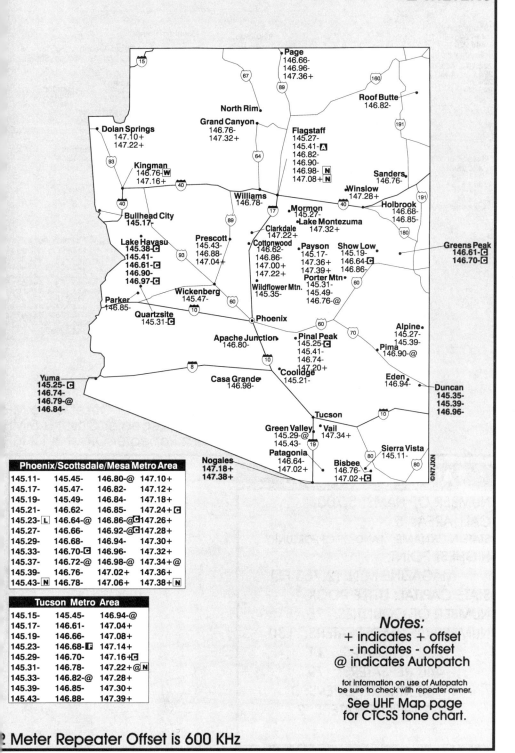
146.70-

Lake Havasu
145.38-
145.41-
146.61-
146.90-
146.97-

Prescott
145.43-
146.88-
147.04+

Porter Mtn
145.31-
145.49-
146.76-@

Wildflower Mtn.
145.35-

Parker
146.85-

Wickenberg
145.47-

Quartzsite
145.31-

Phoenix

Apache Junction
146.80-

Pinal Peak
145.25-
145.41-
146.74-
147.20+

Alpine
145.27-
145.39-

Pima
146.90-@

Coolidge
145.21-

Eden
146.94-

Duncan
145.35-
145.39-
146.96-

Yuma
145.25-
146.74-
146.79-@
146.84-

Casa Grande
146.98-

Tucson

Green Valley
145.29-@
145.43-

Vail
147.34+

Sierra Vista
145.11-

Nogales
147.18+
147.38+

Patagonia
146.64-
147.02+

Bisbee
146.76-
147.02+

Phoenix/Scottsdale/Mesa Metro Area

145.11-	145.45-	146.80-@	147.10+
145.17-	145.47-	146.82-	147.12+
145.19-	145.49-	146.84-	147.18+
145.21-	146.62-	146.85-	147.24+
145.23-	146.64-@	146.86-@	147.26+
145.27-	146.66-	146.92-@	147.28+
145.29-	146.68-	146.94-	147.30+
145.33-	146.70-	146.96-	147.32+
145.37-	146.72-@	146.98-@	147.34+@
145.39-	146.78-	147.02+	147.36+
145.43-	146.78-	147.06+	147.38+

Tucson Metro Area

145.15-	145.45-	146.94-@
145.17-	146.61-	147.04+
145.19-	146.66-	147.08+
145.23-	146.68-	147.14+
145.29-	146.70-	147.16+
145.31-	146.78-	147.22+@
145.33-	146.82-@	147.28+
145.39-	146.85-	147.30+
145.43-	146.88-	147.39+

Notes:
+ indicates + offset
- indicates - offset
@ indicates Autopatch

for information on use of Autopatch
be sure to check with repeater owner.

See UHF Map page
for CTCSS tone chart.

2 Meter Repeater Offset is 600 KHz

17

222 & UP

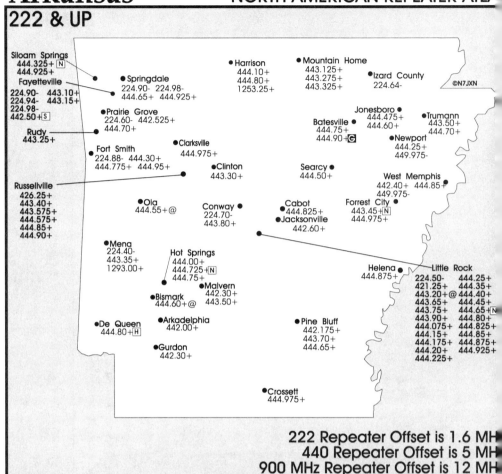

Siloam Springs
444.325+ N
444.925+

Fayetteville
224.90- 443.10+
224.94- 443.15+
224.98-
442.50+ S

Rudy
443.25+

Russellville
426.25+
443.40+
443.575+
444.575+
444.85+
444.90+

Springdale
224.90- 224.98-
444.65+ 444.925+

Prairie Grove
224.60- 442.525+
444.70+

Fort Smith
224.88- 444.30+
444.775+ 444.95+

Clarksville
444.975+

Ola
444.55+@

Mena
224.40-
443.35+
1293.00+

Bismark
444.60+@

De Queen
444.80+ H

Clinton
443.30+

Conway
224.70-
443.80+

Hot Springs
444.00+
444.725+ N
444.75+

Malvern
442.30+
443.50+

Arkadelphia
442.00+

Gurdon
442.30+

Harrison
444.10+
444.80+
1253.25+

Mountain Home
443.125+
443.275+
443.325+

Izard County
224.64-

©N7JXN

Jonesboro
444.475+
444.60+

Batesville
444.75+
444.90+ G

Trumann
443.50+
444.70+

Newport
444.25+
449.975-

Searcy
444.50+

Cabot
444.825+

Jacksonville
442.60+

Forrest City
443.45+ N
444.975+

West Memphis
442.40+ 444.85+
449.975-

Helena
444.875+

Pine Bluff
442.175+
443.70+
444.65+

Little Rock
224.50- 444.25+
421.25+ 444.35+
443.20+@ 444.40+
443.65+ 444.45+
443.75+ 444.65+ N
443.90+ 444.80+
444.075+ 444.825+
444.15+ 444.85+
444.175+ 444.875+
444.20+ 444.925+
444.225+

Crossett
444.975+

222 Repeater Offset is 1.6 MH
440 Repeater Offset is 5 MH
900 MHz Repeater Offset is 12 MH

ARKANSAS FACTS

NUMBER OF HAMS: 5,700
CALL AREA: 5
STATE NICKNAME: LAND OF OPPORTUNITY
HIGHEST POINT:
    MAGAZINE MTN. (2,753 FT.)
STATE CAPITAL: LITTLE ROCK
NUMBER OF COUNTIES: 75
NUMBER OF 2M REPEATERS: 130
    222 REPEATERS: 11
    440 REPEATERS: 79
    900 MHz REPEATERS: 0
    1.2 GHz REPEATERS: 2

CTCSS TONES

A=67.0	Q=107.2	E=173.8
B=69.3	R=110.9	F=179.9
C=71.9	S=114.8	G=186.2
D=74.4	T=118.8	H=192.8
E=77.0	U=123.0	J=203.5
F=79.7	V=127.3	K=206.5
G=82.5	W=131.8	L=210.7
H=85.4	X=136.5	M=218.1
J=88.5	Y=141.3	N=225.7
K=91.5	Z=146.2	P=229.1
L=94.8	A=151.4	Q=233.6
M=97.4	B=156.7	R=241.8
N=100.0	C=162.2	S=250.3
P=103.5	D=167.9	T=254.1

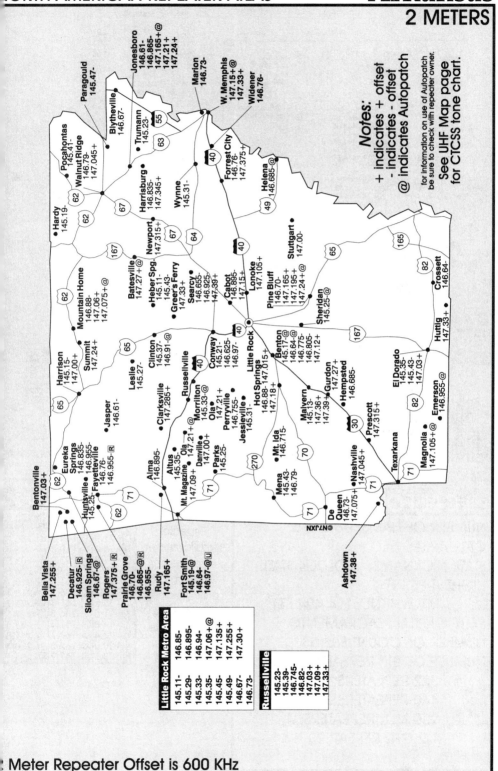

Notes:
+ indicates + offset
- indicates - offset
@ indicates Autopatch

for information on use of Autopatch
be sure to check with repeater owner.

See UHF Map page
for CTCSS tone chart.

Paragould 145.47-

Jonesboro
146.61-
146.865-
147.165+@
147.21+
147.24+

Marion 146.73-

W. Memphis
147.15+@
147.33+

Widener 146.76-

Pocahontas 145.41-
Walnut Ridge 146.79-
147.045+

Blytheville 146.67-

Trumann 145.23-

Hardy 145.19-

Harrisburg 146.835-
147.345+

Forrest City
146.76-
147.375+

Helena 146.685-

Wynne 145.31-

Mountain Home
146.88-
147.06+
147.075+@

Newport 147.315+

Batesville 147.27+@

Heber Spg.
145.11-
145.43-

Greer's Ferry 147.33+

Searcy
146.655-
146.925+
147.39+

Cabot
146.895-
147.15+

Lonoke 147.105+

Stuttgart 147.00-

Pine Bluff
146.70-
147.165+
147.195+
147.24+@

Sheridan 145.25-@

Crossett 146.64-

Huttig 147.33+

Harrison
145.15-
147.00+

Summit 147.24+

Leslie 145.27-

Clinton
145.37-
146.91-@

Russellville

Conway
145.21-
146.625-
146.97-

Little Rock
146.88-147.015+
147.18+

Benton
145.17-@
146.64-@
146.775-
146.805-
147.12+

El Dorado
145.35-
145.43-
147.03+

Emerson 146.955-@

Jasper 146.61-

Clarksville 147.285+

Morrilton 147.21+@

Ola 145.33-@

Perryville 146.755-

Jessieville 145.31-

Hot Springs 147.18+

Malvern
145.13-
147.36+
147.39+

Gurdon 147.27+

Hempsted 146.685-

Prescott 147.315+

Magnolia 147.105+@

Eureka Springs 146.835-

Huntsville 146.955-
145.25+

Fayetteville 146.76-
146.955+ R

Alma 146.895-

Altus 145.35-

Mt. Magazine 147.09+

Danville 147.00+

Parks 145.25-

Mena
145.43-
146.79-

Mt. Ida 146.715-

Nashville 147.045+

De Queen
146.73-
147.075+

Ashdown 147.38+

Texarkana

Bentonville 147.03+

Bella Vista 147.255+

Decatur 146.925+ R

Siloam Springs 146.67-@

Rogers 147.375+ R

Prairie Grove
146.70-
146.865+@ R
146.955-

Rudy 147.165+

Fort Smith
145.15+@
146.64-
146.97+@ U

©N7JXN

Little Rock Metro Area	
145.11-	146.85-
145.29-	146.895-
145.33-	146.94-
145.35-	147.06+@
145.45-	147.135+
145.49-	147.255+
146.67-	147.30+
146.73-	

Russellville
145.23-
145.39-
146.745-
146.82-
147.03+
147.09+
147.33+

222 & UP

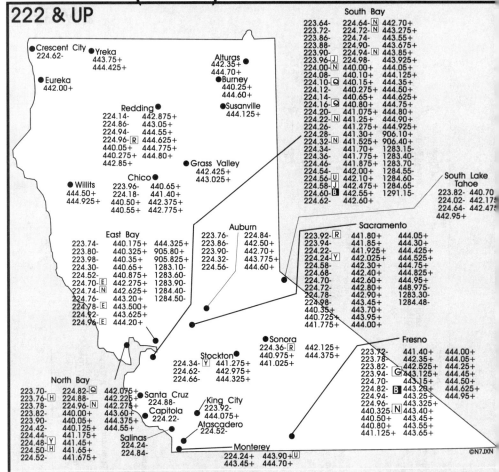

CALIFORNIA FACTS

NUMBER OF HAMS: 98,615

CALL AREA: 6

STATE NICKNAME: GOLDEN STATE

HIGHEST POINT:

    MT. WHITNEY (14,494 FT.)

STATE CAPITAL: SACRAMENTO

NUMBER OF COUNTIES: 58

NUMBER OF 2M REPEATERS: 204

    222 REPEATERS: 100

    440 REPEATERS: 151

    900 MHz REPEATERS: 4

    1.2 GHz REPEATERS: 14

Note: Repeater Statistics shown at left are for Northern CA only. All other Statistics are for entire state.

CTCSS TONES

A=67.0	Q=107.2	E=173.8
B=69.3	R=110.9	F=179.9
C=71.9	S=114.8	G=186.2
D=74.4	T=118.8	H=192.8
E=77.0	U=123.0	J=203.5
F=79.7	V=127.3	K=206.5
G=82.5	W=131.8	L=210.7
H=85.4	X=136.5	M=218.1
J=88.5	Y=141.3	N=225.7
K=91.5	Z=146.2	P=229.1
L=94.8	A=151.4	Q=233.6
M=97.4	B=156.7	R=241.8
N=100.0	C=162.2	S=250.3
P=103.5	D=167.9	T=254.1

California (North)
2 METERS

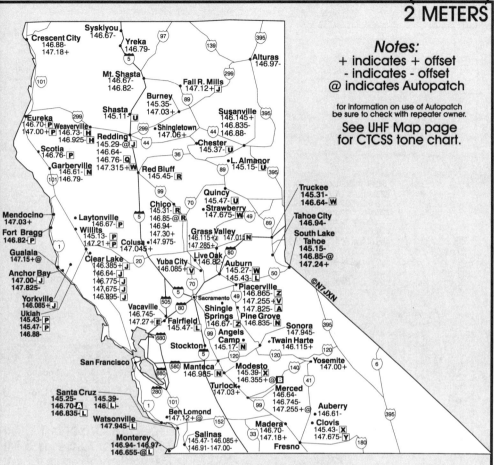

Notes:
+ indicates + offset
- indicates - offset
@ indicates Autopatch

for information on use of Autopatch
be sure to check with repeater owner.

**See UHF Map page
for CTCSS tone chart.**

Map labels:

Crescent City 146.88- 147.18+
Syskiyou 146.67-
Yreka 146.79-
Alturas 146.97-
Mt. Shasta 146.67- 146.82-
Fall R. Mills 147.12+ J
Burney 145.35- 147.03+
Shasta 145.11- U
Susanville 146.145+ 146.835- 146.88-
Eureka 146.70- 147.00+ P
Weaverville 146.73- H 146.925- H
Shingletown 147.06+
Chester 145.37- U
Scotia 146.76- P
Redding 145.29-@ J 146.64- 146.76- Q 147.315+ W
Garberville 146.61- N 146.79-
Red Bluff 145.45- R
L. Almanor 145.15- U
Truckee 145.31- 146.64- W
Mendocino 147.03+
Quincy 145.47- U
Chico 145.31- R 146.85-@ R 146.94- 147.30+ 147.975-
Strawberry 147.675- W
Tahoe City 146.94-
Laytonville 146.67- P
Fort Bragg 146.82- P
Willits 145.13- P 147.21+ P
Colusa 147.045- 147.01- N
Grass Valley 146.115+@ 147.285+
South Lake Tahoe 145.15- 146.85-@ 147.24+
Gualala 147.15+@
Clear Lake 146.385+ J 146.64- J 146.775- J 147.675- J 146.895- J
Live Oak 146.82- J
Anchor Bay 147.00- J 147.825-
Yuba City 146.085+ V
Auburn 145.27- W 145.43- L
Placerville 146.865- V 147.255+ V 147.825- N
Yorkville 146.085+ J
Sacramento
Ukiah 145.43- P 145.47- P 146.88-
Vacaville 146.745- 147.27+ E
Fairfield 145.47- L
Shingle Springs 146.67- Z
Pine Grove 146.835- N
Sonora 147.945-
Angels Camp 145.17- N
Twain Harte 146.115+
Stockton
Yosemite 147.00+
San Francisco
Manteca 146.985- N
Modesto 145.39- X 146.355+@ B
Merced 146.64- 146.745- 147.255+@
Turlock 147.03+
Auberry 146.61-
Santa Cruz 145.25- 146.70- A 146.835- L
145.39- 146. L-
Watsonville 147.945- L
Ben Lomond 147.12+@
Madera 146.70- 147.18+
Clovis 145.43- X 147.675- Y
Monterey 146.94- 146.97- 146.655-@ L
Salinas 145.47-146.085+ 146.91-147.00-
Fresno

©N7JXN

Stockton Area

145.21- N	147.09+ S
146.88- L	147.165+

Fresno Metro Area

145.13-	146.82- Y	147.15+@
145.23- Y	146.85-	147.30+
146.73- Y	146.94-	147.39+ Y
146.79-	147.105+ N	

Sacramento Metro Area

145.13- R	146.085+ V	146.805-	147.105+
145.19- G	146.61-	146.91- N	147.195+
145.23- G	146.625- L	146.97- U	147.30+
145.25- V	146.79- N	147.00- X	147.39+

South Bay

145.15-	146.115+	146.94- U	147.36+ R
145.17- L	146.205+	147.015+	147.39+@
145.19- A	146.385+	147.09+	147.675-@
145.23-@ N	146.64- A	147.165+@	147.825-@
145.27-@	146.76- A	147.285+ P	147.855-
145.37-	146.85-	147.30+	
145.39- L	146.865- S	147.315+ A	
145.45-	146.925-@ S	147.345+ G	

East Bay

145.11-	145.41- V	146.67- E	147.06+ N
145.13- V	145.49- V	146.775- N	147.12+ N
145.29- W	146.025+ N	146.88- E	147.21+ N
145.33- N	146.355+ N	147.03+ B	147.24+
145.35- N	146.655- N	147.045+	147.735- P

North Bay

145.17- J	146.64- J	146.91- J	147.18+ A
145.19- J	146.70- F	146.94- J	147.33+ F
145.31- Q	146.73- J	146.955- J	147.675- J
145.35- J	146.775- J	147.105+@	147.945- J
146.385+ J	146.79- S	147.12+ J	

2 Meter Repeater Offset is 600 KHz

21

222 & UP

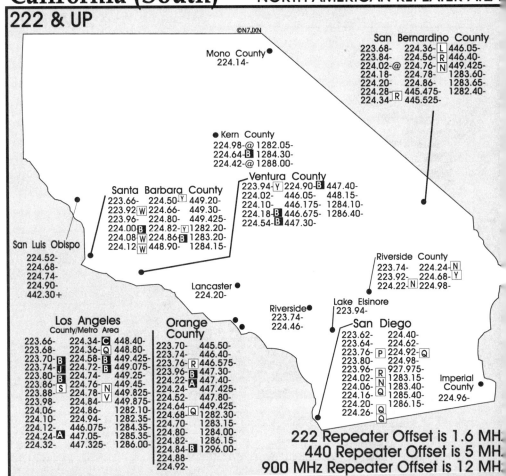

©N7JXN

Mono County
224.14-

San Bernardino County
223.68-	224.36- L	446.05-
223.84-	224.56- R	446.40-
224.02-@	224.76- N	449.425-
224.18-	224.78-	1283.60-
224.20-	224.86-	1283.65-
224.28- R	445.475-	1282.40-
224.34- R	445.525-	

Kern County
224.98-@ 1282.05-
224.64- B 1284.30-
224.42-@ 1288.00-

Ventura County
223.94- Y	224.90- B	447.40-
224.02-	446.05-	448.15-
224.10-	446.175-	1284.10-
224.18- B	446.675-	1286.40-
224.54- B	447.30-	

Santa Barbara County
223.66-	224.50- Y	449.20-
223.92- W	224.66-	449.30-
223.96-	224.80-	449.425-
224.00- B	224.82- Y	1282.20-
224.08- W	224.86- B	1283.20-
224.12- W	448.90-	1284.15-

San Luis Obispo
224.52-
224.68-
224.74-
224.90-
442.30+

Lancaster
224.20-

Riverside
223.74-
224.46-

Riverside County
223.74-	224.24- N	
223.92-	224.68- Y	
224.22- N	224.98-	

Lake Elsinore
223.94-

Los Angeles
County/Metro Area
223.66-	224.34- C	448.40-
223.68-	224.36- Q	448.80-
223.70- B	224.58- B	449.425-
223.74- J	224.72- B	449.075-
223.80- B	224.74-	449.25-
223.86-	224.76- N	449.45-
223.88- S	224.78- V	449.825-
223.98-	224.84-	449.875-
224.06-	224.86-	1282.10-
224.10-	224.94-	1282.35-
224.12-	446.075-	1284.35-
224.24- A	447.05-	1285.35-
224.32-	447.325-	1286.00-

Orange County
223.70-	445.50-
223.74-	446.40-
223.76- R	446.575-
223.96- B	447.30-
224.22- A	447.40-
224.24-	447.425-
224.52-	447.80-
224.64- Q	449.425-
224.68- Q	1282.30-
224.70-	1283.15-
224.80-	1284.00-
224.82-	1286.15-
224.84- B	1296.00-
224.88-	
224.92-	

San Diego
223.62-	224.40-
223.64-	224.62-
223.76- P	224.92- Q
223.80-	224.98-
223.96-	927.975-
224.02- R	1283.15-
224.06- N	1283.40-
224.16- Q	1285.40-
224.20-	1286.15-
224.26- Q	

Imperial County
224.96-

222 Repeater Offset is 1.6 MH.
440 Repeater Offset is 5 MH.
900 MHz Repeater Offset is 12 MH.

CALIFORNIA FACTS

NUMBER OF HAMS: 98,615

CALL AREA: 6

STATE NICKNAME: GOLDEN STATE

HIGHEST POINT:
   MT. WHITNEY (14,494 FT.)

STATE CAPITAL: SACRAMENTO

NUMBER OF COUNTIES: 58

NUMBER OF 2M REPEATERS: 225

   222 REPEATERS: 100

   440 REPEATERS: 134

   900 MHz REPEATERS: 1

   1.2 GHz REPEATERS: 29

Note:
Repeater Statistics shown at left are for Southern CA only. All other Statistics are for entire state.

CTCSS TONES

A = 67.0	Q = 107.2	E = 173.8
B = 69.3	R = 110.9	F = 179.9
C = 71.9	S = 114.8	G = 186.2
D = 74.4	T = 118.8	H = 192.8
E = 77.0	U = 123.0	J = 203.5
F = 79.7	V = 127.3	K = 206.5
G = 82.5	W = 131.8	L = 210.7
H = 85.4	X = 136.5	M = 218.1
J = 88.5	Y = 141.3	N = 225.7
K = 91.5	Z = 146.2	P = 229.1
L = 94.8	A = 151.4	Q = 233.6
M = 97.4	B = 156.7	R = 241.8
N = 100.0	C = 162.2	S = 250.3
P = 103.5	D = 167.9	T = 254.1

California (South)
2 METERS

©N7JXN

Notes:
+ indicates + offset
− indicates − offset
@ indicates Autopatch

for information on use of Autopatch
be sure to check with repeater owner.

See UHF Map page
for CTCSS tone chart.

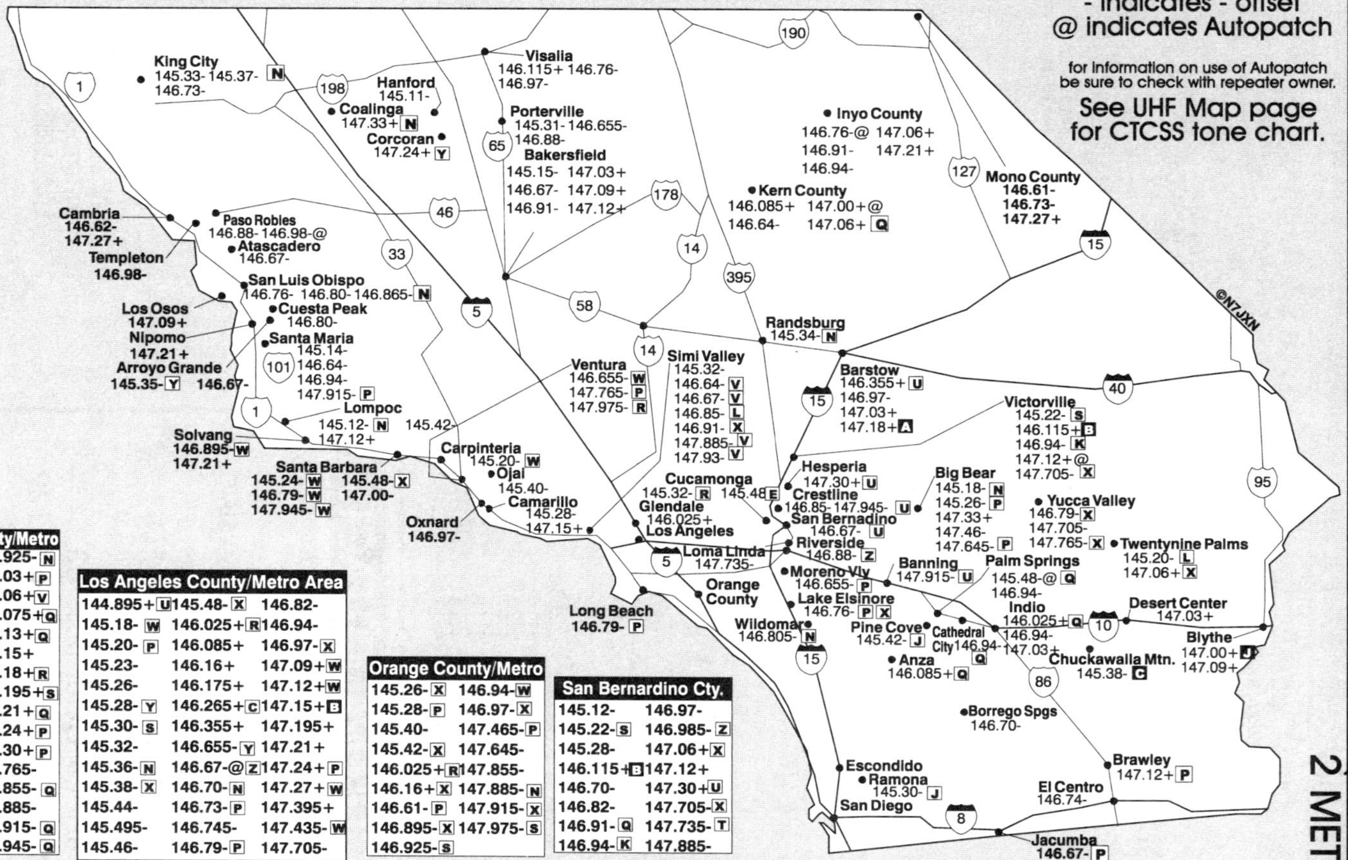

Map place labels

- Mono County: 146.61- / 146.73- / 147.27+
- Inyo County: 146.76-@ 147.06+ / 146.91- 147.21+ / 146.94-
- Kern County: 146.085+ 147.00+@ / 146.64- 147.06+ [Q]
- Randsburg: 145.34- [N]
- Victorville: 145.22- [S] / 146.115+ [B] / 146.94- [K] / 147.12+@ [Q] / 147.705- [X]
- Barstow: 146.355+ [U] / 146.97- / 147.03+ / 147.18+ [A]
- Twentynine Palms: 145.20- [L] / 147.06+ [X]
- Desert Center: 147.03+
- Blythe: 147.03+
- Yucca Valley: 146.79- [X] / 147.705-
- Palm Springs: 145.48-@ [Q] / 146.94-
- Indio: 146.02 [Q] 147.03 / 146.94-
- Chuckawalla Mtn.: 147.00+ [P] 147.09+ [R]
- Cathedral City: 146.94-
- Big Bear: 145.18- / 145.26- [P] / 147.33+ / 147.46-
- Crestline: 147.945- [E]
- San Bernardino: 146.85- / 146.025+
- Banning: 147.915- [U]
- Hesperia: 146.97-
- Moreno Vly: 146.655- / 146.88- [N]
- Riverside: 146.76- [N] / 146.67
- Pine Cove: 145.42- [J]
- Anza: 146.085+
- Brawley: 147.12+ [P]
- El Centro: 146.74-
- Jacumba: 146.67- [P]
- Escondido: 145.30- [J]
- Ramona
- San Diego
- Borrego Spgs: 146.70-
- Loma Linda: 147.735-
- Wildomar: 146.805- [N]
- Lake Elsinore: 146.76- [N]
- Orange County
- Long Beach: 146.79- [P]
- Cucamonga: 145.32- [R] / 145.48- [E]
- Glendale: 146.025+ [Q]
- Los Angeles
- Visalia: 146.115+ 146.76- / 146.97-
- Porterville: 145.31- 146.655- / 146.88-
- Bakersfield: 145.15- 147.03+ / 146.67- 147.09+ / 146.91- 147.12+
- Hanford: 145.11-
- Coalinga: 147.33+ [N]
- Corcoran: 147.24+ [Y]
- King City: 145.33- 145.37- / 146.73-
- Paso Robles: 146.88- 146.98-@
- Atascadero: 146.67-
- Templeton: 146.98-
- Cambria: 146.62- / 147.27+
- San Luis Obispo: 146.76- 146.80- 146.865- [N]
- Cuesta Peak: 146.80-
- Los Osos: 147.09+
- Nipomo: 147.21+
- Arroyo Grande: 145.35- [Y] / 146.6?-
- Santa Maria: 146.14- / 146.94-
- Lompoc: 145.12- [N] / 147.12+
- Solvang: 146.895- [W] / 147.21+
- Santa Barbara: 145.24- [W] 145.48- [X] / 146.79- [W] 147.00- / 147.945- [W]
- Carpinteria: 145.42-
- Ojai: 145.20- [W]
- Camarillo: 145.40- / 147.15+
- Oxnard: 146.97-
- Ventura: 146.655- [W] / 147.765- [P] / 147.975- [R]
- Simi Valley: 145.32- / 146.64- [V] / 146.67- [L] / 146.85- [L] / 146.91- [X] / 147.93- [N]

San Bernardino Cty.

145.12- [X]	146.94- [W]
145.22- [S]	146.985- [Z]
145.28-	147.06+ [X]
145.28-	147.30+ [U]
146.115- [B]	147.12+
146.70-	147.705- [X]
146.82-	147.735- [T]
146.91- [P]	147.885-
146.94- [K]	

Orange County/Metro

145.26- [X]	146.94- [W]
145.28- [P]	146.97- [X]
145.40-	147.465- [P]
145.42- [X]	147.645-
145.48- [X]	147.855-
146.025+ [R]	147.885- [N]
146.16+ [X]	147.915- [X]
146.61- [P]	147.975- [S]
146.925- [S]	

Los Angeles County/Metro Area

144.895+ [U]	145.48- [X]	146.82-
145.18- [W]	146.025+ [R]	146.94- [X]
145.20- [P]	146.085+	146.97- [X]
145.23-	146.16+	147.09+ [W]
145.26-	146.175+	147.12+ [W]
145.28- [Y]	146.265+ [C]	147.15+ [B]
145.30- [S]	146.355+	147.195+
145.32-	146.655+ [Y]	147.21+
145.36- [N]	146.67 @ [Z]	147.24+ [P]
145.38- [X]	146.70- [P]	147.27+ [W]
145.44-	146.73- [P]	147.395+
145.495-	146.745-	147.435- [W]
145.46-	146.79- [P]	147.705-

San Diego County/Metro

145.12- [Q]	146.925- [N]
145.28-	147.03+ [P]
145.32- [Q]	147.06+ [V]
145.36-	147.075+ [Q]
145.38- [Q]	147.13+ [Q]
145.44- [Q]	147.15+
146.16+ [K]	147.18+ [R]
146.175+ [Q]	147.195+ [S]
146.265+ [Q]	147.21+ [Q]
146.61- [Q]	147.24+ [Q]
146.64- [Q]	147.30+ [P]
146.70-	147.765-
146.73- [Q]	147.855-
146.79- [Q]	147.885-
146.88- [Q]	147.915- [Q]
146.91- [P]	147.945- [S]

Colorado

222 & UP

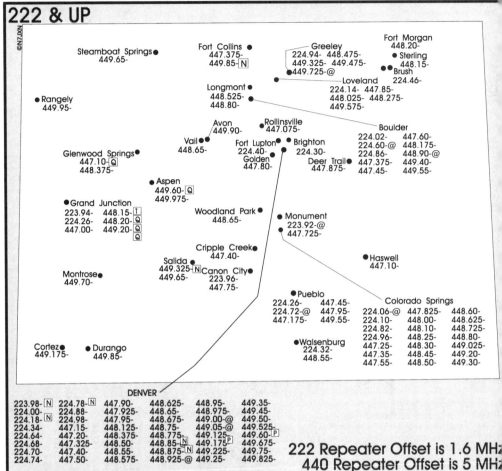

©N7JXN

Steamboat Springs ●
449.65-

Fort Collins ●
447.375-
449.85-[N]

Greeley
224.94- 448.475-
449.325- 449.475-
●449.725-@

Fort Morgan
448.20-
● Sterling
448.15-
●● Brush
224.46-

● Rangely
449.95-

Longmont ●
448.525-
448.80-

Loveland
224.14- 447.85-
448.025- 448.275-
449.575-

Avon
449.90-

Rollinsville
447.075-

Boulder
224.02- 447.60-
224.60-@ 448.175-
224.86- 448.90-@
447.375- 449.40-
447.45- 449.55-

Vail ●●
448.65-

Fort Lupton ●
224.40-
Golden
447.80-

● Brighton
224.30-

Deer Trail ●
447.875-

Glenwood Springs ●
447.10-[Q]
448.375-

● Aspen
449.60-[Q]
449.975-

● Grand Junction
223.94- 448.15-[T]
224.26- 448.20-[Q]
447.00- 449.20-[Q]

Woodland Park ●
448.65-

● Monument
223.92-@
447.725-

Cripple Creek ●
447.40-

● Haswell
447.10-

Salida ●
449.325-[N] Canon City ●
449.65- 223.96-
447.75-

Montrose ●
449.70-

● Pueblo
224.26- 447.45-
224.72-@ 447.95-
447.175- 449.55-

Colorado Springs
224.06-@ 447.825- 448.60-
224.10- 448.00- 448.625-
224.82- 448.10- 448.725-
224.96- 448.25- 448.80-
447.25- 448.30- 449.025-
447.35- 448.45- 449.20-
447.55- 448.50- 449.30-

● Walsenburg
224.32-
448.55-

Cortez ●
449.175-

● Durango
449.85-

DENVER

223.98-[N]	224.78-[N]	447.90-	448.625-	448.95-	449.35-
224.00-[N]	224.88-	447.925-	448.65-	448.975-	449.45-
224.18-[N]	224.98-	447.95-	448.675-	449.00-@	449.50-
224.34-	447.15-	448.125-	448.75-	449.05-@	449.525-
224.64-	447.20-	448.375-	448.775-	449.125-	449.60-[P]
224.68-	447.325-	448.50-	448.85-[N]	449.175-[P]	449.675-
224.70-	447.40-	448.55-	448.875-[N]	449.225-	449.75-
224.74-	447.50-	448.575-	448.925-@	449.25-	449.825-

222 Repeater Offset is 1.6 MHz
440 Repeater Offset is 5 MHz

COLORADO FACTS

NUMBER OF HAMS: 10,577

CALL AREA: 0

STATE NICKNAME: CENTENNIAL STATE

HIGHEST POINT:
MT. ELBERT (14,433 FT.)

STATE CAPITAL: DENVER

NUMBER OF COUNTIES: 63

NUMBER OF 2M REPEATERS: 129

222 REPEATERS: 30

440 REPEATERS: 105

900 MHz REPEATERS: 0

1.2 GHz REPEATERS: 0

CTCSS TONES

A=67.0	Q=107.2	E=173.8
B=69.3	R=110.9	F=179.9
C=71.9	S=114.8	G=186.2
D=74.4	T=118.8	H=192.8
E=77.0	U=123.0	J=203.5
F=79.7	V=127.3	K=206.5
G=82.5	W=131.8	L=210.7
H=85.4	X=136.5	M=218.1
J=88.5	Y=141.3	N=225.7
K=91.5	Z=146.2	P=229.1
L=94.8	A=151.4	Q=233.6
M=97.4	B=156.7	R=241.8
N=100.0	C=162.2	S=250.3
P=103.5	D=167.9	T=254.1

Colorado
2 METERS

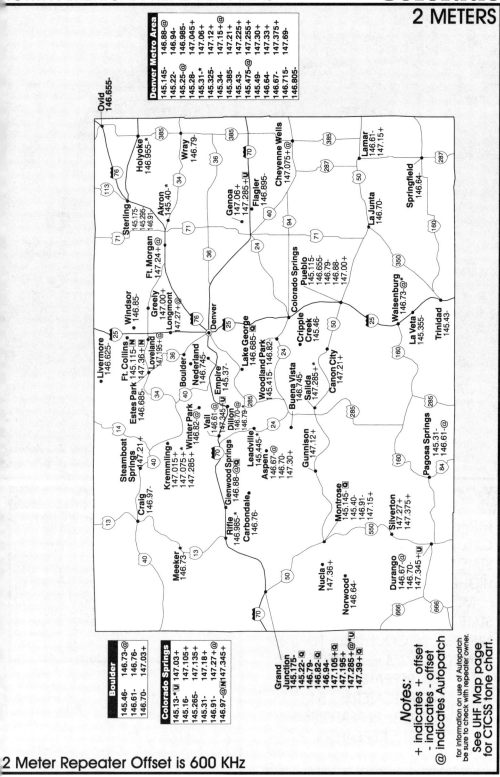

2 Meter Repeater Offset is 600 KHz

222 & UP

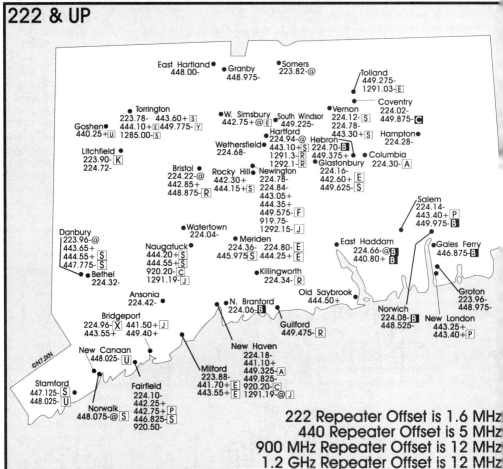

East Hartland ● 448.00-

● Granby 448.975-

● Somers 223.82-@

Tolland 449.275- 1291.03-[E]

Coventry 224.02- 449.875-[C]

● Torrington 223.78- 443.60+[S] 444.10+[E] 449.775-[Y] 1285.00-[S]

Goshen ● 440.25+[U]

Litchfield ● 223.90-[K] 224.72-

● W. Simsbury 442.75+@[E]

South Windsor 449.225-

Vernon 224.12-[S] 224.78- 443.30+[S]

Hampton ● 224.28-

Wethersfield ● 224.68-

Hartford 224.94-@ 443.10+[S] 1291.3-[R] 1292.1-[R]

Hebron 224.70-[B] 449.375+

Columbia 224.30-[A]

Bristol ● 224.22-@ 442.85+ 448.875-[R]

Rocky Hill ● 442.30+ 444.15+[S]

Newington 224.78- 224.84- 443.05+ 444.35+ 449.575+[F] 919.75- 1292.15-[J]

Glastonbury 224.16- 442.60+[E] 449.625-[S]

Salem 224.14- 443.40+[P] 449.975-[B]

● Watertown 224.04-

● Meriden 224.36- 445.975[S]

224.80-[E] 444.25+[E]

East Haddam 224.66-@[B] 440.80+[B]

● Gales Ferry 446.875-[B]

Danbury ● 223.96-@ 443.65+ 444.55+[S] 447.775-[S]

● Bethel 224.32-

Naugatuck ● 444.20+[S] 444.55+[S] 920.20-[C] 1291.19-[J]

● Killingworth 224.34-[S]

Old Saybrook 444.50+

Groton 223.96- 448.975-

Ansonia 224.42- ●

● N. Branford 224.06-[B]

Guilford 449.475-[R]

Norwich 224.08-[B] 448.525-

New London 443.25+ 443.40+[P]

Bridgeport 224.96-[X] 443.55+

441.50+[J] 449.40+

New Haven 224.18- 441.10+ 449.325+[A] 449.825-

New Canaan 448.025-[U]

Milford 223.88- 441.70+[E] 443.55+[E]

920.20-[C] 1291.19-@[J]

©N7JXN

Stamford 447.125-[S] 448.025-[U]

Norwalk 448.075-@[S]

Fairfield 224.10- 442.25+ 442.75+[P] 446.825-[S] 920.50-

222 Repeater Offset is 1.6 MHz
440 Repeater Offset is 5 MHz
900 MHz Repeater Offset is 12 MHz
1.2 GHz Repeater Offset is 12 MHz

CONNECTICUT FACTS

NUMBER OF HAMS: 9,012

CALL AREA: 1

STATE NICKNAME: CONSTITUTION STATE

HIGHEST POINT:
    MT. FRISSELL (S. SLOPE) (2,380 FT.)

STATE CAPITAL: HARTFORD

NUMBER OF COUNTIES: 10

NUMBER OF 2M REPEATERS: 62

222 REPEATERS: 32

440 REPEATERS: 54

900 MHz REPEATERS: 4

1.2 GHz REPEATERS: 7

CTCSS TONES

A=67.0	Q=107.2	E=173.8
B=69.3	R=110.9	F=179.9
C=71.9	S=114.8	G=186.2
D=74.4	T=118.8	H=192.8
E=77.0	U=123.0	J=203.5
F=79.7	V=127.3	K=206.5
G=82.5	W=131.8	L=210.7
H=85.4	X=136.5	M=218.1
J=88.5	Y=141.3	N=225.7
K=91.5	Z=146.2	P=229.1
L=94.8	A=151.4	Q=233.6
M=97.4	B=156.7	R=241.8
N=100.0	C=162.2	S=250.3
P=103.5	D=167.9	T=254.1

Connecticut
2 METERS

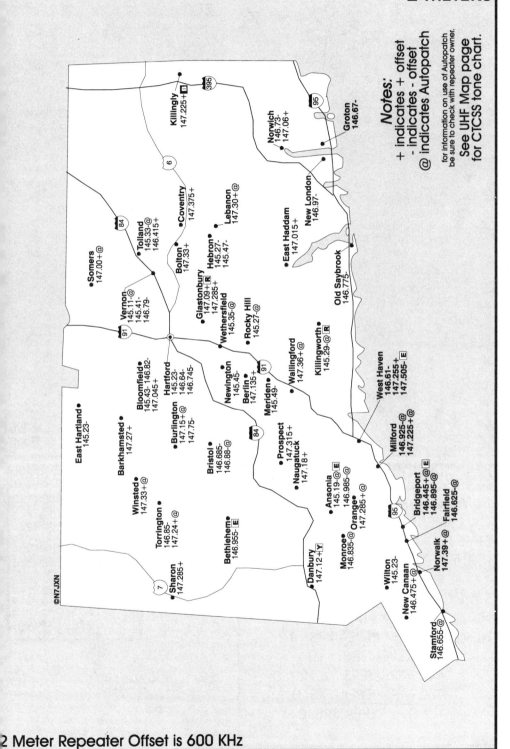

222 & UP

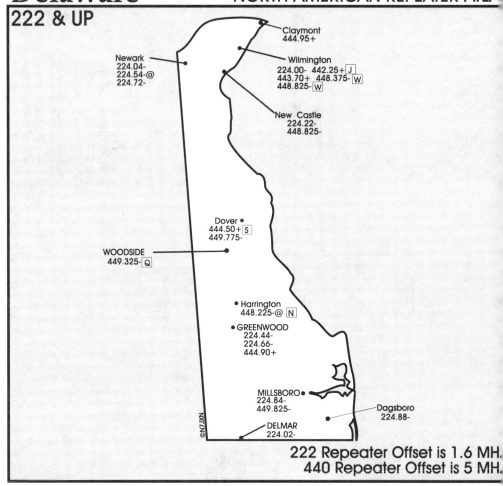

Claymont
444.95+

Newark
224.04-
224.54-@
224.72-

Wilmington
224.00- 442.25+ J
443.70+ 448.375- W
448.825- W

New Castle
224.22-
448.825-

Dover •
444.50+ S
449.775-

WOODSIDE
449.325- Q

Harrington
448.225-@ N

GREENWOOD
224.44-
224.66-
444.90+

MILLSBORO•
224.84-
449.825-

Dagsboro
224.88-

DELMAR
224.02-

NX7ZN©

222 Repeater Offset is 1.6 MH.
440 Repeater Offset is 5 MH.

DELAWARE FACTS

NUMBER OF HAMS: 1,403
CALL AREA: 3
STATE NICKNAME: FIRST STATE
HIGHEST POINT:
   EBRIGHT ROAD (442 FT.)
STATE CAPITAL: DOVER
NUMBER OF COUNTIES: 3
NUMBER OF 2M REPEATERS: 12
   222 REPEATERS: 10
   440 REPEATERS: 12
   900 MHz REPEATERS: 0
   1.2 GHz REPEATERS: 0

CTCSS TONES

A=67.0	Q=107.2	E=173.8
B=69.3	R=110.9	F=179.9
C=71.9	S=114.8	G=186.2
D=74.4	T=118.8	H=192.8
E=77.0	U=123.0	J=203.5
F=79.7	V=127.3	K=206.5
G=82.5	W=131.8	L=210.7
H=85.4	X=136.5	M=218.1
J=88.5	Y=141.3	N=225.7
K=91.5	Z=146.2	P=229.1
L=94.8	A=151.4	Q=233.6
M=97.4	B=156.7	R=241.8
N=100.0	C=162.2	S=250.3
P=103.5	D=167.9	T=254.1

28

Delaware
2 METERS

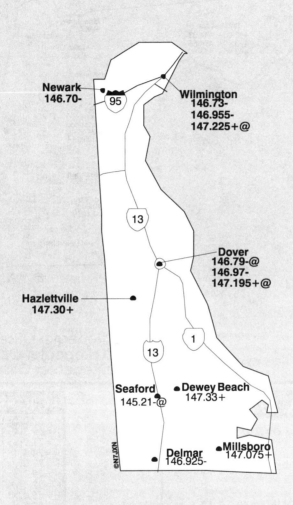

Newark
146.70-

95

Wilmington
146.73-
146.955-
147.225+@

13

Dover
146.79-@
146.97-
147.195+@

Hazlettville
147.30+

13

1

Seaford
145.21-@

Dewey Beach
147.33+

@N7JXN

Delmar
146.925-

Millsboro
147.075+

Notes:
+ indicates + offset
- indicates - offset
@ indicates Autopatch

for information on use of Autopatch
be sure to check with repeater owner.

See UHF Map page
for CTCSS tone chart.

2 Meter Repeater Offset is 600 KHz

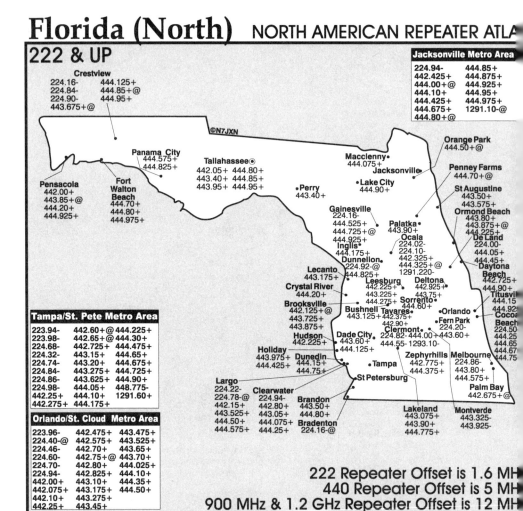

222 & UP

Jacksonville Metro Area

224.94-	444.85+
442.425+	444.875+
444.00+@	444.925+
444.10+	444.95+
444.425+	444.975+
444.675+	1291.10-@
444.80+@	

Crestview
224.16- 444.125+
224.84- 444.85+@
224.90- 444.95+
443.675+@

©N7JXN

Panama City
444.575+
444.825+

Tallahassee⊙
442.05+ 444.80+
443.40+ 444.85+
443.95+ 444.95+

Macclenny•
444.075+

Jacksonville•

Orange Park•
444.50+@

Penney Farms
444.70+@

Pensacola
442.00+
443.85+@
444.20+
444.925+

Fort Walton Beach
444.70+
444.80+
444.975+

•Perry
443.40+

•Lake City
444.90+

St Augustine
443.50+
443.575+

Ormond Beach
443.80+
443.875+@
444.225+

Gainesville
224.16-
444.525+
444.725+@
444.925+

Palatka•
443.90+

Ocala
224.02-
224.10-
442.325+
444.325+@
1291.220-

De Land
224.00-
444.05+
444.45+

Inglis
444.175+

Dunnellon•
224.92-@

Lecanto
443.175+

Leesburg
442.225+
443.225+
444.275+

Deltona
442.925+

Daytona Beach
442.725+
444.90+

Crystal River
444.20+

Brooksville
442.125+@
443.725+
443.875+

Bushnell Tavares•
443.125+ 442.375+
442.90+

Sorrento•
443.75+
444.60+

•Orlando

•Fern Park
224.20-

Titusville
444.15

Cocoa Beach
224.50
444.25
444.65
444.67
444.75

Hudson
442.225+

Dade City•
443.60+
444.125+

Clermont•
224.82- 444.00+ 443.60+
444.55- 1293.10-

Holiday
443.975+
444.425+

Dunedin•
444.15+
444.75+

Zephyrhills
442.775+
444.375+

Melbourne•
224.86-
443.80+
444.575+

•Tampa

Largo
224.22-
224.78-@
442.15+
443.525+
444.50+
444.575+

Clearwater
224.94-
442.80+
443.05+
444.075+
444.25+

St Petersburg•

Brandon
443.50+
444.80+

Bradenton
224.16-@

Palm Bay
442.675+@

Lakeland
443.075+
443.90+
444.775+

Montverde
443.325+
443.925-

Tampa/St. Pete Metro Area

223.94-	442.60+@	444.225+
223.98-	442.65+@	444.30+
224.68-	442.725+	444.475+
224.32-	443.15+	444.65+
224.74-	443.20+	444.675+
224.84-	443.275+	444.725+
224.86-	443.625+	444.90+
224.98-	444.05+	448.775-
442.25+	444.10+	1291.60+
442.275+	444.175+	

Orlando/St. Cloud Metro Area

223.96-	442.475+	443.475+
224.40-@	442.575+	443.525+
224.46-	442.70+	443.65+
224.60-	442.75+@	443.70+
224.70-	442.80+	444.025+
224.94-	442.825+	444.10+
442.00+	443.10+	444.35+
442.075+	443.175+	444.50+
442.10+	443.275+	
442.25+	443.45+	

222 Repeater Offset is 1.6 MH
440 Repeater Offset is 5 MH
900 MHz & 1.2 GHz Repeater Offset is 12 MH

FLORIDA FACTS

NUMBER OF HAMS: 39,959

CALL AREA: 4

STATE NICKNAME: SUNSHINE STATE

HIGHEST POINT:
WALTON COUNTY (345 FT.)

STATE CAPITAL: TALLAHASSEE

NUMBER OF COUNTIES: 67

NUMBER OF 2M REPEATERS: 254

222 REPEATERS: 31

440 REPEATERS: 92

900 MHz REPEATERS: 7

1.2 GHz REPEATERS: 3

CTCSS TONES

A=67.0	Q=107.2	E=173.8
B=69.3	R=110.9	F=179.9
C=71.9	S=114.8	G=186.2
D=74.4	T=118.8	H=192.8
E=77.0	U=123.0	J=203.5
F=79.7	V=127.3	K=206.5
G=82.5	W=131.8	L=210.7
H=85.4	X=136.5	M=218.1
J=88.5	Y=141.3	N=225.7
K=91.5	Z=146.2	P=229.1
L=94.8	A=151.4	Q=233.6
M=97.4	B=156.7	R=241.8
N=100.0	C=162.2	S=250.3
P=103.5	D=167.9	T=254.1

Florida(North)

2 METERS

Melbourne

145.31-	146.715-
145.43-	146.85-
145.47-@	@147.00-|Q|
146.61-	147.105+

Tampa/St. Pete Metro Area

145.15-	146.64-@	146.97-
145.27-@	146.745-	147.06+
145.29-	146.76-	147.075+
145.33-	146.79-	147.105+
145.41-	146.835-	147.21+|P|
145.43-	146.85-	147.24+@
145.47-	146.865-	147.315+
145.49-	146.94-	147.36+@

Orlando/St. Cloud Metro Area

145.11-|P|	146.73-|P|	147.09+
145.15-@	146.76-	147.12+|L|
145.21-|P|	146.79-	147.18+|V|
145.29-@	146.82-|P|	147.195+|P|
145.35-|V|	146.895-|V|	147.225+
145.45-	146.925-|P|	147.255+
146.625-	146.955-|P|	147.285+|P|
146.64-	147.015+|P|	147.30+@
146.70-	147.06+|P|	147.39+

Jacksonville Metropolitan Area

145.13-|P|	146.805-	147.075+
145.29-	146.76-	147.12+@
145.35-	146.88-	147.18+
145.45-|P|	146.925-	147.195+
145.41-	146.955-@	147.225+|P|
146.61-	147.00-	147.33+
146.76-	147.03+|P|	

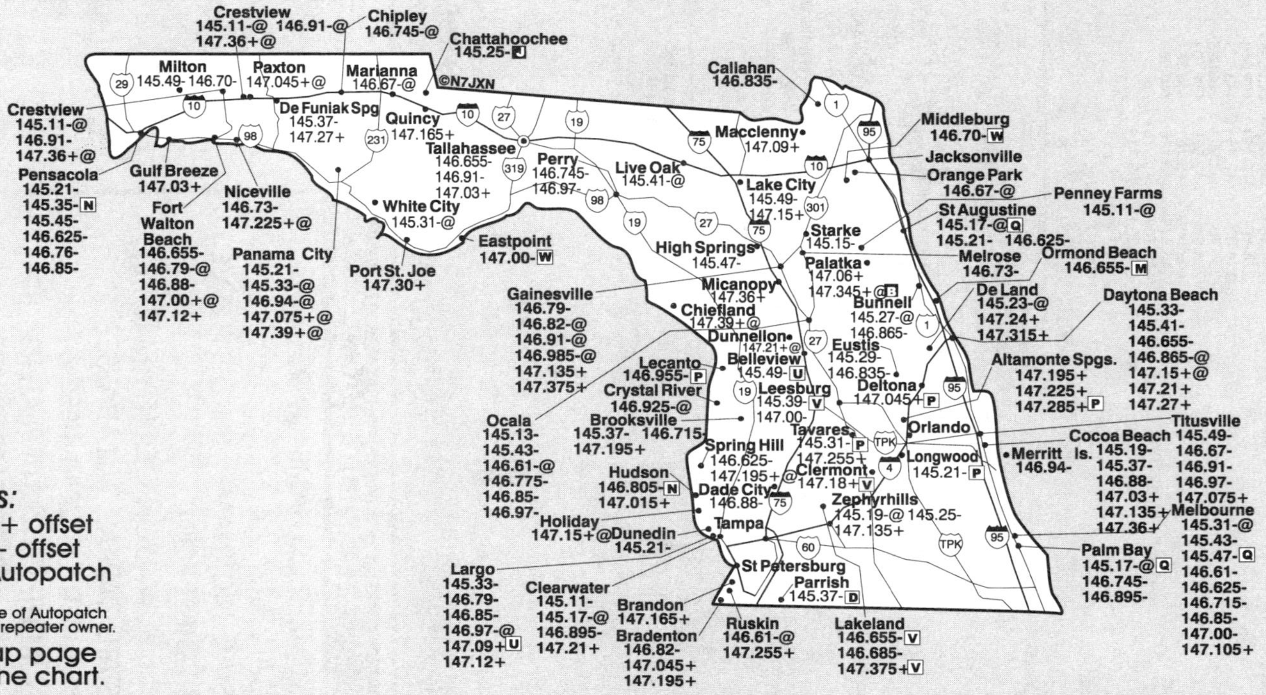

Notes:
+ indicates + offset
- indicates - offset
@ indicates Autopatch

for information on use of Autopatch
be sure to check with repeater owner.

**See UHF Map page
for CTCSS tone chart.**

2 Meter Repeater Offset is 600 KHz

Map location labels:

Titusville 145.49- / 146.67- / 146.61- / 146.625- / 146.91- / 146.97- / 146.715- / 146.85- / 147.00- / 147.105+

Palm Bay 145.17-|Q| / 145.31-@ / 145.47-|Q| / 145.43-/ 146.745- / 146.895-

Cocoa Beach 145.19- / 145.37- / 145.41-

Daytona Beach 145.33- / 146.655-

Ormond Beach 146.655-|M|

Penney Farms 145.11-@

Middleburg 146.70-|W|

Jacksonville 146.67-@

Orange Park 146.67-@

St Augustine 145.21- 146.625-

Melrose 146.73-

Altamonte Spgs. 146.865- / 147.195+ / 147.225+ / 147.285+|P|

De Land 145.23-@ / 147.24+ / 147.315+

Eustis 145.27-@ / 146.665-

Bunnell 146.835-

Deltona 146.835-

Longwood 145.21-|P|

Orlando 147.045+|P|

Zephyrhills 145.19-@ 145.25- / 147.135+

Tavares 145.31-|P|

Leesburg 147.195+ 146.88-|75|

Clermont 147.255+

Lake City 145.49- 147.15-|30|

Starke 145.15-

High Springs 145.47-

Micanopy 147.36+

Chiefland 147.39+@

Belleview 145.25-

Dunnellon 146.625-

Spring Hill 145.625- 146.715+

Macclenny 147.09+

Callahan 146.835-

Crystal River 146.925-

Lecanto 146.955-|P|

Brooksville 145.37- 147.015+

Hudson 146.805-|N|

Dade City 146.82-

Tampa 147.195+

Dunedin 145.21-

Holiday 147.15+

St Petersburg 145.37-|D|

Parrish

Ruskin 146.61-@ 147.255+

Lakeland 146.655-|V| / 146.685- / 147.375+|V|

Bradenton 146.82- / 147.045+ / 147.195+

Brandon 147.165+

Clearwater 145.11- / 145.17-@ / 146.895- / 147.21+

Largo 145.33- / 146.79- / 146.85- / 146.97-@ / 147.09+|U| / 147.12+

Ocala 145.13- / 145.43- / 146.61+@ / 146.775- / 146.85- / 146.97-

Gainesville 146.79- / 146.82-@ / 146.91-@ / 146.985-@ / 147.135+ / 147.375+

Live Oak 145.41-@

Perry 146.745- 146.97-@

Eastpoint 147.00-|W|

Port St.Joe 147.30+

Panama City 145.21- / 145.33-@ / 146.94-@ / 147.075+@ / 147.39+@

Niceville 146.73- / 147.225+@

Fort Walton Beach 146.655- / 146.79-@ / 146.88- / 147.00+@ / 147.12+

Gulf Breeze 147.03+

Milton 145.49- 146.70-

Crestview 145.11-@ 146.91-@ / 147.36+@

Paxton 147.045+@

De Funiak Spg 145.37- / 147.27+

Quincy 147.165+

Marianna 146.67-@

Chipley 146.745-@

Chattahoochee 145.25-|P|

NFJXN

Tallahassee 146.655- / 146.91- / 147.03+

White City 145.31-@

Pensacola 145.21- / 145.35-|N| / 145.45- / 146.625- / 146.76- / 146.85-

Crestview 145.11-@ / 146.91- / 147.36+@

2 Meter Repeater Offset is 600 KHz

31

222 & UP

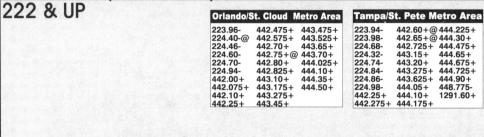

Orlando/St. Cloud Metro Area		
223.96-	442.475+	443.475+
224.40-@	442.575+	443.525+
224.46-	442.70+	443.65+
224.60-	442.75+@	443.70+
224.70-	442.80+	444.025+
224.94-	442.825+	444.10+
442.00+	443.10+	444.35+
442.075+	443.175+	444.50+
442.10+	443.275+	
442.25+	443.45+	

Tampa/St. Pete Metro Area		
223.94-	442.60+@	444.225+
223.98-	442.65+@	444.30+
224.68-	442.725+	444.475+
224.32-	443.15+	444.65+
224.74-	443.20+	444.675+
224.84-	443.275+	444.725+
224.86-	443.625+	444.90+
224.98-	444.05+	448.775-
442.25+	444.10+	1291.60+
442.275+	444.175+	

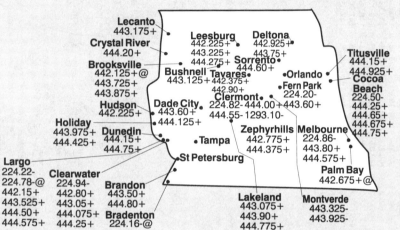

222 Repeater Offset is 1.6 MH
440 Repeater Offset is 5 MH
900 MHz & 1.2 GHz Repeater Offset is 12 MH

FLORIDA FACTS

NUMBER OF HAMS: 39,959

CALL AREA: 4

STATE NICKNAME: SUNSHINE STATE

HIGHEST POINT:
    WALTON COUNTY (345 FT.)

STATE CAPITAL: TALLAHASSEE

NUMBER OF COUNTIES: 67

NUMBER OF 2M REPEATERS: 89

    222 REPEATERS: 23

    440 REPEATERS: 81

    900 MHz REPEATERS: 7

    1.2 GHz REPEATERS: 2

CTCSS TONES

A=67.0	Q=107.2	E=173.8
B=69.3	R=110.9	F=179.9
C=71.9	S=114.8	G=186.2
D=74.4	T=118.8	H=192.8
E=77.0	U=123.0	J=203.5
F=79.7	V=127.3	K=206.5
G=82.5	W=131.8	L=210.7
H=85.4	X=136.5	M=218.1
J=88.5	Y=141.3	N=225.7
K=91.5	Z=146.2	P=229.1
L=94.8	A=151.4	Q=233.6
M=97.4	B=156.7	R=241.8
N=100.0	C=162.2	S=250.3
P=103.5	D=167.9	T=254.1

32

2 METERS

Melbourne	
145.31-	146.715-
145.43-	146.85-
145.47-@ Q	147.00- Q
146.61-	147.105+

Tampa/St. Pete Metro Area		
145.15-	146.64-@	146.97-
145.27-@	146.745-	147.06+
145.29-	146.76-	147.075+
145.33-	146.79-	147.105+
145.41-	146.835-	147.21+ P
145.43-	146.85-	147.24+@
145.47-	146.865-	147.315+
145.49-	146.94-	147.36+@

Orlando/St. Cloud Metro Area		
145.11- P	146.73- P	147.09+
145.15-@	146.76-	147.12+ L
145.21- P	146.79-	147.18+ V
145.29-@	146.82- P	147.195+ P
145.35- V	146.895- V	147.225+
145.45-	146.925- P	147.255+
146.625-	146.955- P	147.285+ P
146.64-	147.015+	147.30+@
146.70-	147.06+ P	147.39+

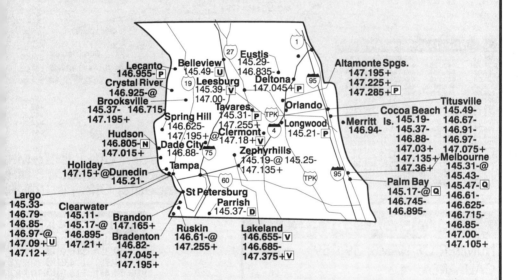

Notes:
+ indicates + offset
- indicates - offset
@ indicates Autopatch

for information on use of Autopatch
be sure to check with repeater owner.

**See UHF Map page
for CTCSS tone chart.**

Florida (South)

222 & UP

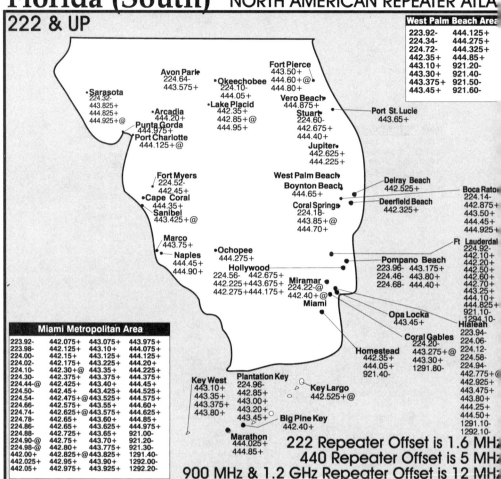

Avon Park
224.64-
443.575+

Okeechobee
224.10-
444.05+

Fort Pierce
443.50+
444.60+@
444.80+

Sarasota
224.32-
443.825+
444.825+
444.925+@

Arcadia
444.20+
Punta Gorda
444.975+
Port Charlotte
444.125+@

Lake Placid
442.35+
442.85+@
444.95+

Vero Beach
444.875+
Stuart
224.60-
442.675+
444.40+

Port St. Lucie
443.65+

Jupiter
442.625+
444.225+

Fort Myers
224.52-
442.45+
Cape Coral
444.35+
Sanibel
443.425+@

West Palm Beach
Boynton Beach
444.65+

Delray Beach
442.525+

Boca Rato
224.14-
442.875+
443.50+
444.45+
444.925+

Coral Springs
224.18-
443.85+@
444.70+

Deerfield Beach
442.325+

Marco
443.75+
Naples
444.45+
444.90+

Ochopee
444.275+

Ft Lauderdal
224.92-
442.10+
442.20+
442.50+
442.60+
442.70+
443.25+
444.10+
444.825+
921.10-
1294.10-

Hollywood
224.56- 442.675+
442.225+443.675+
442.275+444.175+

Miramar
224.22-@
442.40+@

Pompano Beach
223.96- 443.175+
224.46- 443.80+
224.68- 444.40+

Miami

Opa Locka
443.45+

Hialeah
223.94-
224.06-
224.12-
224.58-
224.94-
442.775+@
442.925+
443.475+
443.80+
444.25+
444.50+
1291.10-
1292.10-

Coral Gables
224.20-
443.275+@
443.30+
1291.80-

Homestead
442.35+
444.05+
921.40-

Key West
443.10+
443.35+
443.375+
443.80+

Plantation Key
224.96-
442.85+
443.00+
443.20+
443.45+

Big Pine Key
442.40+

Key Largo
442.525+@

Marathon
444.025+
444.85+

222 Repeater Offset is 1.6 MHz
440 Repeater Offset is 5 MHz
900 MHz & 1.2 GHz Repeater Offset is 12 MHz

FLORIDA FACTS

NUMBER OF HAMS: 39,959

CALL AREA: 4

STATE NICKNAME: SUNSHINE STATE

HIGHEST POINT:
       WALTON COUNTY (345 FT.)

STATE CAPITAL: TALLAHASSEE

NUMBER OF COUNTIES: 67

NUMBER OF 2M REPEATERS: 146

       222 REPEATERS: 39

       440 REPEATERS: 139

       900 MHz REPEATERS: 9

       1.2 GHz REPEATERS: 7

CTCSS TONES

A=67.0	Q=107.2	E=173.8	
B=69.3	R=110.9	F=179.9	
C=71.9	S=114.8	G=186.2	
D=74.4	T=118.8	H=192.8	
E=77.0	U=123.0	J=203.5	
F=79.7	V=127.3	K=206.5	
G=82.5	W=131.8	L=210.7	
H=85.4	X=136.5	M=218.1	
J=88.5	Y=141.3	N=225.7	
K=91.5	Z=146.2	P=229.1	
L=94.8	A=151.4	Q=233.6	
M=97.4	B=156.7	R=241.8	
N=100.0	C=162.2	S=250.3	
P=103.5	D=167.9	T=254.1	

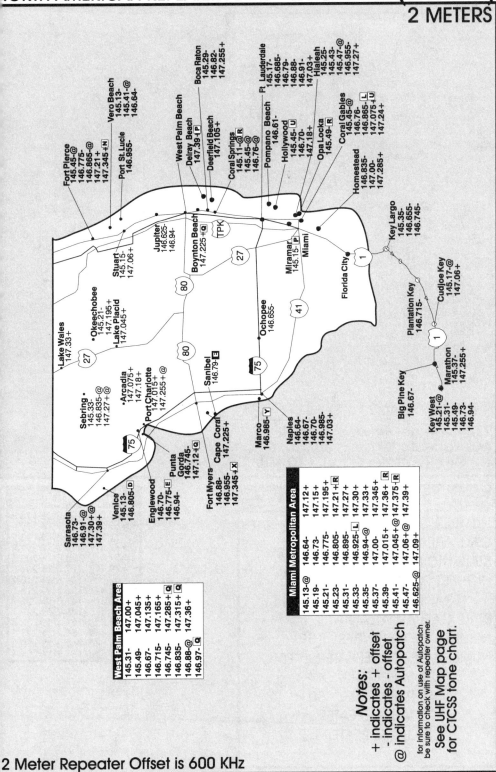

Vero Beach
145.13-
145.41-@
146.64-

Boca Raton
145.29-
146.82-
147.255+

Ft Lauderdale
145.17-
146.685-
146.79-
146.88-
146.91-
147.03+

Hialeah
145.25-
145.43-
145.47-@
146.955-
147.27+

Fort Pierce
145.45-@
146.775-
146.865-@
147.21+
147.345+N

West Palm Beach

Delray Beach
147.39+P

Deerfield Beach
147.105+

Coral Springs
145.11-@R
145.45-@
146.76-@

Pompano Beach
146.61-

Hollywood
145.45-U
146.70-
147.18+

Opa Locka
145.49-R

Coral Gables
145.45-@
146.76-
146.865-L
147.075-U
147.24+

Port St. Lucie
146.955-

Homestead
146.835-
147.00-
147.285+

Key Largo
145.35-
146.655-
146.745-

Stuart
145.15-
147.06+

Jupiter
146.625-
146.94-

Boynton Beach
147.225+Q

TPK

Miramar
145.15-P

Miami

Florida City

Cudjoe Key
145.17-@
147.06+

Plantation Key
146.715-

Lake Wales
147.33+

Okeechobee
145.21-
147.195+

Lake Placid
147.045+

Ochopee
146.655-

Sebring
145.33-
146.835-@
147.27+@

Arcadia
147.075+
147.18+

Port Charlotte
147.015+
147.255+@

Sanibel
146.79 E

Marco
146.985-Y

Naples
146.64-
146.67-
146.70-
146.985-
147.03+

Big Pine Key
146.67-

Key West
145.21-@
145.31-
145.49-
146.73-
146.94-

Marathon
145.37-
147.255+

Sarasota
146.73-
146.91-@
147.30+@
147.39+

Venice
145.13-
146.805-D

Englewood
146.70-
146.775-E
146.94-

Punta Gorda
146.745-
147.12+Q

Cape Coral
147.225+

Fort Myers
146.88-
146.955-
147.345+X

West Palm Beach Area

145.31-	147.00+
145.49-	147.045+
146.67-	147.135+
146.715-	147.165+
146.745-	147.285+Q
146.835-	147.315+Q
146.88-@	147.36+
146.97- Q	

Miami Metropolitan Area

145.13-@	147.12+
145.19-	147.15+
145.21-	147.195+
145.23-	147.21+R
145.31-	147.27+
145.33-	147.30+
145.35-	147.33+
145.37-	147.345+
145.39-	147.015+ 147.36+R
145.41-	147.045+@147.375+R
145.47-	147.06+@ 147.39+
146.625-@	147.09+

Additional column values: 146.64-, 146.73-, 146.775-, 146.805-, 146.895-, 146.925-L, 146.94-@, 147.00-

Notes:
+ indicates + offset
- indicates - offset
@ indicates Autopatch

for information on use of Autopatch
be sure to check with repeater owner.

See UHF Map page
for CTCSS tone chart.

2 Meter Repeater Offset is 600 KHz

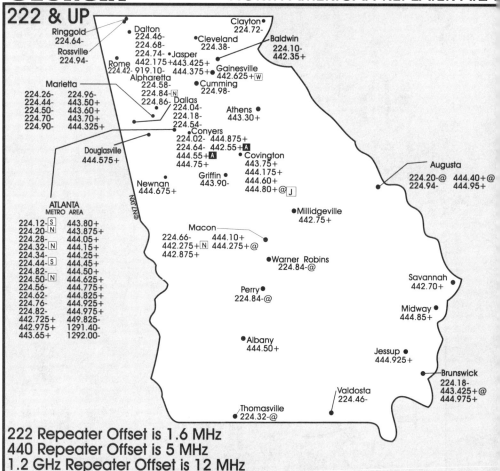

222 & UP

Ringgold
224.64-

Rossville
224.94-

Dalton
224.46-
224.68-
224.74-

Rome
224.42- 919.10-

Marietta
224.26- 224.96-
224.44- 443.50+
224.50- 443.60+
224.70- 443.70+
224.90- 444.325+

Alpharetta
224.58-
224.84-[N]
224.86-

Jasper
442.175+443.425+
444.375+

Clayton
224.72-

Cleveland
224.38-

Gainesville
442.625+[W]

Baldwin
224.10-
442.35+

Cumming
224.98-

Dallas
224.04-
224.18-
224.54-

Athens
443.30+

Conyers
224.02- 444.875+
224.64- 442.55+[A]
444.55+[A]
444.75+

Covington
443.75+
444.175+
444.60+
444.80+@[J]

Douglasville
444.575+

Griffin
443.90-

Newnan
444.675+

Augusta
224.20-@ 444.40+@
224.94-   444.95+

©NZN

ATLANTA
METRO AREA
224.12-[S] 443.80+
224.20-[N] 443.875+
224.28-   444.05+
224.32-[N] 444.15+
224.34-   444.25+
224.44-[S] 444.45+
224.82-   444.50+
224.50-[N] 444.625+
224.56-   444.775+
224.62-   444.825+
224.76-   444.925+
224.82-   444.975+
442.725+ 449.825-
442.975+ 1291.40-
443.65+   1292.00-

Macon
224.66-   444.10+
442.275+[N] 444.275+@
442.875+

Millidgeville
442.75+

Warner Robins
224.84-@

Perry
224.84-@

Savannah
442.70+

Midway
444.85+

Albany
444.50+

Jessup
444.925+

Brunswick
224.18-
443.425+@
444.975+

Valdosta
224.46-

Thomasville
224.32-@

222 Repeater Offset is 1.6 MHz
440 Repeater Offset is 5 MHz
1.2 GHz Repeater Offset is 12 MHz

GEORGIA FACTS

NUMBER OF HAMS: 12,714

CALL AREA: 4

STATE NICKNAME: EMPIRE STATE OF THE SOUTH

HIGHEST POINT:
    BRASSTOWN BALD (4,784 FT.)

STATE CAPITAL: ATLANTA

NUMBER OF COUNTIES: 159

NUMBER OF 2M REPEATERS: 155

222 REPEATERS: 44

440 REPEATERS: 50

900 MHz REPEATERS: 1

1.2 GHz REPEATERS: 2

CTCSS TONES

A=67.0	Q=107.2	E=173.8
B=69.3	R=110.9	F=179.9
C=71.9	S=114.8	G=186.2
D=74.4	T=118.8	H=192.8
E=77.0	U=123.0	J=203.5
F=79.7	V=127.3	K=206.5
G=82.5	W=131.8	L=210.7
H=85.4	X=136.5	M=218.1
J=88.5	Y=141.3	N=225.7
K=91.5	Z=146.2	P=229.1
L=94.8	A=151.4	Q=233.6
M=97.4	B=156.7	R=241.8
N=100.0	C=162.2	S=250.3
P=103.5	D=167.9	T=254.1

GEORGIA
2 METERS

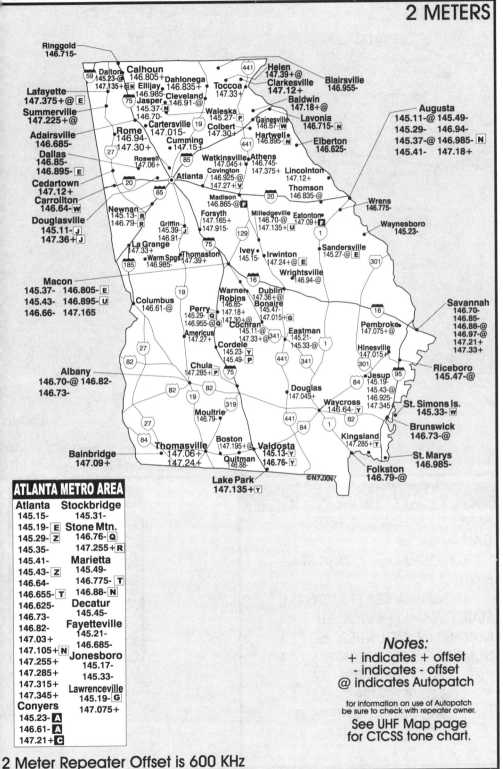

2 Meter Repeater Offset is 600 KHz

222 & UP

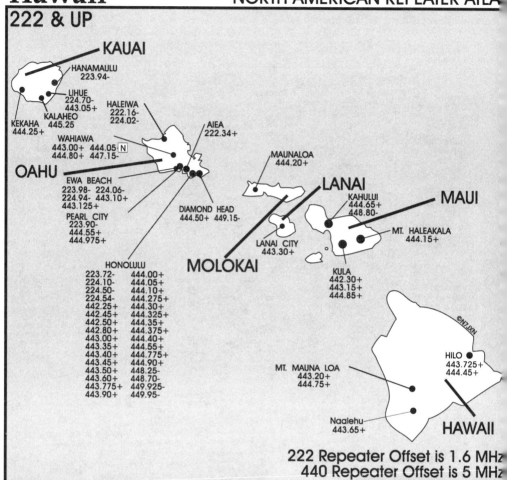

KAUAI

HANAMAULU
223.94-

LIHUE
224.70-
443.05+

KALAHEO
445.25

KEKAHA
444.25+

HALEIWA
222.16-
224.02-

AIEA
222.34+

WAHIAWA
443.00+ 444.05 [N]
444.80+ 447.15-

OAHU

EWA BEACH
223.98- 224.06-
224.94- 443.10+
443.125+

PEARL CITY
223.90-
444.55+
444.975+

DIAMOND HEAD
444.50+ 449.15-

MAUNALOA
444.20+

LANAI

KAHULUI
444.65+
448.80-

MAUI

MT. HALEAKALA
444.15+

LANAI CITY
443.30+

MOLOKAI

KULA
442.30+
443.15+
444.85+

HONOLULU
223.72-   444.00+
224.10-   444.05+
224.50-   444.10+
224.54-   444.275+
442.25+   444.30+
442.45+   444.325+
442.50+   444.35+
442.80+   444.375+
443.00+   444.40+
443.35+   444.55+
443.40+   444.775+
443.45+   444.90+
443.50+   448.25-
443.60+   448.70-
443.775+   449.925-
443.90+   449.95-

MT. MAUNA LOA
443.20+
444.75+

Naalehu
443.65+

HILO
443.725+
444.45+

HAWAII

©N7JXN

222 Repeater Offset is 1.6 MHz
440 Repeater Offset is 5 MHz

HAWAII FACTS

NUMBER OF HAMS: 3,180

CALL AREA: 6

STATE NICKNAME: ALOHA STATE

HIGHEST POINT:
      MAUNA KEA (13,796 FT.)

STATE CAPITAL: HONOLULU

NUMBER OF COUNTIES: 5

NUMBER OF 2M REPEATERS: 64

    222 REPEATERS: 13

    440 REPEATERS: 54

    900 MHz REPEATERS: 0

    1.2 GHz REPEATERS: 0

CTCSS TONES

A=67.0	Q=107.2	E=173.8
B=69.3	R=110.9	F=179.9
C=71.9	S=114.8	G=186.2
D=74.4	T=118.8	H=192.8
E=77.0	U=123.0	J=203.5
F=79.7	V=127.3	K=206.5
G=82.5	W=131.8	L=210.7
H=85.4	X=136.5	M=218.1
J=88.5	Y=141.3	N=225.7
K=91.5	Z=146.2	P=229.1
L=94.8	A=151.4	Q=233.6
M=97.4	B=156.7	R=241.8
N=100.0	C=162.2	S=250.3
P=103.5	D=167.9	T=254.1

Hawaii

2 METERS

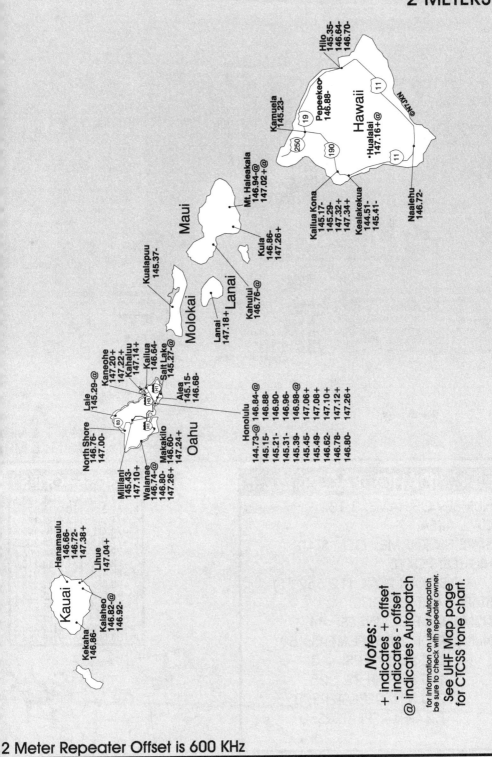

Hawaii

Hilo
145.35-
146.64-
146.70-

Pepeekeo
146.88-

Kamuela
145.23-

*Hualalai
147.16+@

Kailua Kona
145.17-
145.29-
147.32+
147.34+

Kealakekua
144.51-
145.41-

Naalehu
146.72-

11

19

250

190

11

Maui

Mt. Haleakala
146.94-@
147.02+@

Kula
146.86-
147.26+

Kualapuu
145.37-

Molokai

Lanai

Lanai
147.18+

Kahului
146.76-@

Oahu

Laie
145.29-@

Kaneohe
147.20+
147.22+

Kahaluu
147.14+

Kailua
146.64-

Salt Lake
145.27-@

Aiea
145.15-
146.68-

North Shore
146.76-
147.00-

Mililani
145.43-
147.10+

Waianae
146.74-@
146.80-
147.26+

Makakilo
146.60-
147.24+

Honolulu
144.73-@ 146.84-@
145.15-   146.88-
145.21-   146.90-
145.31-   146.96-
145.39-   146.98-@
145.45-   147.06+
145.49-   147.08+
146.62-   147.10+
146.78-   147.12+
146.80-   147.26+

Kauai

Hanamaulu
146.66-
146.72-
147.38+

Lihue
147.04+

Kalaheo
146.82-@
146.92-

Kekaha
146.86-

Notes:
+ indicates + offset
- indicates - offset
@ indicates Autopatch

for information on use of Autopatch
be sure to check with repeater owner.

See UHF Map page
for CTCSS tone chart.

2 Meter Repeater Offset is 600 KHz

Idaho

222 & UP

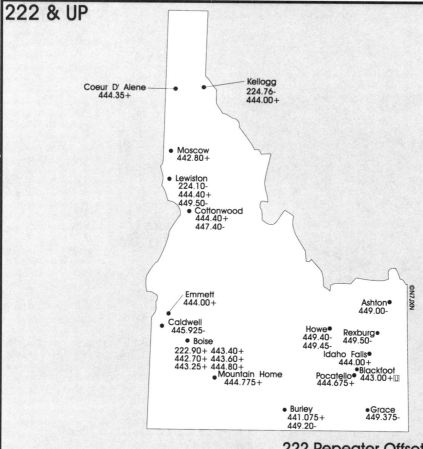

Coeur D' Alene
444.35+

Kellogg
224.76-
444.00+

Moscow
442.80+

Lewiston
224.10-
444.40+
449.50-

Cottonwood
444.40+
447.40-

Emmett
444.00+

Ashton●
449.00-

Caldwell
445.925-

Howe●
449.40-
449.45-

Rexburg●
449.50-

● Boise
222.90+ 443.40+
442.70+ 443.60+
443.25+ 444.80+

Idaho Falls●
444.00+

●Mountain Home
444.775+

Pocatello●
444.675+

●Blackfoot
443.00+

● Burley
441.075+
449.20-

●Grace
449.375-

©N7JXN

222 Repeater Offset is 1.6 MHz
440 Repeater Offset is 5 MHz

IDAHO FACTS

NUMBER OF HAMS: 3,130

CALL AREA: 7

STATE NICKNAME: GEM STATE

HIGHEST POINT:
BORAH PEAK (12,662 FT.)

STATE CAPITAL: BOISE

NUMBER OF COUNTIES: 44

NUMBER OF 2M REPEATERS: 59

222 REPEATERS: 3

440 REPEATERS: 25

900 MHz REPEATERS: 0

1.2 GHz REPEATERS: 0

CTCSS TONES

A=67.0	Q=107.2	E=173.8
B=69.3	R=110.9	F=179.9
C=71.9	S=114.8	G=186.2
D=74.4	T=118.8	H=192.8
E=77.0	U=123.0	J=203.5
F=79.7	V=127.3	K=206.5
G=82.5	W=131.8	L=210.7
H=85.4	X=136.5	M=218.1
J=88.5	Y=141.3	N=225.7
K=91.5	Z=146.2	P=229.1
L=94.8	A=151.4	Q=233.6
M=97.4	B=156.7	R=241.8
N=100.0	C=162.2	S=250.3
P=103.5	D=167.9	T=254.1

Idaho
2 METERS

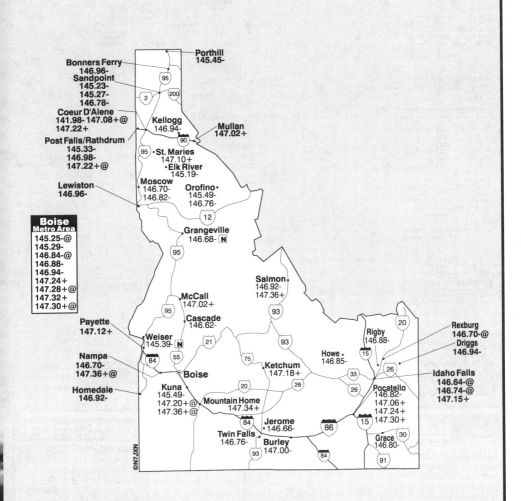

Porthill
145.45-

Bonners Ferry
146.96-
Sandpoint
145.23-
145.27-
146.78-
Coeur D'Alene
141.98- 147.08+@
147.22+
Post Falls/Rathdrum
145.33-
146.98-
147.22+@

Kellogg
146.94-

Mullan
147.02+

St. Maries
147.10+
Elk River
145.19-

Lewiston
146.96-

Moscow
146.70-
146.82-

Orofino
145.49-
146.76-

Boise
Metro Area
145.25-@
145.29-
146.84-@
146.88-
146.94-
147.24+
147.28+@
147.32+
147.30+@

Grangeville
146.68- N

Salmon
146.92-
147.36+

McCall
147.02+

Cascade
146.62-

Payette
147.12+

Weiser
145.39- N

Nampa
146.70-
147.36+@

Homedale
146.92-

Boise

Kuna
145.49-
147.20+@
147.36+@

Mountain Home
147.34+

Ketchum
147.18+

Howe
146.85-

Rigby
146.88-

Rexburg
146.70-@
Driggs
146.94-

Idaho Falls
146.64-@
146.74-@
147.15+

Pocatello
146.82-
147.06+
147.24+
147.30+

Jerome
146.66-

Twin Falls
146.76-

Burley
147.00-

Grace
146.80-

©N7JXN

Notes:
+ indicates + offset
- indicates - offset
@ indicates Autopatch

for information on use of Autopatch
be sure to check with repeater owner.

See UHF Map page
for CTCSS tone chart.

2 Meter Repeater Offset is 600 KHz

Illinois

222 & UP

Chicago Metro Area	
223.84- [R]	443.60+
224.02-	443.675+ [S]
224.06-	443.70+@ [S]
224.10-	443.75+
224.16-@ [R]	443.875+ [S]
224.22- [R]	443.975+
224.24-	444.00+
224.48-	444.375+ [S]
224.86- [Q]	444.50+
224.90- [S]	444.575+ [S]
442.075+ [N]	444.725+
442.175+	444.775+ [S]
442.375+	921.225-@
442.40+ [S]	919.90-
442.45+	1272.00-
442.575+	1292.10-@
442.975+ [S]	1292.30- [S]
443.00+	1292.40-
443.375- [S]	1292.50-

Springfield Metro Area	
224.68-	444.75+ [P]
442.60+@	444.825+
444.10+@	444.90+
444.40+@	1293.00-
444.50+ [P]	

St. Louis Metro Area	
224.06-	443.40+ [P]
224.12-@	443.50+@ [P]
224.20-	443.525+
224.30-	443.60+@ [P]
224.40-	443.70+@ [N]
224.48-	443.90+
224.70-	443.975+
442.075+@	444.225+
442.25+	444.25+
442.40+ [P]	444.375+@ [P]
442.525+	444.425+
442.90+	444.70+@
443.00+@ [P]	444.80+
443.10+	444.95+
443.30+	

Rockford Metro Area	
223.88-	442.25+@
224.04-	442.50+@ [S]
224.28-@	443.45+ [S]
224.44-	444.35+
442.075+@	444.85+

Peoria Metro Area	
443.00+@	444.375+@
444.00+@	444.55+@
444.20+	

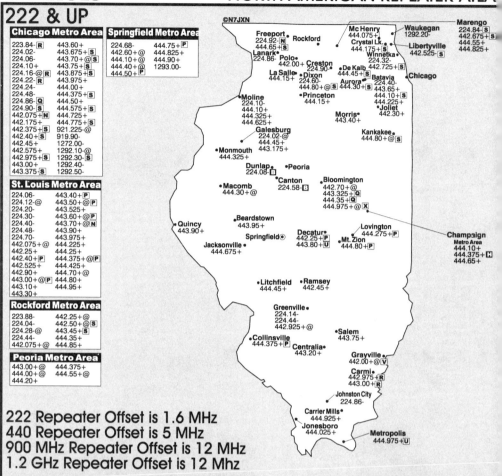

©N7JXN

Marengo 224.84- [S]
Mc Henry 444.075+
Waukegan 1292.20-
Freeport 224.92- [N]
Rockford
Crystal Lk. 444.175+ [S]
Libertyville 442.675+ [S]
442.55+
444.825+
Winnetka 442.525- [S]
Lanark 224.86-
Polo
Creston 442.00+ 224.90-
224.32-
Dixon 224.60-
De Kalb 442.725+ [S]
444.45+ [S]
La Salle 444.15+
Batavia 224.40-
444.80+@ [S]
Aurora 444.30+ [S] 443.65+
Chicago
444.10+ [S]
Moline 224.10- 444.10- 444.325+ 444.625+
Princeton 444.15+
444.225+
Joliet
Morris 443.40+
442.30+
Kankakee 444.80+@ [S]
Galesburg 224.02-@ 444.45+ 443.175+
Monmouth 444.325+
Dunlap 224.08- [B]
Peoria
Canton 224.58- [B]
Macomb 444.30+@
Bloomington 442.70+@ 443.325+ [Q] 444.35+ [Q] 444.975+@ [X]
Quincy 443.90+
Beardstown 443.95+
Lovington 444.275+ [P]
Decatur 442.25+ [P] 443.80+ [U]
Mt. Zion 444.80+ [P]
Springfield
Jacksonville 444.675+
Champaign Metro Area 444.10+ 444.375+ [H] 444.65+
Litchfield 444.45+
Ramsey 442.45+
Greenville 224.14- 224.44- 442.925+@
Salem 443.75+
Collinsville 444.375+ [P]
Centralia 443.20+
Grayville 442.00+@ [V]
Carmi 442.975+ [R] 443.00+ [R]
Johnston City 224.86-
Carrier Mills 444.925+
Jonesboro 444.025+
Metropolis 444.975+ [U]

222 Repeater Offset is 1.6 MHz
440 Repeater Offset is 5 MHz
900 MHz Repeater Offset is 12 MHz
1.2 GHz Repeater Offset is 12 Mhz

ILLINOIS FACTS

NUMBER OF HAMS: 23,043
CALL AREA: 9
STATE NICKNAME: PRAIRIE STATE
HIGHEST POINT:
    CHARLES MOUND (1,235 FT.)
STATE CAPITAL: SPRINGFIELD
NUMBER OF COUNTIES: 102
NUMBER OF 2M REPEATERS: 166
    222 REPEATERS: 36
    440 REPEATERS: 115
    900 MHz REPEATERS: 2
    1.2 GHz REPEATERS: 6

CTCSS TONES

A=67.0	Q=107.2	E=173.8
B=69.3	R=110.9	F=179.9
C=71.9	S=114.8	G=186.2
D=74.4	T=118.8	H=192.8
E=77.0	U=123.0	J=203.5
F=79.7	V=127.3	K=206.5
G=82.5	W=131.8	L=210.7
H=85.4	X=136.5	M=218.1
J=88.5	Y=141.3	N=225.7
K=91.5	Z=146.2	P=229.1
L=94.8	A=151.4	Q=233.6
M=97.4	B=156.7	R=241.8
N=100.0	C=162.2	S=250.3
P=103.5	D=167.9	T=254.1

Illinois
2 METERS

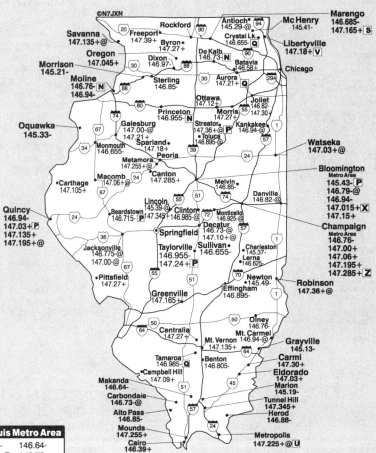

©N7JXN

Antioch• 145.29-@ 94
Rockford 20 Freeport• 147.39+
Marengo 146.685- 147.165+ S
Mc Henry 145.41-
Savanna 147.135+@
Byron• 147.27+
Crystal Lk.• 146.655-@
Libertyville 147.18+ V
Oregon 147.045+ 30
De Kalb 146.73- N 90
Dixon 146.97- 88
Morrison 145.21-
Chicago
Moline 146.76- N 146.94- 88
Sterling 146.85- 30
Batavia 146.58+
Aurora 147.21+ Q 294
Ottawa 147.12+ 80
Joliet 146.82- 55 147.30+
Princeton 146.955- N
Morris 147.27+
Oquawka 145.33- 74
Galesburg 147.00-@ 147.21+
Streator 147.36+@ P
Kankakee 146.94-@ 1
Toluca 146.895-@ 57
Monmouth 146.655- 34
Sparland 147.18+ 39
Peoria
Watseka 147.03+@
67
Metamora 147.255+@
Bloomington
Metro Area
145.43- P
146.79-@
146.94-
147.015+ X
147.15+
Carthage 147.105+ 67
Macomb 147.06+@ 24
Canton 147.285+
Melvin 146.85-
Danville 146.82-@
Champaign
Metro Area
146.76-
147.00+
147.06+
147.195+
147.285+ Z
Quincy 146.94- 147.03+ P 147.135+ 147.195+@ 24
Beardstown 146.715- P
Lincoln 145.39-@
Clinton 147.345+ 146.985-@
Monticello 146.925- 72
Decatur 146.73-@ 57
36
Springfield
Sullivan 146.655-
Charleston 145.37-
Lerna •146.625-
Robinson 147.36+@
Jacksonville 146.775-@ 147.00-@ 67
Taylorville 146.955- 147.24+ P
Newton •145.49-
Pittsfield 147.27+ 55
Greenville 147.165+
Effingham 146.895-
Olney 146.76-
Centralia 147.27+ 50
Mt. Carmel 146.94-@
Grayville 145.13-
Tamaroa 146.985- Q 64
Mt. Vernon 147.135+
Benton 146.805-
Carmi 147.30+
Eldorado 147.03+
Makanda 146.64-
Campbell Hill 147.09+ 51
Marion 145.19-
Tunnel Hill 147.345+
Carbondale 146.73-@
Herod 146.88-
Alto Pass 146.85-
Mounds 147.255+ 24
Cairo 146.39+
Metropolis 147.225+@ U

St. Louis Metro Area	
145.11-	146.64-
145.13-@	146.76-
145.23-@	146.79-
145.29-@	146.82-@
145.31-	146.865-
145.43-	147.12+
145.45-	147.21+ N
145.47-	

Peoria Metro Area	
145.15-	146.85-@
145.27-@	146.91-
145.45-@	146.97-@
146.67-@	147.075+ P
146.76-	147.27+@

Rockford Metro Area	
146.61-@	147.195+
146.805-	147.225+ Q
147.00+	147.375+ N

Springfield Metro Area	
146.64-@	147.045+@
146.685-	147.315+
146.745-	147.375+ R
146.805-@ L	

Chicago Metro Area		
145.11- Q	146.67- Q	147.015+ Q
145.15- Q	146.70- N	147.06
145.19-	146.715- Q	147.09+
145.21-	146.73- Q	147.135+
145.23- Q	146.76- Q	147.15+
145.25-	146.79- Q	147.195+ Q
145.27-	146.805- Q	147.225+ Q
145.31-	146.85-	147.285+ Q
145.33-	146.88- Q	147.315+
145.37-	146.925- Q	147.33+
145.39- Q	146.955- S	147.345+ Q
145.49- Q	146.97- Q	147.36+ X
146.64-	146.985-@ Q	

Notes:
+ indicates + offset
- indicates - offset
@ indicates Autopatch

for information on use of Autopatch
be sure to check with repeater owner.
**See UHF Map page
for CTCSS tone chart.**

2 Meter Repeater Offset is 600 KHz

222 & UP

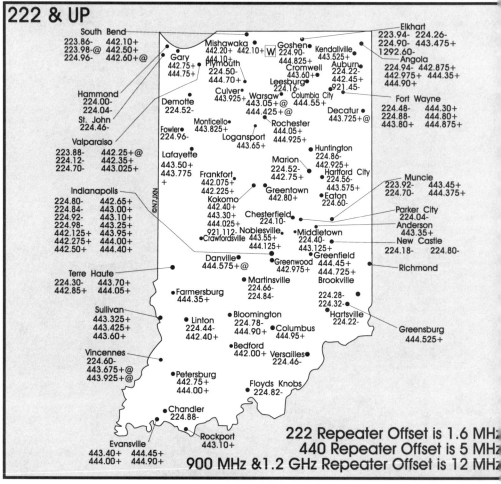

South Bend
223.86- 442.10+
223.98-@ 442.50+
224.96- 442.60+@

Gary
442.75+
444.75+

Mishawaka
442.20+ 442.10+ W

Plymouth
224.50-
444.70+

Leesburg
224.16-

Goshen
224.90-
444.825+

Cromwell
443.60+

Elkhart
223.94- 224.26-
224.90- 443.475+
1292.60-

Kendallville
443.525+

Auburn
224.22-
442.45+
921.45-

Angola
224.94- 442.875+
442.975+ 444.35+
444.90+

Hammond
224.00-
224.04-

St. John
224.46-

Demotte
224.52-

Culver
443.925+

Warsaw
443.05+@
444.425+@

Columbia City
444.55+

Decatur
443.725+@

Fort Wayne
224.48- 444.30+
224.88- 444.80+
443.80+ 444.875+

Valparaiso
223.88- 442.25+@
224.12- 442.35+
224.70- 443.025+

Fowler
224.96-

Monticello
443.825+

Logansport
443.65+

Rochester
444.05+
444.925+

Huntington
224.86-
442.925+

Hartford City
224.56-
443.575+

Muncie
223.92- 443.45+
224.70- 444.375+

Lafayette
443.50+
443.775
+

Frankfort
442.075+
442.225+

Marion
224.52-
442.75+

Eaton
224.60-

Indianapolis
224.80- 442.65+
224.84- 443.00+
224.92- 443.10+
224.98- 443.25+
442.125+ 443.95+
442.275+ 444.00+
442.50+ 444.40+

Kokomo
442.40+
443.30+
444.025+

Greentown
442.80+

Chesterfield
224.10-

Noblesville 443.55+
Crawfordsville 444.125+

Middletown
224.40-
443.125+

Parker City
224.04-

Anderson
443.35+

New Castle
224.18- 224.80-

Terre Haute
224.30- 443.70+
442.85+ 444.05+

Danville
444.575+@

Greenwood
442.975+

Greenfield
444.45+
444.725+

Brookville

Richmond

Sullivan
443.325+
443.425+
443.60+

Farmersburg
444.35+

Martinsville
224.66-
224.84-

224.28-
224.32-

Linton
224.44-
442.40+

Bloomington
224.78-
444.90+

Columbus
444.95+

Hartsville
224.22-

Greensburg
444.525+

Vincennes
224.60-
443.675+@
443.925+@

Bedford
442.00+

Versailles
224.46-

Petersburg
442.75+
444.00+

Floyds Knobs
224.82-

Chandler
224.88-

Rockport
443.10+

Evansville
443.40+ 444.45+
444.00+ 444.90+

222 Repeater Offset is 1.6 MHz
440 Repeater Offset is 5 MHz
900 MHz &1.2 GHz Repeater Offset is 12 MHz

©N7JXN

INDIANA FACTS

NUMBER OF HAMS: 14,392

CALL AREA: 9

STATE NICKNAME: HOOSIER STATE

HIGHEST POINT:
WAYNE COUNTY (1,257 FT.)

STATE CAPITAL: INDIANAPOLIS

NUMBER OF COUNTIES: 92

NUMBER OF 2M REPEATERS: 160

222 REPEATERS: 48

440 REPEATERS: 83

900 MHz REPEATERS: 1

1.2 GHz REPEATERS: 1

CTCSS TONES

A=67.0	Q=107.2	E=173.8
B=69.3	R=110.9	F=179.9
C=71.9	S=114.8	G=186.2
D=74.4	T=118.8	H=192.8
E=77.0	U=123.0	J=203.5
F=79.7	V=127.3	K=206.5
G=82.5	W=131.8	L=210.7
H=85.4	X=136.5	M=218.1
J=88.5	Y=141.3	N=225.7
K=91.5	Z=146.2	P=229.1
L=94.8	A=151.4	Q=233.6
M=97.4	B=156.7	R=241.8
N=100.0	C=162.2	S=250.3
P=103.5	D=167.9	T=254.1

Indiana
2 METERS

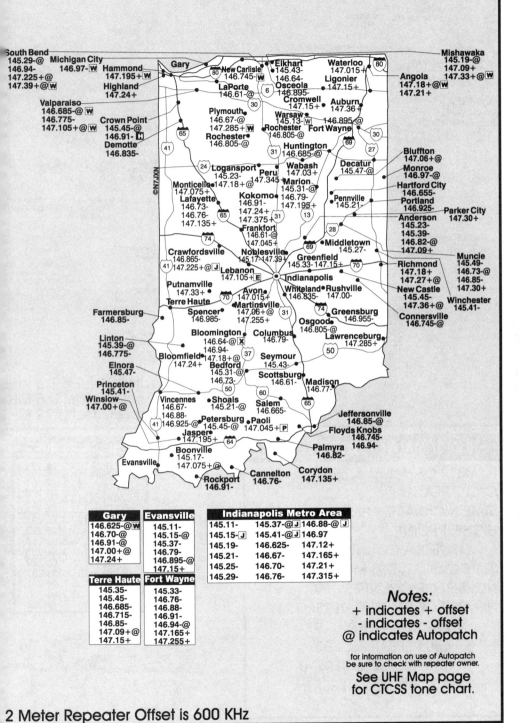

South Bend
145.29-@
146.94-
147.225+@
147.39+@ W

Michigan City
146.97- W

Hammond
147.195+ W

Highland
147.24+

Valparaiso
146.685-@ W
146.775-
147.105+@ W

Crown Point
145.45-@
146.91- H

Demotte
146.835-

Gary

New Carlisle
146.745- W

LaPorte
146.61-@

Plymouth
146.67-@
147.285+ W

Rochester
146.805-@

Elkhart
145.43-
146.64-

Osceola
146.895-

Cromwell
147.15+

Warsaw
145.13- W

Rochester
146.805-@

Waterloo
147.015+

Ligonier
147.15+

Auburn
147.36+

Fort Wayne
146.895-@

Mishawaka
145.19-@
147.09+
147.33+@ W

Angola
147.18+@ W
147.21+

Huntington
146.685-@

Logansport
145.23-

Monticello
147.075+

Lafayette
146.73-
146.76-
147.135+

Frankfort
146.61-@
147.045+

Peru
147.18+@

Wabash
147.03+

Marion
145.31-@
147.345

Kokomo
146.91-
147.24+
147.375+

Decatur
145.47-@

Pennville
145.21-

Middletown
145.27-

Bluffton
147.06+@

Monroe
146.97-@

Hartford City
146.655-

Portland
146.925-

Anderson
145.23-
145.39-
146.82-@
147.09+

Parker City
147.30+

Muncie
145.49-
146.73-@
146.85-
147.30+

Winchester
145.41-

Crawfordsville
146.865-
147.225+@ J

Lebanon
147.105+ E

Putnamville
147.33+

Terre Haute

Noblesville
145.17-147.39+

Greenfield
145.33-147.15+

Avon
147.015+

Whiteland
146.835-

Indianapolis

Rushville
147.00-

Richmond
147.18+
147.27+@

New Castle
145.45-
147.36+@

Connersville
146.745-@

Farmersburg
146.85-

Linton
145.39-@
146.775-

Elnora
145.47-

Princeton
145.41-

Winslow
147.00+@

Spencer
146.985-

Martinsville
147.06+@
147.255+

Bloomington
146.64-@ X
146.94-
147.18+@
147.24+

Bloomfield

Columbus
146.79-

Seymour
145.43-

Bedford
145.31-@
146.73-

Scottsburg
146.61-

Osgood
146.805-@

Greensburg
146.955-

Lawrenceburg
147.285+

Madison
146.77-

Vincennes
146.67-
146.88-
146.925-@

Petersburg
145.45-@

Jasper
147.195+

Boonville
145.17-
147.075+@

Shoals
145.21-@

Paoli
147.045+ P

Salem
146.665-

Jeffersonville
146.85-@

Floyds Knobs
146.745-
146.94-

Palmyra
146.82-

Evansville

Rockport
146.91-

Cannelton
146.76-

Corydon
147.135+

Gary	Evansville
146.625-@ W	145.11-
146.70-@	145.15-@
146.91-@	145.37-
147.00+@	146.79-
147.24+	146.895-@
	147.15+

Terre Haute	Fort Wayne
145.35-	145.33-
145.45-	146.76-
146.685-	146.88-
146.715-	146.91-
146.85-	146.94-@
147.09+@	147.165+
147.15+	147.255+

Indianapolis Metro Area		
145.11-	145.37-@ J	146.88-@ J
145.15- J	145.41-@ J	146.97
145.19-	146.625-	147.12+
145.21-	146.67-	147.165+
145.25-	146.70-	147.21+
145.29-	146.76-	147.315+

Notes:
+ indicates + offset
- indicates - offset
@ indicates Autopatch

for information on use of Autopatch
be sure to check with repeater owner.

See UHF Map page
for CTCSS tone chart.

2 Meter Repeater Offset is 600 KHz

Iowa

222 & UP

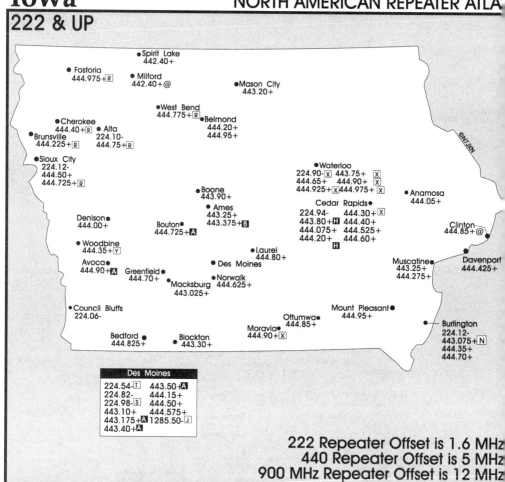

Spirit Lake
442.40+

Fostoria
444.975+ R

Milford
442.40+@

Mason City
443.20+

West Bend
444.775+ R

Cherokee
444.40+ R

Alta
224.10-
444.75+ R

Belmond
444.20+
444.95+

Brunsville
444.225+ R

Sioux City
224.12-
444.50+
444.725+ R

Waterloo
224.90- X   443.75+ X
444.65+   444.90+ X
444.925+ X 444.975+ X

Boone
443.90+

Anamosa
444.05+

Denison
444.00+

Ames
443.25+
443.375+ B

Cedar Rapids
224.94-   444.30+ X
443.80+ H 444.40+
444.075+   444.525+
444.20+   444.60+
H

Clinton
444.85+@

Bouton
444.725+ A

Woodbine
444.35+ Y

Laurel
444.80+

Muscatine
443.25+
444.275+

Davenport
444.425+

Avoca
444.90+ A

Des Moines

Greenfield
444.70+

Macksburg
443.025+

Norwalk
444.625+

Council Bluffs
224.06-

Mount Pleasant
444.95+

Bedford
444.825+

Blockton
443.30+

Moravia
444.90+ X

Ottumwa
444.85+

Burlington
224.12-
443.075+ N
444.35+
444.70+

Des Moines

224.54- T	443.50+ A
224.82-	444.15+
224.98- S	444.50+
443.10+	444.575+
443.175+ A	1285.50- J
443.40+ A	

222 Repeater Offset is 1.6 MHz
440 Repeater Offset is 5 MHz
900 MHz Repeater Offset is 12 MHz

IOWA FACTS

NUMBER OF HAMS: 6,758

CALL AREA: 0

STATE NICKNAME: HAWKEYE STATE

HIGHEST POINT:
    OSCEOLA COUNTY (1,670 FT.)

STATE CAPITAL: DES MOINES

NUMBER OF COUNTIES: 99

NUMBER OF 2M REPEATERS: 121

    222 REPEATERS: 9

    440 REPEATERS: 53

    900 MHz REPEATERS: 0

    1.2 GHz REPEATERS: 1

CTCSS TONES

A=67.0	Q=107.2	E=173.8	
B=69.3	R=110.9	F=179.9	
C=71.9	S=114.8	G=186.2	
D=74.4	T=118.8	H=192.8	
E=77.0	U=123.0	J=203.5	
F=79.7	V=127.3	K=206.5	
G=82.5	W=131.8	L=210.7	
H=85.4	X=136.5	M=218.1	
J=88.5	Y=141.3	N=225.7	
K=91.5	Z=146.2	P=229.1	
L=94.8	A=151.4	Q=233.6	
M=97.4	B=156.7	R=241.8	
N=100.0	C=162.2	S=250.3	
P=103.5	D=167.9	T=254.1	

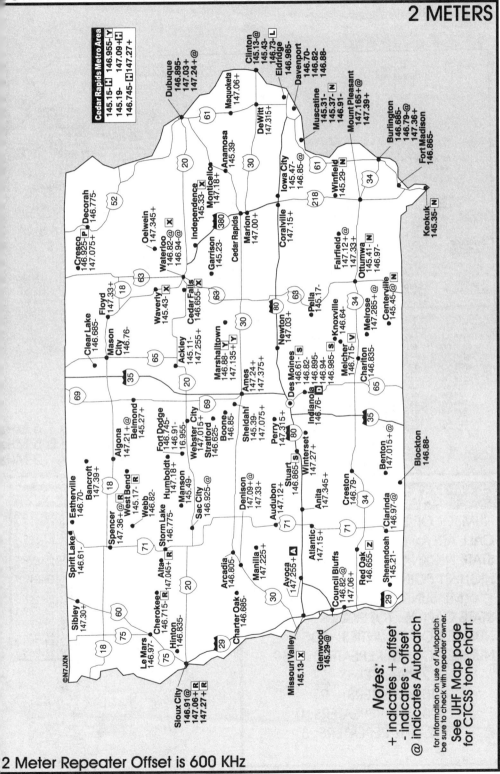

Cedar Rapids Metro Area
145.15- 146.955- Y
145.19- 147.09+ H
146.745- 147.27 +

Dubuque 146.895- 147.03+ 147.24+ @

Clinton 145.13-@ 145.43- L 146.73- Eldridge
Davenport 146.70- 146.82- 146.88-

Maquoketa 147.06+

DeWitt 147.315+

Muscatine 145.31- N 145.37- N 146.91-
Mount Pleasant 147.165+@ 147.39+

Burlington 146.685- 146.79-@ 147.36+

Fort Madison 146.865-

Decorah 146.775-

Cresco 146.925+ P 147.075+

Oelwein 147.345+

Independence 145.33- X Monticello 147.18+

Anamosa 145.39-

Iowa City 145.47- 146.85-@

Winfield 145.29- N

Keokuk 145.35- N

Waterloo 146.82-@ 146.94-@

Garrison 145.23-

Cedar Rapids

Marion 147.00+

Coralville 147.15+

Fairfield 147.12+@ 147.33+

Ottumwa 145.41- N 146.97-

Clear Lake 146.685-

Floyd 147.33+

Mason City 146.76-

Waverly 145.43+ X

Cedar Falls 146.655- X

Ackley 145.11- 147.255+

Marshalltown 147.135+ Y

Newton 147.03+

Pella 145.17-

Knoxville 146.64-

Melcher 146.985- S

Chariton 146.715- V 146.835-

Melrose 147.285+@

Centerville 145.45-@ N

Estherville 146.70-

Bancroft 147.39+

Spencer 147.36+@ R West Bend 145.17- R

Webb 146.82-

Algona 147.21+@

Belmond 145.27+

Fort Dodge 146.745- 146.91-

Humboldt 147.18+

Manson 145.49-

Webster City 147.015+ Stratford 146.625-

Boone 146.85-

Sheldahl 145.39- 147.075+

Perry 147.315+

Ames 147.24+ 147.375+

Des Moines 146.61- S 146.82- 146.94- 146.985- S

Indianola 146.76- D

Benton 147.015+@

Blockton 146.88-

Spirit Lake 146.61-

Sibley 147.30+

Hinton 146.835-

Le Mars 146.97-

Cherokee 146.715- R 146.835-

Altoona 147.045+ R

Storm Lake 146.775- R

Sac City 146.925-@

Arcadia 146.805-

Charter Oak 146.685-

Manilla 147.225+

Avoca 147.255+ A

Denison 147.09+@ 147.33+

Audubon 147.12+

Atlantic 147.15+

Council Bluffs 146.82-@ R

Red Oak 146.655-

Shenandoah 145.21-

Clarinda 146.97-@

Winterset 147.27+

Anita 147.345+

Stuart 146.865- S

Creston 146.79-

Missouri Valley 145.13- X

Glenwood 145.29-@

Sioux City 146.91@ 147.06+ R 147.27+ R

@N7JXN

Notes:
+ indicates + offset
- indicates - offset
@ indicates Autopatch

for information on use of Autopatch
be sure to check with repeater owner.

See UHF Map page
for CTCSS tone chart.

2 Meter Repeater Offset is 600 KHz

47

222 & UP

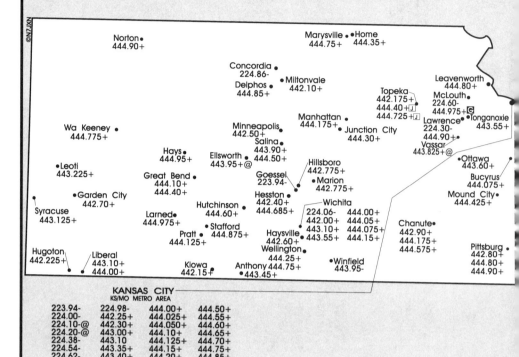

©N7XN

Norton•
444.90+

Marysville •• Home
444.75+ 444.35+

Concordia •
224.86-
Delphos • Miltonvale
444.85+ 442.10+

Leavenworth •
444.80+
Topeka • McLouth •
442.175+ 224.60-
444.40+J 444.975+G
444.725+J Lawrence • • Tonganoxie
224.30- 443.55+
444.90+•
Vassar
443.825+@

Wa Keeney •
444.775+

Minneapolis •
442.50+

Manhattan •
444.175+• Junction City
444.30+

Hays •
444.95+

Salina •
443.90+
Ellsworth • 444.50+
443.95+@

Hillsboro •
442.775+

Ottawa •
443.60+

•Leoti
443.225+

Great Bend •
444.10+
444.40+

Goessel •
223.94- Marion
442.775+

Bucyrus •
444.075+

•Garden City
442.70+

Hesston •
442.40+
Hutchinson • 444.685+
444.60+

Mound City•
444.425+

Syracuse •
443.125+

Larned•
444.975+

Wichita
224.06- 444.00+
442.00+ 444.05+
443.10+ 444.075+
442.60+• 443.55+ 444.15+

Chanute•
442.90+
444.175+
444.575+

Pratt • •Stafford
444.125+ •444.875+

Haysville •

Hugoton •
442.225+

Liberal
443.10+
444.00+

Kiowa
442.15+

Wellington •
444.25+
Anthony 444.75+
•443.45+

•Winfield
443.95-

Pittsburg •
442.80+
444.80+
444.90+

KANSAS CITY
KS/MO METRO AREA

223.94-	224.98-	444.00+	444.50+
224.00-	442.25+	444.025+	444.55+
224.10-@	442.30+	444.050+	444.60+
224.20-@	443.00+	444.10+	444.65+
224.38-	443.10	444.125+	444.70+
224.54-	443.35+	444.15+	444.75+
224.62-	443.40+	444.20+	444.85+
224.66-	443.55+	444.25+	444.875+
224.74-	443.65+	444.30+	444.95+
224.78-	443.725+	444.35+	1283.30-
224.90-	443.85+	444.375+	1284.85-
224.94-	443.95+	444.45+	1284.975-

222 Repeater Offset is 1.6 MHz
440 Repeater Offset is 5 MHz
1.2 GHz Repeater Offset is 12 MHz

KANSAS FACTS

NUMBER OF HAMS: 6,918

CALL AREA: 0

STATE NICKNAME: SUNFLOWER STATE

HIGHEST POINT:
    MT. SUNFLOWER (4,039 FT.)

STATE CAPITAL: TOPEKA

NUMBER OF COUNTIES: 105

NUMBER OF 2M REPEATERS: 139

    222 REPEATERS: 17

    440 REPEATERS: 91

    900 MHz REPEATERS: 0

    1.2 GHz REPEATERS: 3

CTCSS TONES

A=67.0	Q=107.2	E=173.8	
B=69.3	R=110.9	F=179.9	
C=71.9	S=114.8	G=186.2	
D=74.4	T=118.8	H=192.8	
E=77.0	U=123.0	J=203.5	
F=79.7	V=127.3	K=206.5	
G=82.5	W=131.8	L=210.7	
H=85.4	X=136.5	M=218.1	
J=88.5	Y=141.3	N=225.7	
K=91.5	Z=146.2	P=229.1	
L=94.8	A=151.4	Q=233.6	
M=97.4	B=156.7	R=241.8	
N=100.0	C=162.2	S=250.3	
P=103.5	D=167.9	T=254.1	

Kansas
2 METERS

Notes:
+ indicates + offset
- indicates - offset
@ indicates Autopatch

for information on use of Autopatch
be sure to check with repeater owner.

See UHF Map page
for CTCSS tone chart.

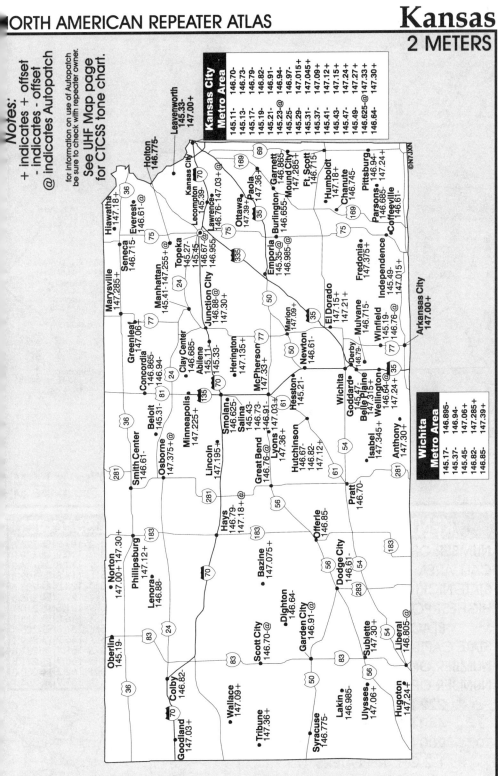

Kansas City Metro Area

145.11-	146.70-
145.13-	146.73-
145.17-	146.79-
145.19-	146.82-
145.21-	146.91-
145.23-@	146.94-
145.25-	146.97-
145.29-	147.015+
145.31-	147.045+
145.37-	147.09+
145.41-	147.12+
145.43-	147.15+
145.47-	147.24+
145.49-	147.27+
146.625-@	147.33+
146.64-	147.30+

Wichita Metro Area

145.17-	146.895-
145.37-	146.94-
145.45-	147.06+
146.82-	147.285+
146.85-	147.39+

Leavenworth 145.33- 147.00+

Holton 146.775-

Hiawatha 147.18+

Everest 146.61-@

Kansas City

Leavenworth

Lecompton 145.39-

Lawrence 146.76-147.03-@

Ottawa 147.39-

Paola 147.36-

Garnett 146.865-

Mound City 147.285+

Ft. Scott 146.715-

Humboldt 147.18+

Chanute 146.745-

Pittsburg 146.685- 147.24+

Parsons 146.94-

Coffeyville 146.61-

Marysville 147.285+

Seneca 146.715-

Greenleaf 147.06

Concordia 146.865-

Manhattan 145.41-147.255+@

Topeka 145.27- 145.35-

Junction City 146.88-@ 147.30+

Emporia 145.35-@ 146.985@

Burlington 146.655-

Fredonia 147.375+

Independence 145.49- 147.015+

Arkansas City 147.00+

Clay Center 146.685-

Abilene 145.11-

Herington 147.135+

McPherson 147.33+

Marion 147.09+

El Dorado 147.15+ 147.21+

Mulvane 146.715-

Winfield 145.19- 146.76-@

Anthony 147.30+

Beloit 145.31-

Minneapolis 147.225+

Smolan 146.625-

Salina 145.43-

Lyons 147.03+

Hutchinson 146.67- 146.82- 147.12+

Hesston 145.21-

Newton 146.61-

Wichita

Goddard 147.24+

Belle Plaine 147.315+

Wellington 147.24+

Isabel 147.345+

Derby 146.79-

Great Bend 146.73- 146.91- 146.76-@

Lincoln 147.195-*

Osborne 147.375+@

Smith Center 146.61-

Hays 146.79- 147.18+@

Offerle 146.85-

Pratt 146.70-

Phillipsburg 147.12+

Norton 147.00+ 147.30+

Lenora 146.88-

Bazine 147.075+

Dodge City 146.61-

Oberlin 145.19-

Colby 146.82-

Goodland 147.03+

Wallace 147.09+

Tribune 147.36+

Scott City 146.70-@

Dighton 146.64-

Garden City 146.91-@

Sublette 147.30+

Liberal 146.805-@

Syracuse 146.775-

Lakin 146.985-

Ulysses 147.06+

Hugoton 147.24+

222 & UP

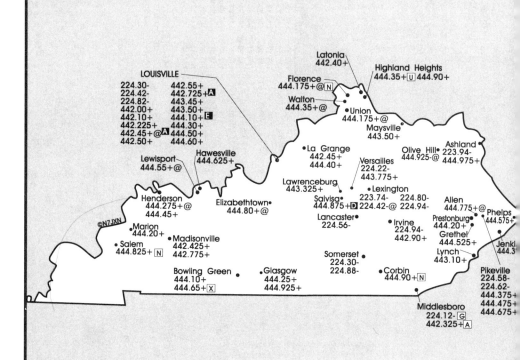

Latonia
442.40+

Highland Heights
444.35+ 444.90+

LOUISVILLE

Florence
444.175+@

Walton
444.35+@

224.30-	442.55+
224.42-	442.725+ A
224.82-	443.45+
442.00+	443.50+
442.10+	444.10+ E
442.225+	444.30+
442.45+@ A	444.50+
442.50+	444.60+

Union
444.175+@

Maysville
443.50+

Olive Hill
444.925-@

Ashland
223.94-
444.975+

Lewisport
444.55+@

Hawesville
444.625+

La Grange
442.45+
444.40+

Versailles
224.22-
443.775+

Lawrenceburg
443.325+

Lexington
223.74-   224.80-
224.42-@ 224.94-

Allen
444.775+@ Phelps
444.575+

Henderson
444.275+@
444.45+

Elizabethtown
444.80+@

Salvisa
444.875+ D

Lancaster
224.56-

Prestonburg
444.20+

Grethel
444.525+

Jenk
444.3

Marion
444.20+

Madisonville
442.425+
442.775+

Irvine
224.94-
442.90+

Lynch
443.10+

Salem
444.825+ N

Somerset
224.30-
224.88-

Corbin
444.90+ N

Pikeville
224.58-
224.62-
444.375+
444.475+
444.675+

Bowling Green
444.10+
444.65+ X

Glasgow
444.25+
444.925+

©N7JXN

Middlesboro
224.12- G
442.325+ A

222 Repeater Offset is 1.6 MH
440 Repeater Offset is 5 MH

KENTUCKY FACTS

NUMBER OF HAMS: 7,699

CALL AREA: 4

STATE NICKNAME: BLUEGRASS STATE

HIGHEST POINT:
        BLACK MTN. (4,145 FT.)

STATE CAPITAL: FRANKFORT

NUMBER OF COUNTIES: 123

NUMBER OF 2M REPEATERS: 113

        222 REPEATERS: 14

        440 REPEATERS: 51

        900 MHz REPEATERS: 0

        1.2 GHz REPEATERS: 0

CTCSS TONES

A=67.0	Q=107.2	E=173.8
B=69.3	R=110.9	F=179.9
C=71.9	S=114.8	G=186.2
D=74.4	T=118.8	H=192.8
E=77.0	U=123.0	J=203.5
F=79.7	V=127.3	K=206.5
G=82.5	W=131.8	L=210.7
H=85.4	X=136.5	M=218.1
J=88.5	Y=141.3	N=225.7
K=91.5	Z=146.2	P=229.1
L=94.8	A=151.4	Q=233.6
M=97.4	B=156.7	R=241.8
N=100.0	C=162.2	S=250.3
P=103.5	D=167.9	T=254.1

KENTUCKY
2 METERS

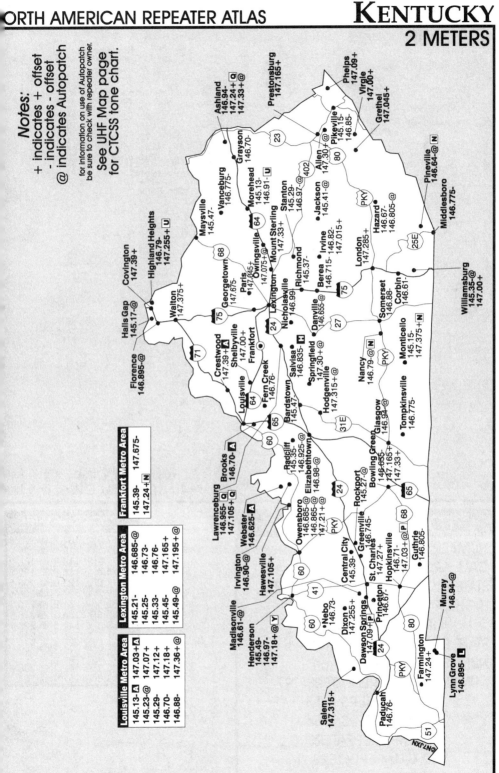

Notes:
+ indicates + offset
- indicates - offset
@ indicates Autopatch

for information on use of Autopatch
be sure to check with repeater owner.

**See UHF Map page
for CTCSS tone chart.**

Louisville Metro Area
145.13- A	147.03+
145.23-@	147.07+
145.29-	147.12+
146.70-	147.18+
146.88-	147.36+@

Lexington Metro Area
145.21-	146.685-@
145.25-	146.73-
145.33-	146.76-
145.45-	147.165+
145.49-@	147.195+@

Frankfort Metro Area
145.39-	147.675-
147.24+ N	

Ashland 146.94-
147.24+ Q
147.33+@

Prestonsburg 147.165+

Phelps 147.09+

Virgle 147.00+

Grethel 147.045+

Pineville 146.64-@ N

Middlesboro 146.775-

Williamsburg 145.35-@ 147.00+

Vanceburg 146.775-

Grayson 146.70-

23

Morehead 145.13
146.91- U

Pikeville 145.15-
146.85

Allen 147.30+
80

402

Hazard 146.67-
146.805-@

Corbin 146.61-

25E

Maysville 145.47-

68

Owingsville 147.075+@

Mount Sterling 147.33+

Stanton 145.29-
146.97-@

Jackson 145.41-@

Irvine 146.82-
147.015+

London 147.285+

75

Somerset 146.88-

Monticello 145.15-
147.375+ N

Georgetown 147.675-

Paris 147.045+

Lexington

Richmond 145.37-

Berea 146.715-

Danville 146.655-

27

Highland Heights 146.79-
147.255+ U

Covington 147.39+

Halls Gap 145.17-@

64

Nicholasville 146.99

Springfield 147.30+@

Nancy 146.79-@ N

PKY

Tompkinsville 146.775-

Walton 147.375+

75

Salvisa 146.835-

Hodgenville 147.315+@

31E

Glasgow 146.94-@

Florence 146.895-@

71

Crestwood 147.39+ A

Shelbyville 147.00+

Frankfort

24

H

Fern Creek 146.76-

Bardstown 145.47-

60

Bowling Green 146.665-
147.165+
147.33+

65

Louisville

64

65

60

Brooks 146.70+ A

Radcliff 145.35-
146.925-@

Elizabethtown 146.98-@

Rockport 145.27-@

68

Greenville 146.745-

Guthrie 146.805-

Lawrenceburg 146.995-Q
147.105+@

Webster 146.625-A

Owensboro 146.685-
146.865-@
147.21+@

24

St. Charles 147.27+

Hopkinsville 146.71-
147.03+@ P

P

Irvington 146.90-@

Hawesville 147.105+

60

Central City 145.39-

Princeton 146.87-

80

Murray 146.94-@

41

Madisonville 146.61-@

Dixon 147.255+

Dawson Springs 147.09+ P

24

PKY

Henderson 145.49-
146.97-
147.18+@ Y

Nebo 146.73-

Farmington 147.24+

Salem 147.315+

Paducah 146.76-

Lynn Grove 146.895-@ L

51

PADUCAH JCN

Louisiana

222 & UP

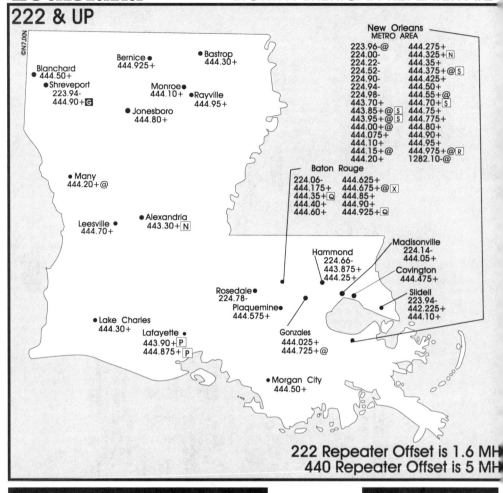

©N7JXN

New Orleans METRO AREA

223.96-@	444.275+
224.00-	444.325+ N
224.22-	444.35+
224.52-	444.375+@ S
224.90-	444.425+
224.94-	444.50+
224.98-	444.55+@
443.70+	444.70+ S
443.85+@ S	444.75+
443.95+@ S	444.775+
444.00+@	444.80+
444.075+	444.90+
444.10+	444.95+
444.15+@	444.975+@ R
444.20+	1282.10-@

Baton Rouge

224.06-	444.625+
444.175+	444.675+@ X
444.35+ Q	444.85+
444.40+	444.90+
444.60+	444.925+ Q

Bernice ● 444.925+

● Bastrop 444.30+

Blanchard ● 444.50+

● Shreveport 223.94- 444.90+ G

Monroe● 444.10+ ●Rayville 444.95+

● Jonesboro 444.80+

● Many 444.20+@

Leesville ● 444.70+

● Alexandria 443.30+ N

Madisonville 224.14- 444.05+

Hammond 224.66- 443.875+ 444.25+

Covington 444.475+

Slidell 223.94- 442.225+ 444.10+

Rosedale● 224.78-

Plaquemine● 444.575+

Gonzales 444.025+ 444.725+@

● Lake Charles 444.30+

Lafayette ● 443.90+ P 444.875+ P

● Morgan City 444.50+

222 Repeater Offset is 1.6 MH
440 Repeater Offset is 5 MH

LOUISIANA FACTS

NUMBER OF HAMS: 7,095

CALL AREA: 5

STATE NICKNAME: PELICAN STATE

HIGHEST POINT:
    DRISKILL MTN. (535 FT.)

STATE CAPITAL: BATON ROUGE

NUMBER OF PARISHES: 64

NUMBER OF 2M REPEATERS: 97

    222 REPEATERS: 13

    440 REPEATERS: 54

    900 MHz REPEATERS: 0

    1.2 GHz REPEATERS: 1

CTCSS TONES

A=67.0	Q=107.2	E=173.8
B=69.3	R=110.9	F=179.9
C=71.9	S=114.8	G=186.2
D=74.4	T=118.8	H=192.8
E=77.0	U=123.0	J=203.5
F=79.7	V=127.3	K=206.5
G=82.5	W=131.8	L=210.7
H=85.4	X=136.5	M=218.1
J=88.5	Y=141.3	N=225.7
K=91.5	Z=146.2	P=229.1
L=94.8	A=151.4	Q=233.6
M=97.4	B=156.7	R=241.8
N=100.0	C=162.2	S=250.3
P=103.5	D=167.9	T=254.1

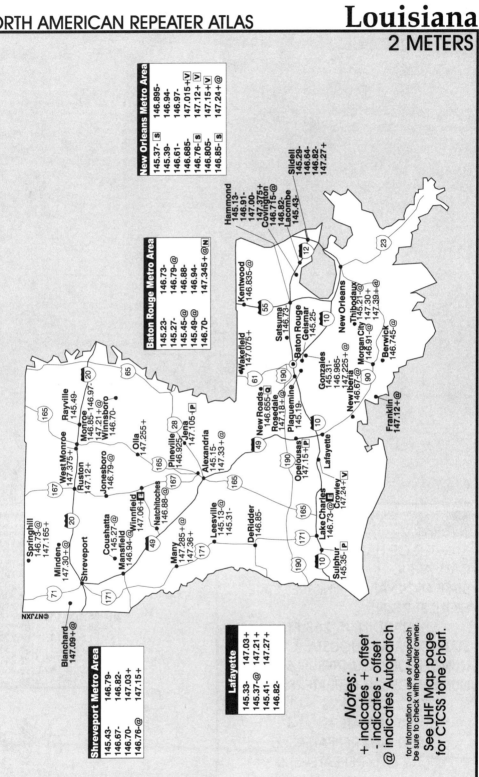

New Orleans Metro Area

145.37- S	146.895-
145.39-	146.94-
146.61-	146.97-
146.685-	147.015+ V
146.76- S	147.12+ V
146.805-	147.15+ V
146.85- S	147.24+ @

Baton Rouge Metro Area

145.23-	146.73-
145.27-	146.79-@
145.45-@	146.88-
145.49-@	146.94-
146.70-	147.345+@N

Shreveport Metro Area

145.43-	146.79-
146.67-	146.82-
146.70-	147.03+
146.76-@	147.15+

Lafayette

145.33-	147.03+
145.37-@	147.21+
145.41-	147.27+
146.82-	

Slidell
145.29-
146.64-
146.82-
147.27+

Hammond
145.13-
146.91-
147.00-
Covington 147.375+
146.715-@
Lacombe
145.43-

Kentwood
146.835-@

Wakefield
147.075+

Satsuma
146.73-

Baton Rouge

Geismar
145.25-

New Orleans

Thibodaux 145.21-@
Morgan City
146.91-@ 147.30+
147.39+@

Berwick
146.745-@

Franklin
147.12+@

Gonzales
145.31-
146.985-
147.225+@

New Iberia
146.67-

Opelousas
147.15+ P

Lafayette

Crowley
147.24+ V

Lake Charles
146.73-@ E

Sulphur
145.35- P

Plaquemine
145.19-

Rosedale
147.18+@

New Roads
146.655-Q

Leesville
145.13-@
145.31-

DeRidder
146.85-

Many
147.285+@
147.36+

Natchitoches
146.88-@

Winnfield
147.06+@ E

Coushatta
145.27-@

Mansfield
146.94-@

Shreveport

Minden
147.30+@

Springhill
146.73-@
147.165+

Blanchard
147.09+@

West Monroe
147.375+

Ruston
147.12+

Jonesboro
146.79-@

Monroe
146.85-146.97-
147.21+@
Winnsboro
146.70-

Rayville
145.49-

Olla
147.255+

Pineville
146.925-

Jena
147.105+ P

Alexandria
145.15-
147.33+@

Springhill
146.73-@
147.165+

©N7JXN

Kentwood ... (SH 12, 55, 10, 23, 20, 65, 165, 167, 71, 171, 49, 28, 61, 190, 90, 49, 165)

Notes:
+ indicates + offset
- indicates - offset
@ indicates Autopatch

for information on use of Autopatch
be sure to check with repeater owner.

**See UHF Map page
for CTCSS tone chart.**

222 & UP

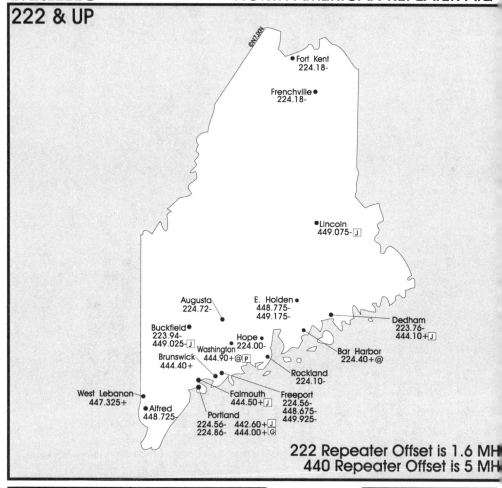

Fort Kent
224.18-

Frenchville ●
224.18-

● Lincoln
449.075- J

Augusta
224.72-

E. Holden ●
448.775-
449.175-

Dedham
223.76-
444.10+ J

Buckfield ●
223.94-
449.025- J

Hope ● 224.00-
Washington 444.90+@ P

Brunswick 444.40+
444.40+

Bar Harbor
224.40+@

Rockland
224.10-

West Lebanon
447.325+

● Alfred
448.725-

Falmouth
444.50+ J

Freeport
224.56-
448.675-
449.925-

Portland
224.56-   442.60+ J
224.86-   444.00+ G

222 Repeater Offset is 1.6 MH
440 Repeater Offset is 5 MH

MAINE FACTS

NUMBER OF HAMS: 4,059

CALL AREA: 1

STATE NICKNAME: PINE TREE STATE

HIGHEST POINT:
          KATAHDIN (5,268 FT.)

STATE CAPITAL: AUGUSTA

NUMBER OF COUNTIES: 16

NUMBER OF 2M REPEATERS: 60

          222 REPEATERS: 11

          440 REPEATERS: 14

          900 MHz REPEATERS: 0

          1.2 GHz REPEATERS: 0

CTCSS TONES

A=67.0	Q=107.2	E=173.8
B=69.3	R=110.9	F=179.9
C=71.9	S=114.8	G=186.2
D=74.4	T=118.8	H=192.8
E=77.0	U=123.0	J=203.5
F=79.7	V=127.3	K=206.5
G=82.5	W=131.8	L=210.7
H=85.4	X=136.5	M=218.1
J=88.5	Y=141.3	N=225.7
K=91.5	Z=146.2	P=229.1
L=94.8	A=151.4	Q=233.6
M=97.4	B=156.7	R=241.8
N=100.0	C=162.2	S=250.3
P=103.5	D=167.9	T=254.1

Maine
2 METERS

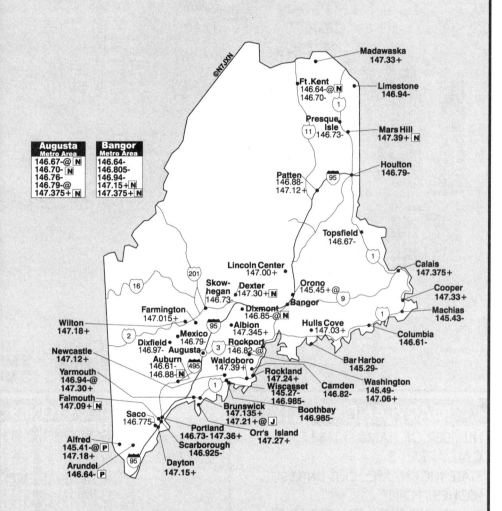

Madawaska
147.33+

Ft.Kent
146.64-@
146.70-

Limestone
146.94-

Presque Isle
146.73-

Mars Hill
147.39+

Houlton
146.79-

Patten
146.88-
147.12+

Topsfield
146.67-

Calais
147.375+

Lincoln Center
147.00+

Orono
145.45+@

Cooper
147.33+

Skowhegan
146.73-

Dexter
147.30+

Bangor

Machias
145.43-

Farmington
147.015+

Dixmont
146.85-@

Hulls Cove
147.03+

Columbia
146.61-

Wilton
147.18+

Albion
147.345+

Dixfield
146.97-

Mexico
146.79-

Augusta

Rockport
146.82-@

Bar Harbor
145.29-

Newcastle
147.12+

Auburn
146.61-
146.88-

Waldoboro
147.39+

Rockland
147.24+

Washington
145.49-
147.06+

Yarmouth
146.94-@
147.30+

Wiscasset
145.27-
146.985-

Camden
146.82-

Falmouth
147.09+

Brunswick
147.135+
147.21+@

Boothbay
146.985-

Saco
146.775-

Portland
146.73-147.36+

Orr's Island
147.27+

Alfred
145.41-@
147.18+

Scarborough
146.925-

Arundel
146.64-

Dayton
147.15+

Augusta Metro Area
146.67-@
146.70-
146.76-
146.79-@
147.375+

Bangor Metro Area
146.64-
146.805-
146.94-
147.15+
147.375+

Notes:
+ indicates + offset
- indicates - offset
@ indicates Autopatch

for information on use of Autopatch
be sure to check with repeater owner.
See UHF Map page
for CTCSS tone chart.

2 Meter Repeater Offset is 600 KHz

55

222 & UP

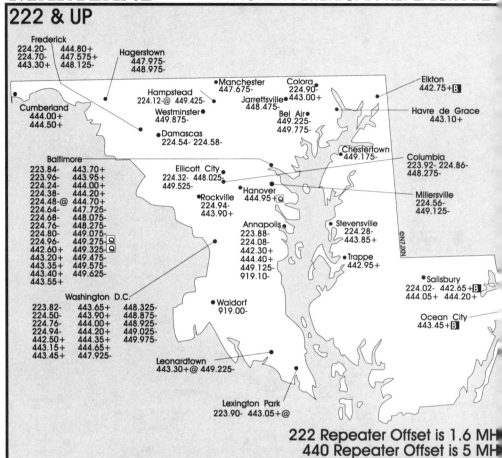

Frederick
224.20-   444.80+
224.70-   447.575+
443.30+   448.125-

Hagerstown
447.975-
448.975-

Manchester
447.675-

Colora
224.90-

Elkton
442.75+B

Cumberland
444.00+
444.50+

Hampstead
224.12-@ 449.425-

Jarrettsville•443.00+
448.475-

Havre de Grace
443.10+

Westminster•
449.875-

Bel Air•
449.225-
449.775-

Damascas
224.54- 224.58-

Chestertown
•449.175-

Columbia
223.92- 224.86-
448.275-

Baltimore
223.84-   443.70+
223.96-   443.95+
224.24-   444.00+
224.38-   444.20+
224.48-@ 444.70+
224.64-   447.725-
224.68-   448.075-
224.76-   448.275-
224.80-   449.075-
224.96-   449.275-Q
442.60+   449.325-Q
443.20+   449.475-
443.35+   449.575-
443.40+   449.625-
443.55+

Ellicott City
224.32- 448.025-
449.525-

Hanover
444.95+Q

Rockville
224.94-
443.90+

Millersville
224.56-
449.125-

Annapolis•
223.88-
224.08-
442.30+
444.40+
449.125-
919.10-

Stevensville
224.28-
443.85+

Trappe
442.95+

Salisbury
224.02- 442.65+B
444.05+ 444.20+

Washington D.C.
223.82-   443.65+   448.325-
224.50-   443.90+   448.875-
224.76-   444.00+   448.925-
224.94-   444.20+   449.025-
442.50+   444.35+   449.975-
443.15+   444.65+
443.45+   447.925-

Waldorf
919.00-

Ocean City
443.45+B

Leonardtown
443.30+@ 449.225-

Lexington Park
223.90- 443.05+@

222 Repeater Offset is 1.6 MH
440 Repeater Offset is 5 MH
900 MHz Repeater Offset is 12 MH

MARYLAND FACTS

NUMBER OF HAMS: 11,344

CALL AREA: 3

STATE NICKNAME: OLD LINE STATE

HIGHEST POINT:
  BACKBONE MTN. (3,360 FT.)

STATE CAPITAL: ANNAPOLIS

NUMBER OF COUNTIES: 24

NUMBER OF 2M REPEATERS: 83

222 REPEATERS: 30

440 REPEATERS: 69

900 MHz REPEATERS: 2

1.2 GHz REPEATERS: 0

CTCSS TONES

A=67.0	Q=107.2	E=173.8
B=69.3	R=110.9	F=179.9
C=71.9	S=114.8	G=186.2
D=74.4	T=118.8	H=192.8
E=77.0	U=123.0	J=203.5
F=79.7	V=127.3	K=206.5
G=82.5	W=131.8	L=210.7
H=85.4	X=136.5	M=218.1
J=88.5	Y=141.3	N=225.7
K=91.5	Z=146.2	P=229.1
L=94.8	A=151.4	Q=233.6
M=97.4	B=156.7	R=241.8
N=100.0	C=162.2	S=250.3
P=103.5	D=167.9	T=254.1

MARYLAND
2 METERS

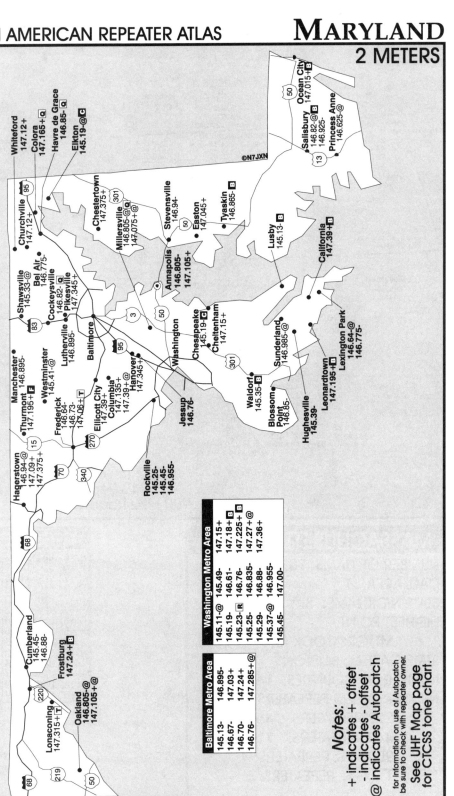

Whiteford 147.12+
Colora 147.165+ Q
Havre de Grace 146.85- Q
Elkton 145.19-@ C

Ocean City 147.015+ B
Salisbury 146.82-@ B
Princess Anne 146.625-@
146.925-

©N7JXN

Churchville 147.12+
95

Chestertown 147.375+
301
Millersville 146.805-@ Q
147.075+@

Stevensville 146.94-
Easton 147.045+
50
Tyaskin 146.865+ B

Lusby 145.13- B
California 147.39+ B

Shawsville 145.33-@
Bel Air 146.775-
Cockeysville
83
Pikesville 147.345+

Lutherville 146.895-
Baltimore
Annapolis 146.805- 147.105+

Washington
3
50

Chesapeake 145.19- C
Cheltenham 147.15+

Sunderland 146.985-@
301

Lexington Park 146.64-@ 146.775-

Manchester 146.895-
Thurmont 147.195+ F
147.09+
Westminster 145.41-@

Frederick 146.64- 146.73- 147.06+ T
Columbia 147.135+
Ellicott City 147.39+
Hanover 147.39+@ 147.345+
95

Jessup 146.76-

Waldorf 145.35- B

Blossom Point 146.85-
Hughesville 145.39-

Leonardtown 147.195+ B

Hagerstown 146.94-@
147.09+
147.375+
15
270

Rockville 145.25- 145.45- 146.955-

70
340

68

Cumberland 145.45- 146.88-
Frostburg 147.24+ B

Oakland 146.805-@ 147.105+@

Lonaconing 147.315+ T
220

68
219
50

Notes:
+ indicates + offset
- indicates - offset
@ indicates Autopatch

for information on use of Autopatch
be sure to check with repeater owner.

See UHF Map page
for CTCSS tone chart.

Meter Repeater Offset is 600 KHz

222 & UP

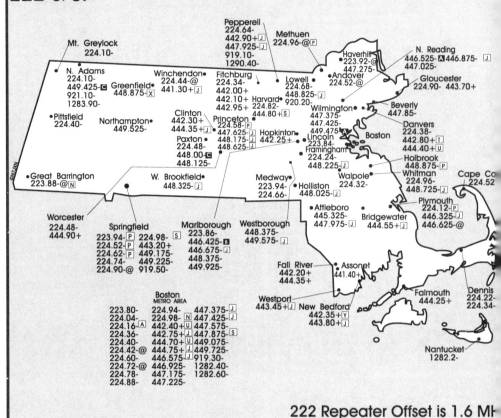

Mt. Greylock
224.10-

N. Adams
224.10-
449.425-☐
921.10-
1283.90-

Pittsfield
224.40-

Northampton•
449.525-

Winchendon•
224.44-@
441.30+☐

Greenfield•
448.875-☐

Pepperell
224.64-
442.90+☐
447.925-☐
919.10-
1290.40-

Methuen
224.96-@☐

Fitchburg
224.34-
442.00+
442.10+
442.95+

Harvard•
224.82-
444.80+☐

Lowell
224.68-
448.825-☐
920.20-

Haverhill
223.92-@
447.275-

Andover
224.52-@

N. Reading
446.525-☒ 446.875- ☐
447.025-

Gloucester
224.90- 443.70+

Clinton
442.30+
444.35+☐

Princeton
224.58-☐
447.625-☐
448.625-☐

Hopkinton•
442.25+

Wilmington•
447.375-
447.425-
449.475-

Beverly
447.85-

Danvers
224.38-
442.80+☐
444.40+☐

Paxton•
224.48-
448.00-☐
448.125-

Lincoln
223.84-
Framingham
224.24-
448.225-☐

Boston

Holbrook
448.875-☐

Great Barrington
223.88-@☐

W. Brookfield•
448.325-☐

Medway•
223.94-
224.66-

Holliston
448.025-☐

Walpole•
224.32-

Whitman
224.96-
448.725-☐

Cape Co
224.52

Worcester
224.48-
444.90+

Springfield
223.94-☐ 224.98-☐
224.52-☐ 443.20+
224.62-☐ 449.175-
224.74- 449.225-
224.90-@ 919.50-

Marlborough
223.86-
446.425-☐
446.675-☐
448.375-
449.925-

Westborough
448.375-
449.575-☐

Attleboro
445.325-
447.975-☐

Bridgewater
444.55+☐

Plymouth
224.12-☐
446.325-☐
446.625-@

Fall River
442.20+
444.35+

Assonet
441.40+

Falmouth
444.25+

Dennis
224.22-
224.34-

Westport
443.45+☐

New Bedford•
442.35+☐
443.80+☐

Nantucket
1282.2-

Boston
METRO AREA

223.80-   224.94-   447.375-☐
224.04-   224.98-☐   447.425-☐
224.16-☐   442.40+☐   447.575-
224.36-   442.75+☐   447.875-☐
224.40-   444.70+☐   449.075-
224.42-@   444.75+☐   449.725-
224.60-   446.575-☐   919.30-
224.72-@   446.925-   1282.40-
224.78-   447.175-   1282.60-
224.88-   447.225-

222 Repeater Offset is 1.6 MH
440 Repeater Offset is 5 MH
900 MHz Repeater Offset is 12 MH

MASSACHUSETTS FACTS

NUMBER OF HAMS: 15,510

CALL AREA: 1

STATE NICKNAME: BAY STATE

HIGHEST POINT:
    MT. GREYLOCK (3,491 FT.)

STATE CAPITAL: BOSTON

NUMBER OF COUNTIES: 14

NUMBER OF 2M REPEATERS: 86

    222 REPEATERS: 45

    440 REPEATERS: 71

    900 MHz REPEATERS: 4

    1.2 GHz REPEATERS: 5

CTCSS TONES

A=67.0	Q=107.2	E=173.8
B=69.3	R=110.9	F=179.9
C=71.9	S=114.8	G=186.2
D=74.4	T=118.8	H=192.8
E=77.0	U=123.0	J=203.5
F=79.7	V=127.3	K=206.5
G=82.5	W=131.8	L=210.7
H=85.4	X=136.5	M=218.1
J=88.5	Y=141.3	N=225.7
K=91.5	Z=146.2	P=229.1
L=94.8	A=151.4	Q=233.6
M=97.4	B=156.7	R=241.8
N=100.0	C=162.2	S=250.3
P=103.5	D=167.9	T=254.1

Massachusetts

2 METERS

E. Harwich
147.33+

Yarmouth
147.045+

Nantucket
145.31-

Provincetown
147.255-

Plymouth
146.685-

E. Sandwich
146.73-

Falmouth
146.655-

Weymouth
147.30+

Stoughton
146.775-

Fairhaven
145.49-

Topsfield
147.285+ Q

Beverly
147.39+

Lynn
145.33-

Danvers
147.015+

Scituate
145.39-

Gloucester
145.13- Q

Whitman
147.225+

Bridgewater
147.18+@ A

Wareham
147.315+

Andover
145.29- D
146.835-

Norwell
145.25-

Sharon
146.865-

Fall River
145.15-@ U

Haverhill
145.35-
146.625-

Boston

Framingham
147.15+@

Walpole
146.895-
147.09+

Attleboro
147.195+ N

Taunton
147.135+

Chelmsford
145.49- C

Billerica
147.12+

Maynard
147.24+ C

Foxboro
147.375+

Carlisle
146.955-

Southboro
145.27-

Medway
147.06+

Harvard
145.41-

Marlboro
146.61-
147.27+

Fitchburg
145.45-
147.315+

Clinton
146.655-@ D

Oxford
147.255+

Templeton
145.37-@

Warren
147.21+
Monson
147.105+

Paxton
146.97-

Worcester
146.925-

Greenfield
146.985- X

W. Brookfield
145.31-

Springfield
146.67-@
146.70-

Northampton
145.13- Y

North Adams
145.49-

Washington
146.715-

Great Barrington
145.27- N

Mt. Greylock
145.21-
146.91-

Pittsfield
145.29-
147.03+

Notes:
+ indicates + offset
- indicates - offset
@ indicates Autopatch

for information on use of Autopatch
be sure to check with repeater owner.

See UHF Map page
for CTCSS tone chart.

Boston Metropolitan Area	
145.11-	146.67-
145.21-@	146.715-
145.23- J	146.79-
145.27-	146.82-
145.31-	146.88-@
145.33-	146.91-
145.43-	146.985-
146.64-	147.015+
147.03+	
147.075+ A	
147.195+ N	
147.21+ N	
147.33+	
147.36+	
147.39+	

2 Meter Repeater Offset is 600 KHz

59

222 & UP

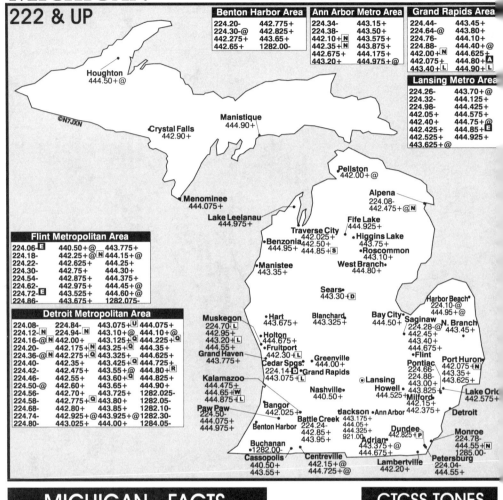

Benton Harbor Area

224.20-	442.775+
224.30-@	442.825+
442.275+	443.65+
442.65+	1282.00-

Ann Arbor Metro Area

224.34-	443.15+
224.38-	443.50+
442.10+[N]	443.575+
442.35+[N]	443.875+
442.675+	444.175+
443.20+	444.975+@

Grand Rapids Area

224.44-	443.45+
224.64-@	443.80+
224.76-	444.10+
224.88-	444.40+@
442.00+[N]	444.625+
442.075+	444.80+[A]
443.40+[L]	444.90+

Lansing Metro Area

224.26-	443.70+@
224.32-	444.125+
224.98-	444.425+
442.05+	444.575+
442.40+	444.75+@
442.425+	444.85+[E]
442.525+	444.925+
443.625+@	

Houghton
444.50+@

©N7JXN

Manistique
444.90+

Crystal Falls
442.90+

Pellston
442.00+@

Menominee
444.075+

Alpena
224.08-
442.475+@[N]

Lake Leelanau
444.975+

Fife Lake
444.925+

Traverse City
442.025+
Benzonia 442.50+
444.95+ 444.85+[S]

Higgins Lake
443.75+
Roscommon
West Branch•
444.80+

Manistee
443.35+

Sears•
443.30+[D]

Harbor Beach•
224.10-@
444.95+@

Flint Metropolitan Area

224.06-[E]	440.50+@	443.775+
224.18-	442.25+@[N]	444.15+@
224.22-	442.625+	444.25+
224.30-	442.75+	444.30+
224.54-	442.875+	444.375+
224.62-	442.975+	444.45+@
224.72-[E]	443.525+	444.60+@
224.86-	443.675+	1282.075-

Detroit Metropolitan Area

224.08-	224.84-	443.075+[U]	444.075+
224.12-[N]	224.94-[N]	443.10+@	444.10+@
224.16-@[N]	442.00+	443.125+@[Q]	444.225+[Q]
224.20-	442.175+[N]	443.25+[Q]	444.35+
224.36-@[N]	442.275+[Q]	443.325+	444.625+
224.40-	442.35+	443.55+@[Q]	444.725+
224.42-	442.475+	443.60+[Q]	444.80+[R]
224.46-	442.55+	443.60+[Q]	444.825+
224.50-@	442.60+	443.65+	444.90+
224.56-	442.70+	443.725+	1282.025-
224.58-	442.775+[Q]	443.80+	1282.05-
224.68-	442.80+	443.825+	1282.10-
224.74-	442.925+@	443.925+@	1282.30-
224.80-	443.025+	444.00+	1284.05-

Muskegon
224.70-[L]
442.95+
443.20+[L]
444.55+

• Hart
443.675+

Blanchard•
443.325+

Bay City•
444.50+

Saginaw
224.28-@
442.45+
443.40+
444.675+

N. Branch•
443.45+

Holton•
444.675+
Fruitport•

Greenville•
444.00+

Flint•

Grand Haven
443.775+

Cedar Spgs•
442.30+[L]

Pontiac
442.075+[N]

Port Huron
224.88-
443.00+

443.35+
443.625+

Grand Rapids
443.075+[L]

224.14-[D]

Kalamazoo
444.475+
444.65+[W]
444.875+[L]

Nashville•
440.50+

Lansing
Howell
444.525+

443.825+
Milford•
442.15+

Lake Ori[c]
442.575+

Bangor
442.025+

Paw Paw
224.50-
444.075+
444.975+

Jackson
443.175+
444.05+
444.325+
921.00

Ann Arbor 442.375+

Detroit

Battle Creek
224.24-
442.85+
443.95+

Dundee
442.825+[P]

Benton Harbor

Buchanan•
•1282.00-

Adrian•
443.375+@
444.675+

Monroe
224.78-
444.55+[N]
1285.00-

Cassopolis
440.50+
443.55+

Centreville•
442.15+@
444.725+@

Lambertville•
442.20+

Petersburg
224.04-
444.55+

MICHIGAN FACTS

NUMBER OF HAMS: 19,980

CALL AREA: 8

STATE NICKNAME: WOLVERINE STATE

HIGHEST POINT:
   MT. CURWOOD (1,980 FT.)

STATE CAPITAL: LANSING

NUMBER OF COUNTIES: 83

NUMBER OF 2M REPEATERS: 155

   222 REPEATERS: 39

   440 REPEATERS: 151

   900 MHz REPEATERS: 1

   1.2 GHz REPEATERS: 8

CTCSS TONES

[A]=67.0	[Q]=107.2	[E]=173.8
[B]=69.3	[R]=110.9	[F]=179.9
[C]=71.9	[S]=114.8	[G]=186.2
[D]=74.4	[T]=118.8	[H]=192.8
[E]=77.0	[U]=123.0	[J]=203.5
[F]=79.7	[V]=127.3	[K]=206.5
[G]=82.5	[W]=131.8	[L]=210.7
[H]=85.4	[X]=136.5	[M]=218.1
[J]=88.5	[Y]=141.3	[N]=225.7
[K]=91.5	[Z]=146.2	[P]=229.1
[L]=94.8	[A]=151.4	[Q]=233.6
[M]=97.4	[B]=156.7	[R]=241.8
[N]=100.0	[C]=162.2	[S]=250.3
[P]=103.5	[D]=167.9	[T]=254.1

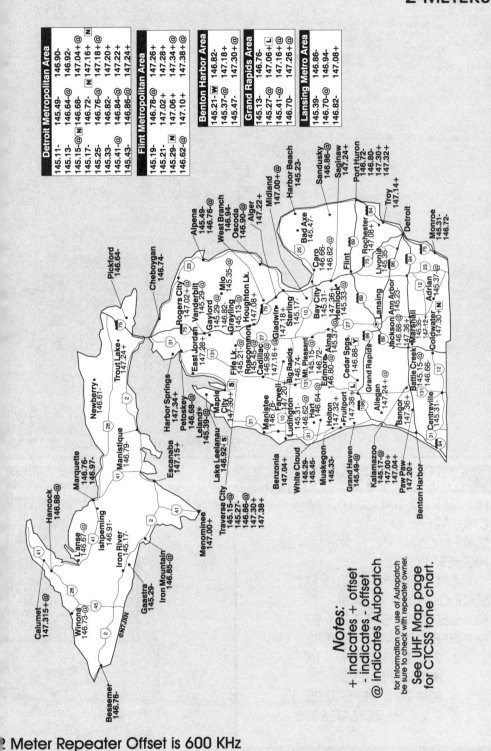

Detroit Metropolitan Area	
145.11-	146.90-
145.13-	146.92-
145.15-@	147.04+ @
145.17-	147.16+ [N]
145.25-	147.18+ @
145.33-	147.20+
145.41-@	147.22+
145.43-	147.24+

Flint Metropolitan Area	
145.19-	147.26+
145.21-	147.28+
145.29- [N]	147.34+ @
146.62-@	147.38+ @

Benton Harbor Area	
145.21- [W]	146.82-
145.37-@	147.18+
145.47-	147.30+ @

Grand Rapids Area	
145.13-	146.76-
145.27-@	147.06+ [L]
145.41-@	147.16+ @
146.70-	147.26+ @

Lansing Metro Area	
145.39-	146.86-
146.70-@	146.94-
146.82-	147.08+

Notes:
+ indicates + offset
- indicates - offset
@ indicates Autopatch

for information on use of Autopatch
be sure to check with repeater owner.

**See UHF Map page
for CTCSS tone chart.**

Meter Repeater Offset is 600 KHz

Minnesota

222 & UP

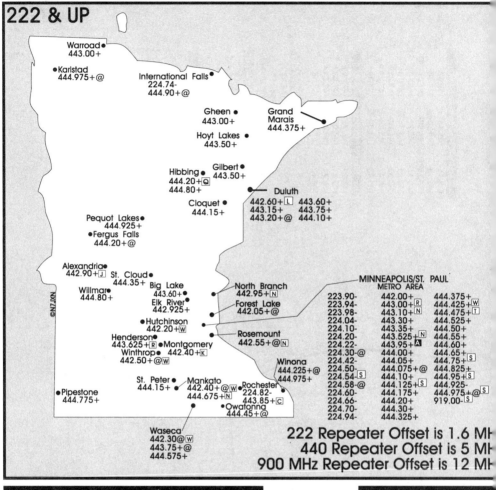

Warroad
443.00+

Karlstad
444.975+@

International Falls
224.74-
444.90+@

Gheen
443.00+

Grand Marais
444.375+

Hoyt Lakes
443.50+

Hibbing
444.20+Q
444.80+

Gilbert
443.50+

Cloquet
444.15+

Duluth
442.60+L 443.60+
443.15+   443.75+
443.20+@ 444.10+

Pequot Lakes
444.925+

Fergus Falls
444.20+@

Alexandria
442.90+J

St. Cloud
444.35+

Willmar
444.80+

Big Lake
443.60+

Elk River
442.925+

North Branch
442.95+N

Forest Lake
442.05+@

MINNEAPOLIS/ST. PAUL
METRO AREA

Hutchinson
442.20+W

Henderson
443.625+R

Winthrop
442.50+@W

Montgomery
442.40+K

Rosemount
442.55+@N

Winona
444.225+@
444.975+

223.90-	442.00+	444.375+
223.94-	443.00+R	444.425+W
223.98-	443.10+N	444.475+T
224.04-	443.30+	444.525+
224.10-	443.35+	444.50+
224.20-	443.525+N	444.55+
224.22-	443.95+A	444.60+
224.30-@	444.00+	444.65+S
224.42-	444.05+	444.75+S
224.50-	444.075+@	444.825+S
224.54-S	444.10+	444.95+S
224.58-@	444.125+S	444.925+
224.60-	444.175+	444.975+@S
224.66-	444.20+	919.00-S
224.70-	444.30+	
224.94-	444.325+	

St. Peter
444.15+

Mankato
442.40+@W
444.675+N

Rochester
224.82-
443.85+C

Owatonna
444.45+@

Pipestone
444.775+

Waseca
442.30+@W
443.75+@
444.575+

©N7XN

222 Repeater Offset is 1.6 MH
440 Repeater Offset is 5 MH
900 MHz Repeater Offset is 12 MH

MINNESOTA FACTS

NUMBER OF HAMS: 10,116

CALL AREA: 0

STATE NICKNAME: NORTH STAR STATE

HIGHEST POINT:
    EAGLE MTN. (2,301 FT.)

STATE CAPITAL: ST. PAUL

NUMBER OF COUNTIES: 87

NUMBER OF 2M REPEATERS: 136

    222 REPEATERS: 18

    440 REPEATERS: 70

    900 MHz REPEATERS: 1

    1.2 GHz REPEATERS: 0

CTCSS TONES

A=67.0	Q=107.2	E=173.8
B=69.3	R=110.9	F=179.9
C=71.9	S=114.8	G=186.2
D=74.4	T=118.8	H=192.8
E=77.0	U=123.0	J=203.5
F=79.7	V=127.3	K=206.5
G=82.5	W=131.8	L=210.7
H=85.4	X=136.5	M=218.1
J=88.5	Y=141.3	N=225.7
K=91.5	Z=146.2	P=229.1
L=94.8	A=151.4	Q=233.6
M=97.4	B=156.7	R=241.8
N=100.0	C=162.2	S=250.3
P=103.5	D=167.9	T=254.1

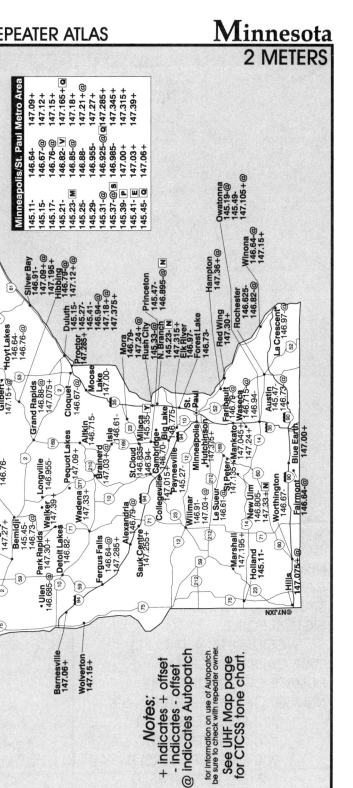

Minneapolis/St. Paul Metro Area			
145.11-		146.64-	147.09+
145.15-		146.67-@	147.12+
145.17-		146.76-@	147.15+
145.21-		146.82-🆅	147.165+🆀
145.23-Ⓜ		146.85-@	147.18+
145.25-		146.88-	147.21+@
145.29-		146.955-	147.27+
145.31-@		146.925-@Ⓠ	147.285+
145.37-@Ⓢ		146.985-	147.345+
145.39-Ⓟ		147.00+	147.315+
145.41-Ⓔ		147.03+	147.39+
145.45-Ⓠ		147.06+	

Grand Marais 146.895-

Silver Bay 146.91-
147.09+@
147.195+
Hibbing 146.79@
147.12+@

Ely 147.24+
Hoyt Lakes 146.76-@

Duluth 145.15-
145.27-
Proctor 145.41-
147.285+ 146.94-@
147.18+@
147.375+

Virginia 147.15+
Gilbert 147.21+ 147.15+@

Green 147.21+
147.15+@

Grand Rapids 146.88-@
147.075+

Cloquet 146.67-@

Moose Lake 147.00-

Mora 146.79-
147.24+@

Rush City 145.33-@
N.Branch 145.23-Ⓝ
147.315+
Elk River 146.97-
Forest Lake 146.73-

Princeton 145.47-
146.895-@ Ⓝ

Hampton 147.36+@

Owatonna 145.19-@
145.49-
147.105+@

Winona 146.64-@
147.15+

International Falls 146.61-@
146.97-

Roosevelt 147.00-

Big Falls 146.91-

Loman 146.67-
147.345+

Northome 146.76-

Longville 146.955-

Aitkin 146.715-

Brainerd 147.03+@

Isle 146.61-

Milaca 146.94-
147.015+

Cambridge 146.70-

Big Lake 146.775-

Minneapolis/St. Paul

Red Wing 147.30+

Rochester 146.625-
146.82-@

La Crescent 146.97-@

Wannaska 147.09+@

Greenbush 147.06+

Thief River Falls 146.85-

Lengby 147.27+

Bemidji 145.45-
146.73-@

Walker 147.39+

Park Rapids 147.30+

Ulen 146.685-@

Detroit Lakes 146.82-@

Pequot Lakes 147.09+

Wadena 147.33+

St.Cloud 146.835-Ⓨ
146.94-
145.35-Ⓥ

Paynesville 145.27-

Hutchinson 147.375+

Faribault 146.79-
Waseca 146.715-
146.94-

Austin 145.47
146.73-@

Karlstad 145.47-

Fisher 146.70-

Barnesville 147.06+

Wolverton 147.15+

Fergus Falls 146.64-@
147.285+

Alexandria 146.79-@

Sauk Centre 147.255+

Collegeville 147.015-

Willmar 146.91-
147.03-@

Le Sueur 146.61-@

Mankato 147.045+
147.24+

St.Peter 147.183+@

New Ulm 146.805-
147.33+Ⓝ

Worthington 146.67-

Blue Earth 147.00+

Fairmont 146.64-@

Hills 147.075+

Marshall 147.195+

Holland 145.11-

Notes:
\+ indicates + offset
\- indicates - offset
@ indicates Autopatch

for information on use of Autopatch
be sure to check with repeater owner.

See UHF Map page
for CTCSS tone chart.

222 & UP

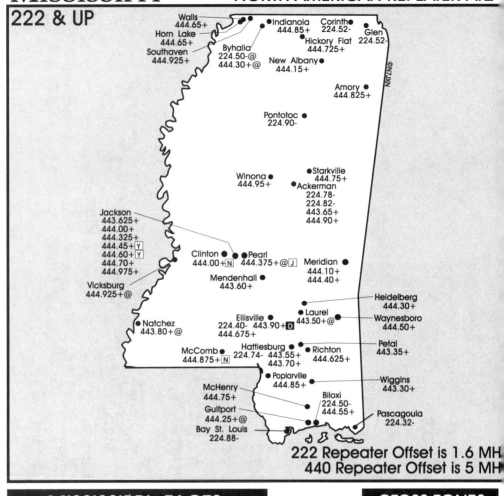

Walls
444.65+

Horn Lake
444.65+

Southaven
444.925+

Byhalia
224.50-@
444.30+@

Indianola
444.85+

Corinth
224.52-

Glen
224.52-

Hickory Flat
444.725+

New Albany
444.15+

Amory
444.825+

Pontotoc
224.90-

Winona
444.95+

Starkville
444.75+

Ackerman
224.78-
224.82-
443.65+
444.90+

Jackson
443.625+
444.00+
444.325+
444.45+ Y
444.60+ Y
444.70+
444.975+

Vicksburg
444.925+@

Clinton
444.00+ N

Pearl
444.375+@ J

Meridian
444.10+
444.40+

Mendenhall
443.60+

Heidelberg
444.30+

Natchez
443.80+@

Ellisville
224.40- 443.90+ D
444.675+

Laurel
443.50+@

Waynesboro
444.50+

Petal
443.35+

McComb
444.875+ N

Hattiesburg
224.74- 443.55+
443.70+

Richton
444.625+

Poplarville
444.85+

Wiggins
443.30+

McHenry
444.75+

Gulfport
444.25+@

Bay St. Louis
224.88-

Biloxi
224.50-
444.55+

Pascagoula
224.32-

222 Repeater Offset is 1.6 MH
440 Repeater Offset is 5 MH

MISSISSIPPI FACTS

NUMBER OF HAMS: 4,284

CALL AREA: 5

STATE NICKNAME: MAGNOLIA STATE

HIGHEST POINT:
    WOODALL MTN. (806 FT.)

STATE CAPITAL: JACKSON

NUMBER OF COUNTIES: 82

NUMBER OF 2M REPEATERS: 89

    222 REPEATERS: 11

    440 REPEATERS: 41

    900 MHz REPEATERS: 0

    1.2 GHz REPEATERS: 0

CTCSS TONES

A=67.0	Q=107.2	E=173.8
B=69.3	R=110.9	F=179.9
C=71.9	S=114.8	G=186.2
D=74.4	T=118.8	H=192.8
E=77.0	U=123.0	J=203.5
F=79.7	V=127.3	K=206.5
G=82.5	W=131.8	L=210.7
H=85.4	X=136.5	M=218.1
J=88.5	Y=141.3	N=225.7
K=91.5	Z=146.2	P=229.1
L=94.8	A=151.4	Q=233.6
M=97.4	B=156.7	R=241.8
N=100.0	C=162.2	S=250.3
P=103.5	D=167.9	T=254.1

MISSISSIPPI
2 METERS

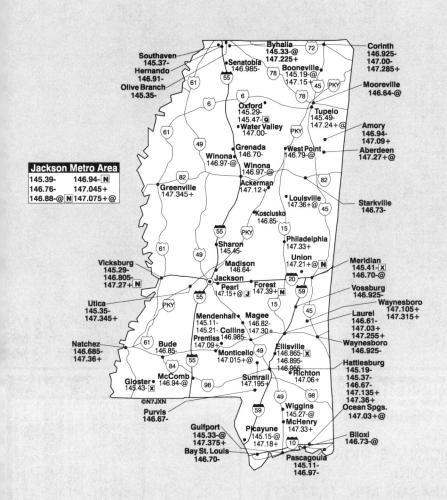

Byhalia 145.33-@ 147.225+

Corinth 146.925- 147.00- 147.285+

Southaven 145.37- **Hernando** 146.91- **Olive Branch** 145.35-

Senatobia 146.985-

Booneville 145.19-@ 147.15+

Mooreville 146.64-@

Oxford 145.29- 145.47-

Tupelo 145.49- 147.24+@

Amory 146.94- 147.09+

Water Valley 147.00-

Grenada 146.70-

West Point 146.79-@

Aberdeen 147.27+@

Winona 146.97-@

Winona 146.97-@

Greenville 147.345+

Ackerman 147.12+

Louisville 147.36+@

Starkville 146.73-

Kosciusko 146.85-

Jackson Metro Area
145.39-	146.94- N
146.76-	147.045+
146.88-@ N	147.075+@

Sharon 145.45-

Philadelphia 147.33+

Union 147.21+@ N

Meridian 145.41- X 146.70-@

Vicksburg 145.29- 146.805- 147.27+ N

Madison 146.64-

Jackson

Pearl 147.15+@ J

Forest 147.39+ N

Vossburg 146.925-

Utica 145.35- 147.345+

Mendenhall 145.11- 145.21-

Magee 146.82-

Collins 147.30+

Waynesboro 147.105+ 147.315+

Laurel 146.61- 147.03+ 147.255+

Natchez 146.685- 147.36+

Bude 146.85-

Prentiss 146.985-

Monticello 147.015+@

Ellisville 146.865- X 146.895- 146.955-

Waynesboro 146.925-

Hattiesburg 145.19- 145.37- 146.67- 147.135+ 147.36+

Gloster 145.43- X

McComb 146.94-@

Sumrall 147.195+

Richton 147.06+

Purvis 146.67-

©N7JXN

Wiggins 145.27-@

McHenry 147.33+

Ocean Spgs. 147.03+@

Gulfport 145.33-@ 147.375+

Picayune 145.15-@ 147.18+

Bay St. Louis 146.70-

Biloxi 146.73-@

Pascagoula 145.11- 146.97-

Notes:
+ indicates + offset
- indicates - offset
@ indicates Autopatch

for information on use of Autopatch
be sure to check with repeater owner.

**See UHF Map page
for CTCSS tone chart.**

2 Meter Repeater Offset is 600 KHz

222 & UP

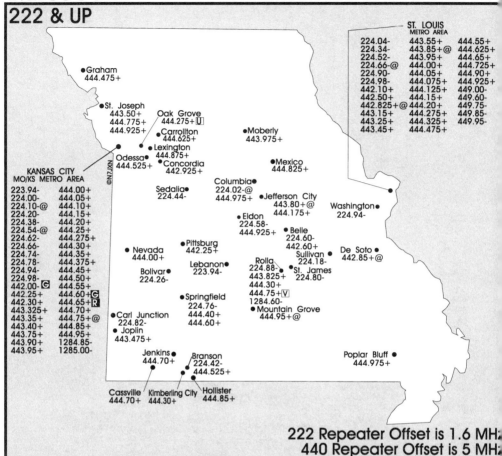

St. LOUIS
METRO AREA

224.04-	443.55+	444.55+
224.34-	443.85+@	444.625+
224.52-	443.95+	444.65+
224.66-@	444.00+	444.725+
224.90-	444.05+	444.90+
224.98-	444.075+	444.925+
442.10+	444.125+	449.00-
442.50+	444.15+	449.60-
442.825+@	444.20+	449.75-
443.15+	444.275+	449.85-
443.25+	444.325+	449.95-
443.45+	444.475+	

Graham
444.475+

St. Joseph
443.50+
444.775+
444.925+

Oak Grove
444.275+ U

Carrollton
444.625+

Lexington
444.875+

Odessa
444.525+

Concordia
442.925+

Moberly
443.975+

Mexico
444.825+

KANSAS CITY
MO/KS METRO AREA

223.94-	444.00+
224.00-	444.05+
224.10-@	444.10+
224.20-	444.15+
224.38-	444.20+
224.54-@	444.25+
224.62-	444.275+
224.66-	444.30+
224.74-	444.35+
224.78-	444.375+
224.94-	444.45+
224.98- G	444.50+
442.00- G	444.55+
442.25+	444.60- G
442.30+	444.65+ R
443.325+	444.70+
443.35+	444.75+@
443.40+	444.85+
443.75+	444.95+
443.90+	1284.85-
443.95+	1285.00-

Sedalia
224.44-

Columbia
224.02-@
444.975+

Jefferson City
443.80+@
444.175+

Washington
224.94-

Eldon
224.58-
444.925+

Belle
224.60-
442.60+

Sullivan
224.18-

De Soto
442.85+@

Nevada
444.00+

Pittsburg
442.25+

Lebanon
223.94-

Rolla
224.88-
443.825+
444.30+
444.75+ V
1284.60-

St. James
224.80-

Bolivar
224.26-

Springfield
224.76-
444.40+
444.60+

Mountain Grove
444.95+@

Carl Junction
224.82-

Joplin
443.475+

Jenkins
444.70+

Branson
224.42-
444.525+

Poplar Bluff
444.975+

Cassville
444.70+

Kimberling City
444.30+

Hollister
444.85+

222 Repeater Offset is 1.6 MH
440 Repeater Offset is 5 MH
1.2 GHz Repeater Offset is 12 MH

MISSOURI FACTS

NUMBER OF HAMS: 11,758

CALL AREA: 0

STATE NICKNAME: SHOW ME STATE

HIGHEST POINT:
    TAUM SAUK MTN. (1,772 FT.)

STATE CAPITAL: JEFFERSON CITY

NUMBER OF COUNTIES: 115

NUMBER OF 2M REPEATERS: 177

    222 REPEATERS: 30

    440 REPEATERS: 88

    900 MHz REPEATERS: 0

    1.2 GHz REPEATERS: 3

CTCSS TONES

A=67.0	Q=107.2	E=173.8
B=69.3	R=110.9	F=179.9
C=71.9	S=114.8	G=186.2
D=74.4	T=118.8	H=192.8
E=77.0	U=123.0	J=203.5
F=79.7	V=127.3	K=206.5
G=82.5	W=131.8	L=210.7
H=85.4	X=136.5	M=218.1
J=88.5	Y=141.3	N=225.7
K=91.5	Z=146.2	P=229.1
L=94.8	A=151.4	Q=233.6
M=97.4	B=156.7	R=241.8
N=100.0	C=162.2	S=250.3
P=103.5	D=167.9	T=254.1

Missouri
2 METERS

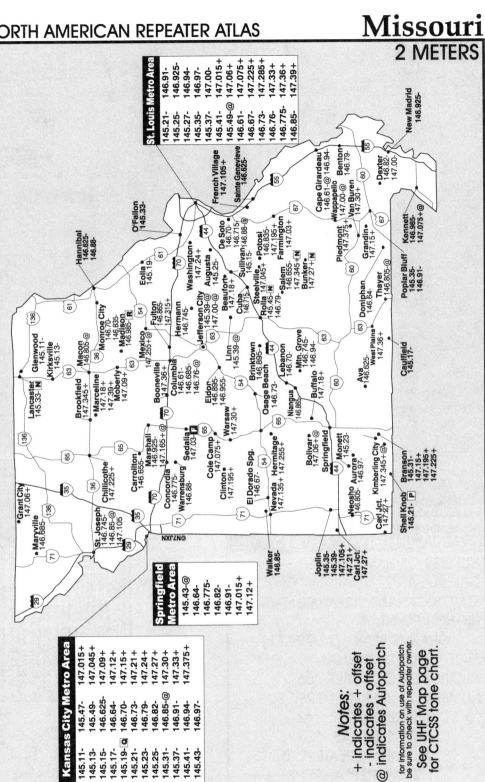

St. Louis Metro Area

145.21-	146.91-
145.25-	146.925-
145.27-	146.94-
145.35-	146.97-
145.37-	147.00-
145.41-	147.015+
145.49-@	147.06+
146.61-	147.075+
146.67-	147.225+
146.73-	147.285+
146.76-	147.33+
146.775-	147.36+
146.85-	147.39+

Springfield Metro Area

145.43-@
146.64-
146.775-
146.82-
146.91-
147.015+
147.12+

Kansas City Metro Area

145.11-	147.015+
145.13-	147.045+
145.15-	147.09+
145.17-	147.12+
145.19- Q	147.15+
145.21-	147.21+
145.23-	147.24+
145.25-	147.27+
145.31-	147.30+
145.37-	147.33+
145.41-	147.375+
145.43-	
146.70-	
146.73-	
146.79-	
146.82-	
146.85-@	
146.91-	
146.94-	
146.97-	

See UHF Map page
for CTCSS tone chart.

Notes:
+ indicates + offset
- indicates - offset
@ indicates Autopatch

for information on use of Autopatch
be sure to check with repeater owner.

2 Meter Repeater Offset is 600 KHz

222 & UP

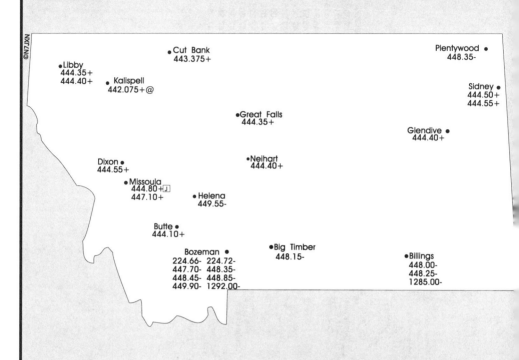

©N7JXN

Cut Bank
443.375+

Plentywood •
448.35-

• Libby
444.35+
444.40+

• Kalispell
442.075+@

Sidney •
444.50+
444.55+

•Great Falls
444.35+

Glendive •
444.40+

Dixon •
444.55+

•Neihart
444.40+

• Missoula
444.80+J
447.10+

• Helena
449.55-

Butte •
444.10+

Bozeman •
224.66- 224.72-
447.70- 448.35-
448.45- 448.85-
449.90- 1292.00-

•Big Timber
448.15-

•Billings
448.00-
448.25-
1285.00-

222 Repeater Offset is 1.6 MH:
440 Repeater Offset is 5 MH:
1.2 GHz Repeater Offset is 12 MH:

MONTANA FACTS

NUMBER OF HAMS: 2,518

CALL AREA: 7

STATE NICKNAME: TREASURE STATE

HIGHEST POINT:

GRANITE PEAK (12,799 FT.)

STATE CAPITAL: HELENA

NUMBER OF COUNTIES: 56

NUMBER OF 2M REPEATERS: 72

222 REPEATERS: 2

440 REPEATERS: 23

900 MHz REPEATERS: 0

1.2 GHz REPEATERS: 2

CTCSS TONES

A=67.0	Q=107.2	E=173.8
B=69.3	R=110.9	F=179.9
C=71.9	S=114.8	G=186.2
D=74.4	T=118.8	H=192.8
E=77.0	U=123.0	J=203.5
F=79.7	V=127.3	K=206.5
G=82.5	W=131.8	L=210.7
H=85.4	X=136.5	M=218.1
J=88.5	Y=141.3	N=225.7
K=91.5	Z=146.2	P=229.1
L=94.8	A=151.4	Q=233.6
M=97.4	B=156.7	R=241.8
N=100.0	C=162.2	S=250.3
P=103.5	D=167.9	T=254.1

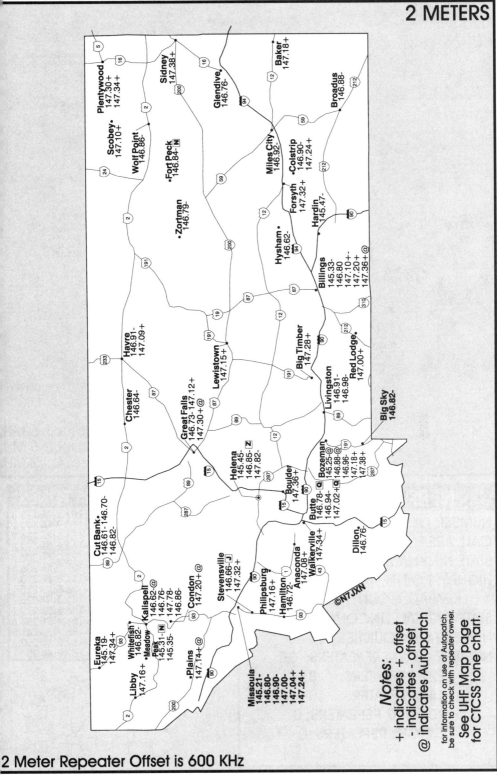

Plentywood•
147.30+
147.34+

Sidney•
147.38+

Baker•
147.18+

Scobey•
147.10+

Wolf Point•
146.86•

Glendive•
146.76•

•Broadus
146.88-

•Fort Peck N
146.84-

Miles City•
146.92

•Colstrip
146.90-
147.24+

•Zortman
146.79-

Forsyth•
147.32+

Hardin•
145.47-

Hysham•
146.62-

Billings
145.33-
146.80
147.10+-
147.20+
147.36+ @

Havre•
146.91-
147.09+

Chester•
146.64-

Lewistown•
147.15+

Big Timber•
147.28+

Red Lodge•
147.00+

Great Falls•
146.73- 147.12+
147.30+ @

Livingston•
146.91-
146.98-

Big Sky•
146.82-

Cut Bank•
146.61- 146.70-
146.82-

Helena•
145.45-
146.85- Z
147.82-

Bozeman•
145.25 @
146.88 @
146.96-
147.18+
147.38+

Boulder•
147.36+

Butte•
146.78- Q
146.94-
147.02- @

Dillon•
146.76-

Stevensville•
146.66- J
147.32+

Anaconda•
147.08+

Walkerville•
147.34+

Philipsburg•
147.16+

Hamilton•
146.72-

Eureka•
145.19-
147.34+

Whitefish•
146.82-

Kalispell•
146.62- @
147.78-
146.86-

Condon•
147.20+ @

Libby•
147.16+

Meadow Peak• N
145.31-
145.35-

•Plains
147.14+ @

Missoula
145.21-
146.80-
146.90-
147.00-
147.04+
147.24+

©N7JXN

Notes:
+ indicates + offset
- indicates - offset
@ indicates Autopatch

for information on use of Autopatch
be sure to check with repeater owner.

See UHF Map page
for CTCSS tone chart.

2 Meter Repeater Offset is 600 KHz

Nebraska

222 & UP

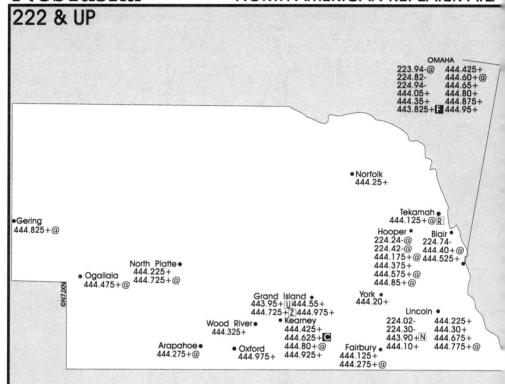

OMAHA
223.94-@	444.425+
224.82-	444.60+@
224.94-	444.65+
444.05+	444.80+
444.35+	444.875+
443.825+**F**	444.95+

• Norfolk
444.25+

• Gering
444.825+@

Tekamah •
444.125+@**R**

Hooper •   Blair •
224.24-@   224.74-
224.42-@   444.40+@
444.175+@ 444.525+
444.375+
444.575+@
444.85+@

North Platte •
444.225+

• Ogallala   444.725+@
444.475+@

Grand Island •
443.95+**U** 444.55+
444.725+**Z** 444.975+

York •
444.20+

Lincoln •
224.02-   444.225+
224.30-   444.30+
443.90+**N**   444.675+
444.10+   444.775+@

Wood River •
444.325+

• Kearney
444.425+
444.625+**C**
444.80+@
444.925+

Fairbury •
444.125+
444.275+@

Arapahoe •
444.275+@

• Oxford
444.975+

©N7JXN

222 Repeater Offset is 1.6 MH.
440 Repeater Offset is 5 MH
900 MHz Repeater Offset is 12 MH

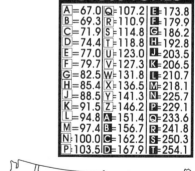

NEBRASKA FACTS

NUMBER OF HAMS: 3,866

CALL AREA: 0

STATE NICKNAME: CORNHUSKER STATE

HIGHEST POINT:
    KIMBALL COUNTY (5,246 FT.)

STATE CAPITAL: LINCOLN

NUMBER OF COUNTIES: 93

NUMBER OF 2M REPEATERS: 70

    222 REPEATERS: 8

    440 REPEATERS: 40

    900 MHz REPEATERS: 0

    1.2 GHz REPEATERS: 0

CTCSS TONES

A=67.0	**Q**=107.2	**E**=173.8
B=69.3	**R**=110.9	**F**=179.9
C=71.9	**S**=114.8	**G**=186.2
D=74.4	**T**=118.8	**H**=192.8
E=77.0	**U**=123.0	**J**=203.5
F=79.7	**V**=127.3	**K**=206.5
G=82.5	**W**=131.8	**L**=210.7
H=85.4	**X**=136.5	**M**=218.1
J=88.5	**Y**=141.3	**N**=225.7
K=91.5	**Z**=146.2	**P**=229.1
L=94.8	**A**=151.4	**Q**=233.6
M=97.4	**B**=156.7	**R**=241.8
N=100.0	**C**=162.2	**S**=250.3
P=103.5	**D**=167.9	**T**=254.1

Nebraska
2 METERS

Omaha
Blair 146.61-
Fremont 145.265-@ 146.67-@ 147.105+@ 147.165+
Ashland 145.31-
Bellevue 145.115- 147.39+
Lincoln 147.39+
Nebraska City 146.70-@ 146.73-@
Johnson 146.885-@
Falls City 147.36+

Wayne 147.03+
Columbus 146.64-@ 146.775-
Waco 147.27+@
Beaver Xing 146.76-
Wilber 146.985-@
Fairbury 147.12+@

Norfolk 146.73-
Osceola 147.015+
Grand Island 145.205- 146.94-
Aurora 147.18+
Hastings 145.13-@

Neligh 146.79-
Elba 147.24+
Heartwell 146.82-

Chambers 147.30+
Burwell 147.09+
Kearny 146.625-@ 146.91-@ 147.135+ 147.315+
Oxford 146.715-

Ainsworth 147.36+
Broken Bow 146.865- 147.06+
Maywood 147.345+
Arapahoe 146.745-@
Cambridge 146.97-@
McCook 147.27+@

Cody 146.745-
North Platte 145.37- 146.70- 146.94-
Hayes Center 146.67-
Culbertson 147.15+

Gordon 146.67-
Ogallala 146.76-

Chadron 147.36+@
Angora 147.285+
Scottsbluff 147.075+@

Lincoln Metropolitan Area	
145.145-	145.49-
145.19-	146.76-
145.235-	146.85-@
145.33-	147.045+@
147.195+	
147.33+	

Omaha Metro Area	
145.37-	147.00+@
145.45-	147.30+@
146.94-	147.36+
147.00-@	

2 Meter Repeater Offset is 600 KHz

71

222 & UP

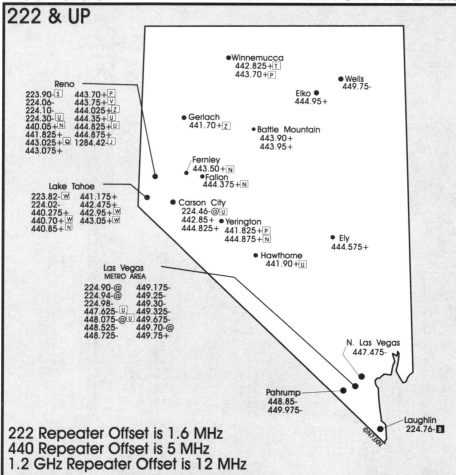

Winnemucca
442.825+T
443.70+P

Wells
449.75-

Reno
223.90-S   443.70+P
224.06-   443.75+V
224.10-   444.025+Z
224.30-U   444.35+U
440.05+N   444.825+U
441.825+   444.875+
443.025+Q   1284.42-J
443.075+

Elko
444.95+

Gerlach
441.70+Z

Battle Mountain
443.90+
443.95+

Fernley
443.50+N
Fallon
444.375+N

Lake Tahoe
223.82-W   441.175+
224.02-   442.475+
440.275+   442.95+W
440.70+W   443.05+W
440.85+N

Carson City
224.46-@U
442.85+   **Yerington**
444.825+   441.825+P
             444.875+N

Ely
444.575+

Hawthorne
441.90+U

Las Vegas
METRO AREA

224.90-@   449.175-
224.94-@   449.25-
224.98-   449.30-
447.625-U   449.325-
448.075-@U   449.675-
448.525-   449.70-@
448.725-   449.75+

N. Las Vegas
447.475-

Pahrump
448.85-
449.975-

Laughlin
224.76-B

©N7JXN

222 Repeater Offset is 1.6 MHz
440 Repeater Offset is 5 MHz
1.2 GHz Repeater Offset is 12 MHz

NEVADA FACTS

NUMBER OF HAMS: 3,538
CALL AREA: 7
STATE NICKNAME: SILVER STATE
HIGHEST POINT:
      BOUNDARY PEAK (13,143 FT.)
STATE CAPITAL: CARSON CITY
NUMBER OF COUNTIES: 16
NUMBER OF 2M REPEATERS: 56
      222 REPEATERS: 11
      440 REPEATERS: 45
      900 MHz REPEATERS: 0
      1.2 GHz REPEATERS: 1

CTCSS TONES

A=67.0	Q=107.2	E=173.8
B=69.3	R=110.9	F=179.9
C=71.9	S=114.8	G=186.2
D=74.4	T=118.8	H=192.8
E=77.0	U=123.0	J=203.5
F=79.7	V=127.3	K=206.5
G=82.5	W=131.8	L=210.7
H=85.4	X=136.5	M=218.1
J=88.5	Y=141.3	N=225.7
K=91.5	Z=146.2	P=229.1
L=94.8	A=151.4	Q=233.6
M=97.4	B=156.7	R=241.8
N=100.0	C=162.2	S=250.3
P=103.5	D=167.9	T=254.1

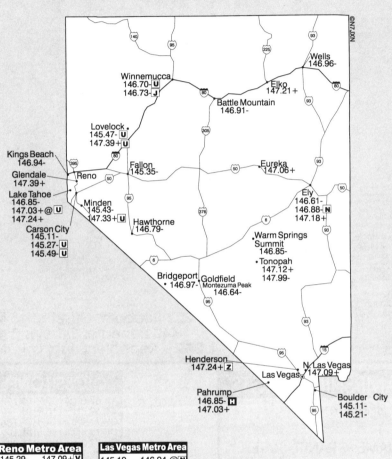

©N7JXN

Wells
146.96-

Winnemucca
146.70- U
146.73- J

Elko
147.21+

Battle Mountain
146.91-

Lovelock
145.47- U
147.39+ U

Kings Beach
146.94-

Glendale
147.39+

Fallon
145.35-

Reno

Eureka
147.06+

Lake Tahoe
146.85-
147.03+@ U
147.24+

Minden
145.43-
147.33+ U

Hawthorne
146.79-

Ely
146.61-
146.88- N
147.18+

Carson City
145.11-
145.27- U
145.49- U

Warm Springs
Summit
146.85-

Tonopah
147.12+
147.99-

Bridgeport
146.97-

Goldfield
Montezuma Peak
146.64-

Henderson
147.24+ Z

N Las Vegas
147.09+

Las Vegas

Pahrump
146.85- H
147.03+

Boulder City
145.11-
145.21-

Reno Metro Area	
145.29-	147.09+ V
145.33- A	147.12+ U
145.45- U	147.15+ U
146.61- U	147.18+
146.67- U	147.21+ U
146.76- U	147.30+@

Las Vegas Metro Area	
145.19-	146.94-@ N
145.39-	147.06+
146.67-	147.09+
146.79-	147.18+ N
146.88- N	147.27+

Notes:
+ indicates + offset
- indicates - offset
@ indicates Autopatch

for information on use of Autopatch
be sure to check with repeater owner.

See UHF Map page
for CTCSS tone chart.

2 Meter Repeater Offset is 600 KHz

222 & UP

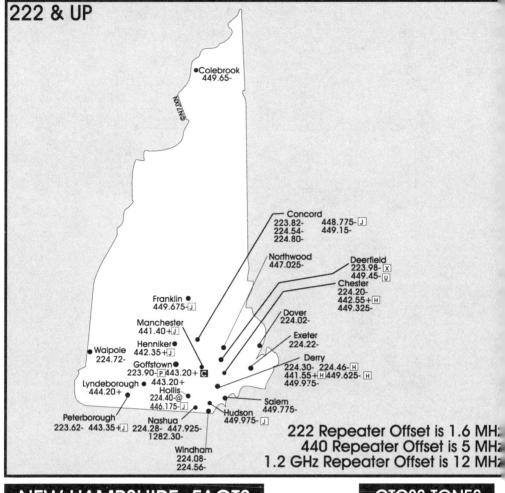

Colebrook
449.65-

NY/ZN©

Concord
223.82-   448.775-[J]
224.54-   449.15-
224.80-

Northwood
447.025-

Deerfield
223.98- [X]
449.45- [U]

Chester
224.20-
442.55+[H]
449.325-

Franklin ●
449.675-[J]

Dover
224.02-

Manchester
441.40+[J]

Exeter
224.22-

Henniker●
442.35+[J]

Derry
224.30- 224.46-[H]
441.55+[H]449.625- [H]
449.975-

Walpole
224.72-

Goffstown●
223.90-[P]443.20+ [C]

Lyndeborough ●
444.20+

443.20+

Hollis
224.40-@
446.175-[J]

Salem
449.775-

Peterborough
223.62- 443.35+[J]

Nashua
224.28- 447.925-
1282.30-

Hudson
449.975- [J]

Windham
224.08-
224.56-

222 Repeater Offset is 1.6 MH.
440 Repeater Offset is 5 MH.
1.2 GHz Repeater Offset is 12 MH.

NEW HAMPSHIRE FACTS

NUMBER OF HAMS: 4,472

CALL AREA: 1

STATE NICKNAME: GRANITE STATE

HIGHEST POINT:
MT. WASHINGTON (6,288 FT.)

STATE CAPITAL: CONCORD

NUMBER OF COUNTIES: 10

NUMBER OF 2M REPEATERS: 34

222 REPEATERS: 16

440 REPEATERS: 21

900 MHz REPEATERS: 0

1.2 GHz REPEATERS: 1

CTCSS TONES

A=67.0	Q=107.2	E=173.8
B=69.3	R=110.9	F=179.9
C=71.9	S=114.8	G=186.2
D=74.4	T=118.8	H=192.8
E=77.0	U=123.0	J=203.5
F=79.7	V=127.3	K=206.5
G=82.5	W=131.8	L=210.7
H=85.4	X=136.5	M=218.1
J=88.5	Y=141.3	N=225.7
K=91.5	Z=146.2	P=229.1
L=94.8	A=151.4	Q=233.6
M=97.4	B=156.7	R=241.8
N=100.0	C=162.2	S=250.3
P=103.5	D=167.9	T=254.1

NEW HAMPSHIRE
2 METERS

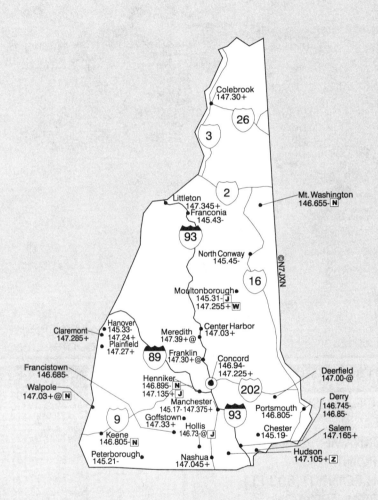

Colebrook
147.30+

26

3

2

Littleton
147.345+
Franconia
145.43-

93

Mt. Washington
146.655-[N]

North Conway
145.45-

16

Moultonborough•
145.31-[J]
147.255+[W]

Hanover
•145.33-
147.24+
Plainfield
147.27+

Claremont
147.285+

Meredith
147.39+@

Center Harbor
147.03+

Francistown
146.685-

Walpole
147.03+@[N]

89

Franklin
147.30+@

Concord
146.94-
147.225+

Deerfield
147.00-@

Henniker
146.895-[N]
147.135+[J]

202

Derry
146.745-
146.85-

Manchester
145.17-147.375+

Goffstown•
147.33+

9

Portsmouth
146.805-

93

Hollis
146.73-@[J]

Chester
•145.19-

Salem
147.165+

Keene
146.805-[N]

Peterborough•
145.21-

Nashua
147.045+

Hudson
147.105+[Z]

@N7JXN

Notes:
+ indicates + offset
- indicates - offset
@ indicates Autopatch

for information on use of Autopatch
be sure to check with repeater owner.

See UHF Map page
for CTCSS tone chart.

2 Meter Repeater Offset is 600 KHz

222 & UP

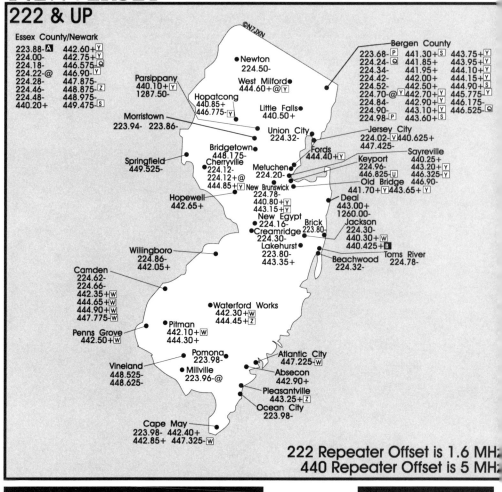

©N7JXN

Essex County/Newark

223.88-Ⓐ	442.60+Ⓨ
224.00-	442.75+Ⓨ
224.18-	446.575-Ⓠ
224.22-@	446.90-Ⓨ
224.28-	447.875-
224.46-	448.875-Ⓩ
224.48-	448.975-
440.20+	449.475-Ⓢ

Bergen County

223.68-Ⓟ	441.30+Ⓢ	443.75+Ⓨ
224.24-Ⓠ	441.85+	443.95+Ⓨ
224.34-	441.95+	444.10+Ⓨ
224.42-	442.00+	444.15+Ⓨ
224.52-	442.50+	444.90+Ⓢ
224.70-@Ⓨ	442.70+Ⓨ	445.775-Ⓨ
224.84-	442.90+Ⓨ	446.175-
224.90-	443.10+Ⓨ	446.525-Ⓠ
224.98-Ⓟ	443.60+Ⓢ	

• Newton
224.50-

West Milford•
444.60+@Ⓨ

Parsippany
440.10+Ⓨ
1287.50-

Hopatcong
440.85+
446.775-Ⓨ

Little Falls•
440.50+

Morristown
223.94- 223.86-

Union City
224.32-

Jersey City
224.02-Ⓥ 440.625+
447.425-

Bridgetown
448.175-
Cherryville
224.12-
224.12+@
444.85+Ⓨ

Springfield
449.525-

Metuchen
224.20-

Fords
444.40+Ⓨ

Sayreville
440.25+
Keyport 443.20+Ⓨ
224.96- 446.325-Ⓨ
446.825-Ⓤ
Old Bridge 446.90-
441.70+Ⓨ 443.65+Ⓨ

Hopewell
442.65+

New Brunswick
224.78-
440.80+Ⓨ
443.15+Ⓨ

New Egypt
• 224.16-
•Creamridge
224.30-

Brick
223.80-

Deal
443.00+
1260.00-

Jackson
224.30-
440.30+Ⓦ
440.425+Ⓑ

Willingboro
224.86-
442.05+

Lakehurst •
223.80-
443.35+

Beachwood
224.32-

Toms River
224.78-

Camden
224.62-
224.66-
442.35+Ⓦ
444.65+Ⓦ
444.90+Ⓦ
447.775-Ⓦ

•Waterford Works
442.30+Ⓦ
444.45+Ⓩ

•Pitman
442.10+Ⓦ
444.30+

Penns Grove
442.50+Ⓦ

Pomona
223.98-

Atlantic City
447.225-Ⓦ

Vineland
448.525-
448.625-

•Millville
223.96-@

Absecon
442.90+

Pleasantville
443.25+Ⓩ

Ocean City
223.98-

Cape May
223.98- 442.40+
442.85+ 447.325-Ⓦ

222 Repeater Offset is 1.6 MH:
440 Repeater Offset is 5 MH:

NEW JERSEY FACTS

NUMBER OF HAMS: 17,250

CALL AREA: 2

STATE NICKNAME: GARDEN STATE

HIGHEST POINT:

HIGH POINT (1,803 FT.)

STATE CAPITAL: TRENTON

NUMBER OF COUNTIES: 21

NUMBER OF 2M REPEATERS: 95

222 REPEATERS: 38

440 REPEATERS: 69

900 MHz REPEATERS: 0

1.2 GHz REPEATERS: 2

CTCSS TONES

Ⓐ=67.0	Ⓠ=107.2	Ⓔ=173.8
Ⓑ=69.3	Ⓡ=110.9	Ⓕ=179.9
Ⓒ=71.9	Ⓢ=114.8	Ⓖ=186.2
Ⓓ=74.4	Ⓣ=118.8	Ⓗ=192.8
Ⓔ=77.0	Ⓤ=123.0	Ⓙ=203.5
Ⓕ=79.7	Ⓥ=127.3	Ⓚ=206.5
Ⓖ=82.5	Ⓦ=131.8	Ⓛ=210.7
Ⓗ=85.4	Ⓧ=136.5	Ⓜ=218.1
Ⓙ=88.5	Ⓨ=141.3	Ⓝ=225.7
Ⓚ=91.5	Ⓩ=146.2	Ⓟ=229.1
Ⓛ=94.8	Ⓐ=151.4	Ⓠ=233.6
Ⓜ=97.4	Ⓑ=156.7	Ⓡ=241.8
Ⓝ=100.0	Ⓒ=162.2	Ⓢ=250.3
Ⓟ=103.5	Ⓓ=167.9	Ⓣ=254.1

NEW JERSEY
2 METERS

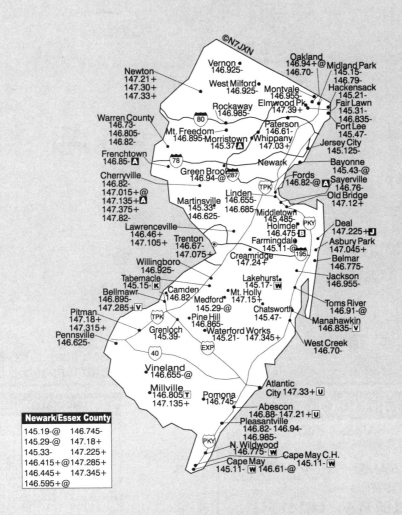

©N7JXN

Newton
147.21+
147.30+
147.33+

Vernon •
146.925-

West Milford •
146.925-

Rockaway •
146.985-

Oakland
146.94+@
146.70-

Midland Park
145.15-
146.79-
Hackensack
145.21-
Fair Lawn
145.31-
146.835-
Fort Lee
145.47-
Jersey City
145.125-

Montvale
146.955-
Elmwood Pk
147.39+

Warren County
146.73-
146.805-
146.82-

Mt. Freedom •
146.895-Morristown
145.37 [A]

Paterson
146.61-
Whippany
147.03+

Newark

Frenchtown
146.85- [A]

80

78

Green Brook
146.94-@

287

Bayonne
145.43-@
Sayerville
146.76-
Old Bridge
147.12+

Fords
146.82-@ [A]

Cherryville
146.82-
147.015+@
147.135+[A]
147.375+
147.82-

Martinsville
145.33-
146.625-

Linden
146.655-
146.685-

TPK

Middletown
145.485-
Holmdel
146.475 [B]
Farmingdale
145.11-@

PKY

Deal
147.225+ [J]
Asbury Park
147.045+
Belmar
146.775-

Lawrenceville
146.46+
147.105+

Trenton
146.67-
147.075+

Creamridge
147.24+

195

Jackson
146.955-

Willingboro
146.925-

Tabernacle
145.15- [K]

Bellmawr
146.895-
147.285+ [V]

Camden •
146.82

Lakehurst •
145.17- [W]

Mt. Holly
Medford • 147.15+
145.29-@

Chatsworth
145.47-

Toms River
146.91-@

Manahawkin
146.835- [V]

Pitman
147.18+
147.315+
Pennsville
146.625-

TPK

Grenloch
145.39-

Pine Hill
146.865-

Waterford Works
145.21- 147.345+

West Creek
146.70-

40

EXP

Vineland •
146.655-@

Millville •
146.805 [T]
147.135+

Pomona
146.745-

Atlantic
City 147.33+ [U]

Abescon
146.88- 147.21+ [U]
Pleasantville
146.82- 146.94-
146.985-
N. Wildwood
146.775- [W]

PKY

Cape May
145.11- [W] 146.61-@

Cape May C.H.
145.11- [W]

Newark/Essex County	
145.19-@	146.745-
145.29-@	147.18+
145.33-	147.225+
146.415+@	147.285+
146.445+	147.345+
146.595+@	

Notes:
+ indicates + offset
- indicates - offset
@ indicates Autopatch

for information on use of Autopatch
be sure to check with repeater owner.

See UHF Map page
for CTCSS tone chart.

2 Meter Repeater Offset is 600 KHz

222 & UP

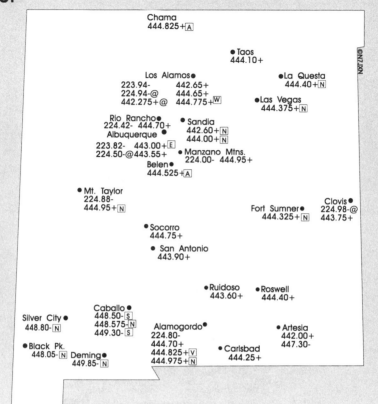

Chama
444.825+Ⓐ

● Taos
444.10+

Los Alamos●
223.94-   442.65+
224.94-@   444.65+
442.275+@ 444.775+Ⓦ

●La Questa
444.40+Ⓝ

●Las Vegas
444.375+Ⓝ

Rio Rancho●
224.42- 444.70+
Albuquerque ●
223.82   443.00+Ⓔ
224.50-@443.55+

● Sandia
442.60+Ⓝ
444.00+Ⓝ

● Manzano Mtns.
224.00- 444.95+

Belen●
444.525+Ⓐ

● Mt. Taylor
224.88-
444.95+Ⓝ

Fort Sumner●
444.325+Ⓝ

Clovis ●
224.98-@
443.75+

● Socorro
444.75+

● San Antonio
443.90+

● Ruidoso
443.60+

● Roswell
444.40+

Caballo ●
448.50-Ⓢ
448.575-Ⓝ
449.30-Ⓢ

Silver City ●
448.80-Ⓝ

Alamogordo●
224.80-
444.70+
444.825+Ⓥ
444.975+Ⓝ

● Artesia
442.00+
447.30-

● Black Pk.
448.05-Ⓝ Deming●
449.85-Ⓝ

● Carlsbad
444.25+

©N7JXN

222 Repeater Offset is 1.6 MHz
440 Repeater Offset is 5 MHz

NEW MEXICO FACTS

NUMBER OF HAMS: 4,443

CALL AREA: 5

STATE NICKNAME: LAND OF ENCHANTMENT

HIGHEST POINT:
    WHEELER PEAK (13,161 FT.)

STATE CAPITAL: SANTA FE

NUMBER OF COUNTIES: 33

NUMBER OF 2M REPEATERS: 85

    222 REPEATERS: 8

    440 REPEATERS: 34

    900 MHz REPEATERS: 0

    1.2 GHz REPEATERS: 0

CTCSS TONES

A=67.0	Q=107.2	E=173.8
B=69.3	R=110.9	F=179.9
C=71.9	S=114.8	G=186.2
D=74.4	T=118.8	H=192.8
E=77.0	U=123.0	J=203.5
F=79.7	V=127.3	K=206.5
G=82.5	W=131.8	L=210.7
H=85.4	X=136.5	M=218.1
J=88.5	Y=141.3	N=225.7
K=91.5	Z=146.2	P=229.1
L=94.8	A=151.4	Q=233.6
M=97.4	B=156.7	R=241.8
N=100.0	C=162.2	S=250.3
P=103.5	D=167.9	T=254.1

New Mexico
2 METERS

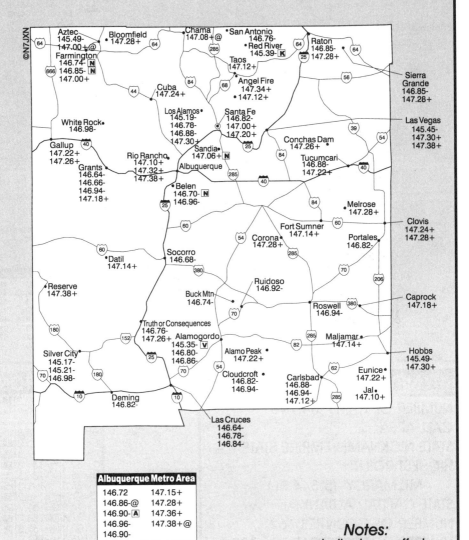

©N7ZN

Aztec- 145.49- 147.00+@
64

Bloomfield • 147.28+
64

Chama 147.08+@
285

• **San Antonio** 146.76-
• **Red River** 145.39- K
64

Raton 146.85- • 147.28+
25
64

Farmington 146.74 N
666 146.85- N
147.00+

Taos 147.12+
84

Angel Fire 147.34+
68 • 147.12+

Sierra Grande 146.85- 147.28+
56

Cuba 147.24+

White Rock • 146.98-

Los Alamos • 145.19- 146.78- 146.88- 147.30+

Santa Fe 146.82- 147.00+ 147.20+
25

Las Vegas 145.45- 147.30+ 147.38+
39

Gallup 147.22+ 147.26+
40

Rio Rancho 147.10+ 147.32+ 147.38+

Sandia • 147.06+ N
Albuquerque
285

Conchas Dam 147.26+ •
84
54

Grants 146.64- 146.66- 146.94- 147.18+

Tucumcari 146.88- 147.22+
40

Belen 146.70- N
25 146.96-

Melrose • 147.28+
84

Clovis 147.24+ 147.28+

Datil • 147.14+
60

Socorro 146.68-

60

Corona 147.28+
54

Fort Sumner 147.14+
60

Portales 146.82-
285

70
206

Reserve • 147.38+

Buck Mtn 146.74-

Ruidoso 146.92-

Roswell 146.94-
380

Caprock 147.18+

180

Truth or Consequences 146.76- 147.26+ •
152
25

Alamogordo 145.35- V 146.80- 146.86-
70

Alamo Peak • 147.22+
54

Maljamar • 147.14+
82
285

Hobbs 145.49- 147.30+

Silver City • 145.17- 145.21- 146.98-
70 180

Cloudcroft 146.82- 146.94-

Carlsbad 146.88- 146.94- 147.12+
62

Eunice • 147.22+

Jal • 147.10+
285

Deming 146.82-
10 10

Las Cruces 146.64- 146.78- 146.84-

Albuquerque Metro Area

146.72	147.15+
146.86-@	147.28+
146.90- A	147.36+
146.96-	147.38+@
146.90-	

Notes:
+ indicates + offset
- indicates - offset
@ indicates Autopatch

for information on use of Autopatch
be sure to check with repeater owner.

See UHF Map page for CTCSS tone chart.

2 Meter Repeater Offset is 600 KHz

New York (Northeast) NORTH AMERICAN REPEATER ATLAS

222 & UP

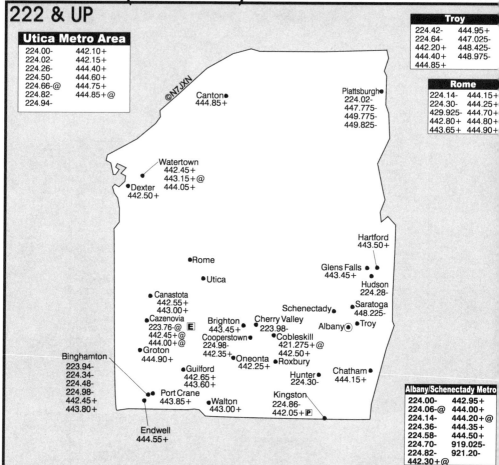

Troy

224.42-	444.95+
224.64-	447.025-
442.20+	448.425-
444.40+	448.975-
444.85+	

Utica Metro Area

224.00-	442.10+
224.02-	442.15+
224.26-	444.40+
224.50-	444.60+
224.66-@	444.75+
224.82-	444.85+@
224.94-	

Rome

224.14-	444.15+
224.30-	444.25+
429.925-	444.70+
442.80+	444.80+
443.65+	444.90+

@N7JXN

Canton●
444.85+

Plattsburgh●
224.02-
447.775-
449.775-
449.825-

Watertown
442.45+
443.15+@
●Dexter 444.05+
442.50+

Hartford
443.50+

●Rome

●Utica

Glens Falls ● ●
443.45+

Hudson
224.28-

● Canastota
442.55+
443.00+

Schenectady● ●Saratoga
448.225-

●Cazenovia
223.76-@ **E**
442.45+@
444.00+@
●Groton
444.90+

Brighton Cherry Valley
443.45+ 223.98-
Cooperstown●
224.98-
442.35+ ●Oneonta
442.25+

Albany◉ ●Troy

●Cobleskill
421.275+@
442.50+
●Roxbury

Binghamton
223.94-
224.34-
224.48-
224.98-
442.45+
443.80+

●Guilford
442.65+
443.60+

Hunter●
224.30-

Chatham●
444.15+

● Port Crane
443.85+

●Walton
443.00+

Kingston
224.86-
442.05+ **P**

Albany/Schenectady Metro

224.00-	442.95+
224.06-@	444.00+
224.14-	444.20+@
224.36-	444.35+
224.58-	444.50+
224.70-	919.025-
224.82-	921.20-
442.30+@	

Endwell
444.55+

NEW YORK FACTS

NUMBER OF HAMS: 34,793

CALL AREA: 2

STATE NICKNAME: EMPIRE STATE

HIGHEST POINT:
   MT. MARCY (5,344 FT.)

STATE CAPITAL: ALBANY

NUMBER OF COUNTIES: 62

NUMBER OF 2M REPEATERS: 139

   222 REPEATERS: 31

   440 REPEATERS: 46

   900 MHz REPEATERS: 4

   1.2 GHz REPEATERS: 3

CTCSS TONES

A=67.0	Q=107.2	E=173.8
B=69.3	R=110.9	F=179.9
C=71.9	S=114.8	G=186.2
D=74.4	T=118.8	H=192.8
E=77.0	U=123.0	J=203.5
F=79.7	V=127.3	K=206.5
G=82.5	W=131.8	L=210.7
H=85.4	X=136.5	M=218.1
J=88.5	Y=141.3	N=225.7
K=91.5	Z=146.2	P=229.1
L=94.8	A=151.4	Q=233.6
M=97.4	B=156.7	R=241.8
N=100.0	C=162.2	S=250.3
P=103.5	D=167.9	T=254.1

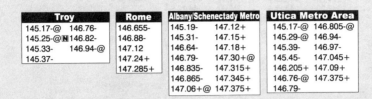

Troy		Rome	Albany/Schenectady Metro		Utica Metro Area	
145.17-@	146.76-	146.655-	145.19-	147.12+	145.17-@	146.805-@
145.25-@	146.82-	146.88-	145.31-	147.15+	145.29-@	146.94-
145.33-	146.94-@	147.12	146.64-	147.18+	145.39-	146.97-
145.37-		147.24+	146.79-	147.30+@	145.45-	147.045+
		147.285+	146.835-	147.315+	146.205+	147.09+
			146.865-	147.345+	146.76-@	147.375+
			147.06+@	147.375+	146.79-	

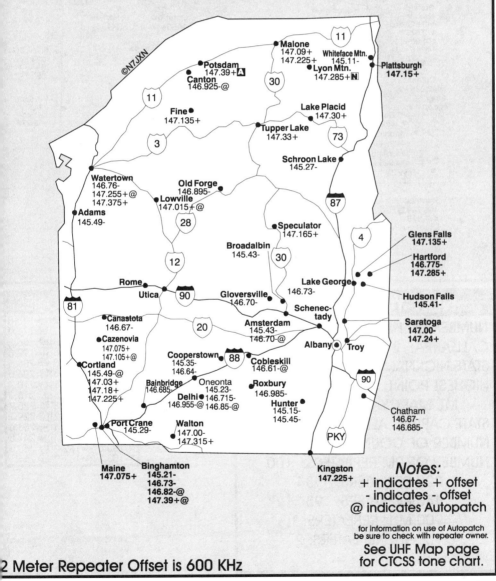

Malone
147.09+
147.225+

Whiteface Mtn.
145.11-

Lyon Mtn.
147.285+ N

Plattsburgh
147.15+

©N7JXN

Potsdam
147.39+ A

Canton
146.925-@

Fine
147.135+

Lake Placid
147.30+

Tupper Lake
147.33+

Schroon Lake
145.27-

Watertown
146.76-
147.255+@
147.375+

Old Forge
146.895-
Lowville
147.015+@

Adams
145.49-

Speculator
147.165+

Broadalbin
145.43-

Glens Falls
147.135+

Hartford
146.775-
147.285+

Rome

Utica

Gloversville
146.70-

Lake George
146.73-

Hudson Falls
145.41-

Canastota
146.67-

Cazenovia
147.075+
147.105+@

Cortland
145.49-@
147.03+
147.18+
147.225+

Amsterdam
145.43-
146.70-@

**Schenec-
tady**

Albany **Troy**

Saratoga
147.00-
147.24+

Cooperstown
145.35-
146.64-

Cobleskill
146.61-

Bainbridge
146.685-

Oneonta
145.23-

Delhi
146.955-@

Roxbury
146.985-

146.715-
146.85-@

Hunter
145.15-
145.45-

Chatham
146.67-
146.685-

Port Crane
145.29-

Walton
147.00-
147.315+

Maine
147.075+

Binghamton
145.21-
146.73-
146.82-@
147.39+@

Kingston
147.225+

Notes:
+ indicates + offset
- indicates - offset
@ indicates Autopatch

for information on use of Autopatch
be sure to check with repeater owner.

**See UHF Map page
for CTCSS tone chart.**

2 Meter Repeater Offset is 600 KHz

New York (Northwest) NORTH AMERICAN REPEATER ATLAS

222 & UP

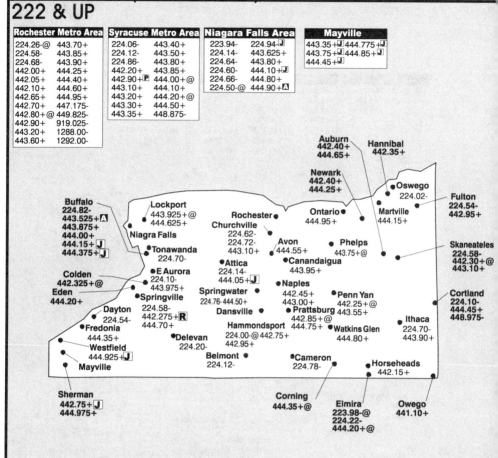

Rochester Metro Area

224.26-@	443.70+
224.58-	443.85+
224.68-	443.90+
442.00+	444.25+
442.05+	444.40+
442.10+	444.60+
442.65+	444.95+
442.70+	447.175-
442.80+@	449.825-
442.90+	919.025-
443.20+	1288.00-
443.60+	1292.00-

Syracuse Metro Area

224.06-	443.40+
224.12-	443.50+
224.86-	443.80+
442.20+	443.85+
442.90+ℙ	444.00+@
443.10+	444.10+
443.20+	444.20+@
443.30+	444.50+
443.35+	448.875-

Niagara Falls Area

223.94-	224.94-◩
224.14-	443.625+
224.64-	443.80+
224.60-	444.10+◩
224.66-	444.80+
224.50-@	444.90+🅐

Mayville

443.35+◩	444.775+◩
443.75+◩	444.85+◩
444.45+◩	

Map labels:

Auburn 442.40+ 444.65+
Hannibal 442.35+
Newark 442.40+ 444.25+
Oswego 224.02-
Fulton 224.54- 442.95+
Buffalo 224.82- 443.525+🅐 443.875+ 444.00+ 444.15+◩ 444.375+◩
Lockport 443.925+@ 444.625+
Rochester
Churchville 224.62- 224.72- 443.10+
Ontario 444.95+
Martville 444.15+
Skaneateles 224.58- 442.30+@ 443.10+
Niagra Falls
Tonawanda 224.70-
Avon 444.55+
Phelps 443.75+@
Colden 442.325+@
E Aurora 224.10- 443.975+
Attica 224.14- 444.05+◩
Canandaigua 443.95+
Eden 444.20+
Springwater 224.76- 444.50+
Naples 442.45+ 443.00+
Penn Yan 442.25+@ 443.55+
Cortland 224.10- 444.45+ 448.975-
Springville 224.58- 442.275+🆁 444.70+
Dayton 224.54-
Dansville
Prattsburg 442.85+@
Fredonia 444.35+
Hammondsport 224.00-@ 442.75+ 442.95+
Watkins Glen 444.75+ 444.80+
Ithaca 224.70- 443.90+
Westfield 444.925+◩
Delevan 224.20-
Belmont 224.12-
Cameron 224.78-
Horseheads 442.15+
Mayville
Sherman 442.75+◩ 444.975+
Corning 444.35+@
Elmira 223.98-@ 224.22- 444.20+@
Owego 441.10+

NEW YORK FACTS

NUMBER OF HAMS: 34,793
CALL AREA: 2
STATE NICKNAME: EMPIRE STATE
HIGHEST POINT:
    MT. MARCY (5,344 FT.)
STATE CAPITAL: ALBANY
NUMBER OF COUNTIES: 62
NUMBER OF 2M REPEATERS: 100
    222 REPEATERS: 34
    440 REPEATERS: 93
    900 MHz REPEATERS: 1
    1.2 GHz REPEATERS: 2

CTCSS TONES

A=67.0	Q=107.2	E=173.8
B=69.3	R=110.9	F=179.9
C=71.9	S=114.8	G=186.2
D=74.4	T=118.8	H=192.8
E=77.0	U=123.0	I=203.5
F=79.7	V=127.3	K=206.5
G=82.5	W=131.8	L=210.7
H=85.4	X=136.5	M=218.1
J=88.5	Y=141.3	N=225.7
K=91.5	Z=146.2	P=229.1
L=94.8	A=151.4	Q=233.6
M=97.4	B=156.7	R=241.8
N=100.0	C=162.2	S=250.3
P=103.5	D=167.9	T=254.1

Niagara Falls Area	
146.73-	147.045+
146.685-	147.09+
146.775-	147.255+
146.82-	147.36+
146.955-	

Syracuse Metro Area	
145.21-	147.06+
145.27-	147.105+ @
145.43-	147.21+
146.625-	147.30+
146.685-	147.33+
146.745-	147.345+
146.91-	147.39+

Rochester Metro Area	
145.11- R	146.88-@
145.29-@	146.94-
146.67-	147.075+
146.715-	147.09+
146.79-@	147.135+
146.82-	147.30+

Notes:

+ indicates + offset
- indicates - offset
@ indicates Autopatch

for information on use of Autopatch
be sure to check with repeater owner.

See UHF Map page
for CTCSS tone chart.

Dexter 146.70-

81

Syracuse

81

Oswego 146.85-

Fulton● 145.33-@ 147.15+

Skaneateles 147.195+

Cortland

Ithaca 146.61-@ 146.775- 146.97-

Breesport 147.285+

Owego 146.76-

Endicott 145.47-

Auburn 145.13-@ 145.35-@ 147.00-@ 147.27+@

Clyde 145.47

Seneca Falls 147.075+

Penn Yan 145.37- 146.835- 147.12+

Watkins Glen 147.165+

17

Elmira 147.36+@

Lyons 146.745-

Phelps 146.655-

Canandaigua 146.82- R

Naples 146.925-

Groveland 147.03+

Hornell 146.865-

Alfred 146.955-

Corning 146.70- 147.015+

Prattsburg 145.41- 147.24+

Greece 147.18+ Rochester

Churchville 145.21-

Springwater 146.76-

Dansville 147.33+

Hammondsport 145.19-@ 146.805-

Wellsville 147.135+ 147.21+

Prattsburg 145.41- 147.12+

Albion 145.27-

380

20

Batavia 147.15+@ 147.285+

90

104

Colden 146.97- 147.09+

219

Delevan 145.39-

Little Valley 147.195+

Alma 145.49-

Niagra Falls

Boston 146.91-

81

17

Frewsburg 146.79-

Tonawanda 146.955- 146.97- 147.045+

Grand Island 146.73-

Buffalo 146.865- A

Dayton 146.655-

Cherry Creek

Jamestown 146.88-146.94-@

Lancaster 147.255+ A

Fredonia 146.625-

Stockton 147.00+ 146.88-

Mayville 145.29-

Sherman 147.33+

Meter Repeater Offset is 600 KHz

222 & UP

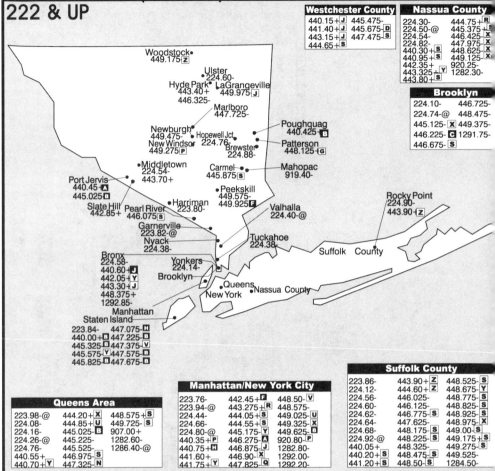

Westchester County

440.15+ J	445.475-
441.40+ J	445.675- D
443.15+ J	447.475- S
444.65+ S	

Nassua County

224.30-	444.75+ R
224.50-@	445.375- S
224.54-	446.425- X
224.82-	447.975- X
440.30+ S	448.625- X
440.95+ S	449.125- X
442.35+	920.25-
443.325+ Y	1282.30-
443.80+ S	

Brooklyn

224.10-	446.725-
224.74-@	448.475-
445.125- X	449.375-
446.225- C	1291.75-
446.675- S	

Woodstock•
449.175 Z

Ulster
•224.60-

Hyde Park• LaGrangeville
443.40+ 449.975 J
446.325-

Marlboro
447.725-

Newburgh•
449.475- Hopewell Jct
New Windsor 224.76-
449.275 P Brewster•
224.88-

Poughquag
440.425- B

Patterson
448.125+ G

Middletown
•224.54-
443.70+

Carmel•
445.875 S

Mahopac
919.40-

Port Jervis•
440.45- A
445.025- B

Peekskill
449.575-
449.925 F

Rocky Point
224.90-
443.90+ Z

Slate Hill• Pearl River Harriman
442.85+ 446.075 S 223.80-

Valhalla
224.40-@

Garnerville
223.82-@
Nyack
224.38-

Tuckahoe
224.38-

Suffolk County

Bronx
224.58-
440.60+ J
442.05+ Y
443.30+ J
448.375+
1292.85-

Yonkers
224.14-

Brooklyn•

Queens
New York •Nassua County

Manhattan
Staten Island

223.84-	447.075- H
440.00+ B	447.225- B
445.325- B	447.375- V
445.575- Y	447.575- B
445.825- B	447.675- B

Suffolk County

223.86-	443.90+ Z	448.525- S
224.12-	444.60+ Z	448.675- Y
224.56-	446.025-	448.775- S
224.60-	446.125-	448.825- S
224.62-	446.775- S	448.925- X
224.64-	447.625-	448.975- X
224.68-	448.175- S	449.00- S
224.92-@	448.225- S	449.175+ S
440.05+	448.325-	449.275- S
440.20+ S	448.475- S	449.525-
441.20+ S	448.50- S	1284.50-

Manhattan/New York City

223.76-	442.45+ F	448.50- V
223.94-@	443.275+ R	448.575-
224.44-	444.05+ S	449.025- U
224.66-	444.55+ S	449.325- X
224.80-@	445.175- Y	449.625- B
440.35+ P	446.275- A	920.80- P
440.75+ H	446.875- X	1282.80-
441.60+	446.90- X	1292.00-
441.75+ Y	447.825- Q	1292.20-

Queens Area

223.98-@	444.20+ X	448.575+ S
224.08-	444.85+ U	449.725- S
224.16-	445.025- B	907.00+
224.26-@	445.225-	1282.60-
224.76-	445.525-	1286.40-@
440.55+	446.975- S	
440.70+ Y	447.325- N	

NEW YORK FACTS

NUMBER OF HAMS: 34,793

CALL AREA: 2

STATE NICKNAME: EMPIRE STATE

HIGHEST POINT:
   MT. MARCY (5,344 FT.)

STATE CAPITAL: ALBANY

NUMBER OF COUNTIES: 62

NUMBER OF 2M REPEATERS: 77

   222 REPEATERS: 6375

   440 REPEATERS: 109

   900 MHz REPEATERS: 3

   1.2 GHz REPEATERS: 9

CTCSS TONES

A=67.0	Q=107.2	E=173.8	
B=69.3	R=110.9	F=179.9	
C=71.9	S=114.8	G=186.2	
D=74.4	T=118.8	H=192.8	
E=77.0	U=123.0	J=203.5	
F=79.7	V=127.3	K=206.5	
G=82.5	W=131.8	L=210.7	
H=85.4	X=136.5	M=218.1	
J=88.5	Y=141.3	N=225.7	
K=91.5	Z=146.2	P=229.1	
L=94.8	A=151.4	Q=233.6	
M=97.4	B=156.7	R=241.8	
N=100.0	C=162.2	S=250.3	
P=103.5	D=167.9	T=254.1	

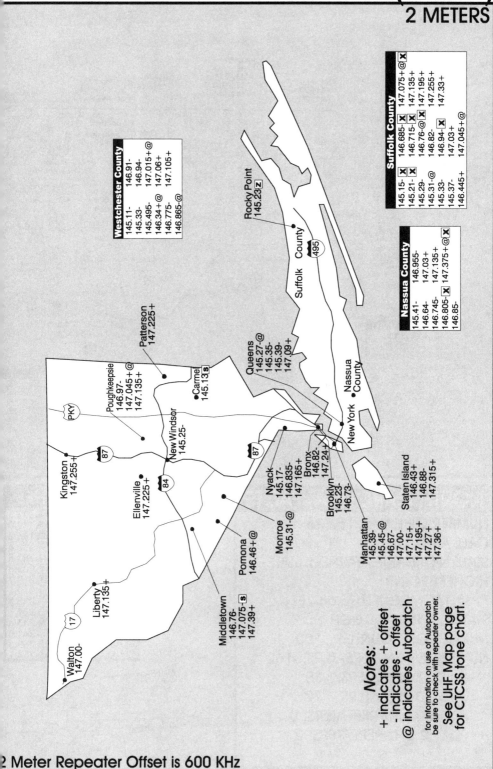

2 METERS

Westchester County

145.11-	146.91-
145.33-	146.94-
145.495-	147.015+@
146.34+@	147.06+
146.775+	147.105+
146.865-@	

Suffolk County

145.15-	☒	147.075+@☒
145.21-	☒	147.135+
145.29-	146.685-☒	147.195+
145.31-@	146.715-☒	147.255+
145.33-	146.76-@☒	147.33+
145.37-	146.82-	
146.445-	146.94-☒	
	147.03+	
	147.045+@	

Nassua County

145.41-	146.955-
145.64-	147.03+
146.745-	147.135+
146.805-☒	147.375+@☒
146.85-	

Rocky Point
145.23☒

Suffolk County

495

Patterson
147.225+

Poughkeepsie
146.97-
147.045+@
147.135+

Carmel
145.13s

Queens
145.27-@
145.35-
145.39-
147.09+

PKY

New Windsor
145.25-

Nassua
County

New York

Kingston
147.255+

87

87

Nyack
145.17-
146.835-
147.165+

Bronx
146.82-
147.24-

Staten Island
146.43+
146.88-
147.315+

Ellenville
147.225+

84

Monroe
145.31-@

Brooklyn
145.23-
146.73-

Pomona
146.46+@

Manhattan
145.39-
145.45-@
146.67-
147.00-
147.15+
147.195+
147.27+
147.36+

17

Liberty
147.135+

Middletown
146.76-
147.075-s
147.39+

Walton
147.00-

Notes:
+ indicates + offset
- indicates - offset
@ indicates Autopatch

for information on use of Autopatch
be sure to check with repeater owner.

See UHF Map page
for CTCSS tone chart.

2 Meter Repeater Offset is 600 KHz

222 & UP

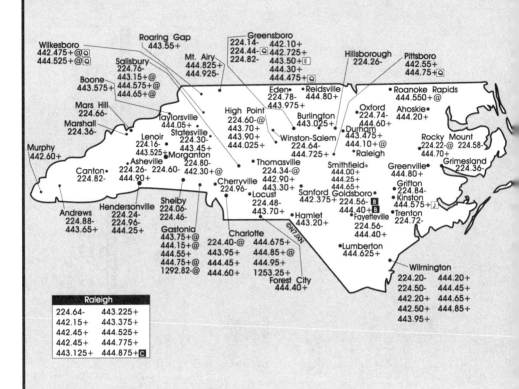

Wilkesboro
442.475+@▢
444.525+@▢

Roaring Gap
443.55+

Salisbury
224.76-
443.15+@
444.575+@
444.65+@

Mt. Airy
444.825+
444.925-

Greensboro
224.14-
224.44-▢
224.82-

442.10+
442.725+
443.50+Ⓔ
444.30+
444.475+▢

Hillsborough
224.26-

Pittsboro
442.55+
444.75+▢

Boone
443.575+

Mars Hill
224.66-

Marshall
224.36-

Taylorsville
444.05+

High Point
224.60-@
443.70+
443.90+
444.025+

Eden
224.78-
443.975+

Reidsville
444.80+

Burlington
443.025+

Oxford
224.74-
444.60+

Durham
443.475+
444.10+@
Raleigh

Ahoskie
444.20+

Roanoke Rapids
444.550+@

Murphy
442.60+

Lenoir
224.16-
443.525+

Statesville
224.30-
443.45+

Morganton
224.80-

Asheville
224.26- 224.60-
444.90+

Winston-Salem
224.64-
444.725+

Thomasville
224.34-@
442.90+
443.30+

Smithfield
444.00+
444.25+
444.65+

Rocky Mount
224.22-@ 224.58-
444.70+

Greenville
444.80+

Grimesland
224.36-

Canton
224.82-

442.30+@

Cherryville
224.96-

Locust
224.48-
443.70+

Sanford
442.375+

Goldsboro
224.56-Ⓑ
444.40+Ⓑ

Grifton
224.84-

Kinston
444.575+Ⓙ

Andrews
224.88-
443.65+

Hendersonville
224.24-
224.96-
444.25+

Shelby
224.06-
224.46-

Hamlet
443.20+

Fayetteville
224.56-
444.40+

Trenton
224.72-

Gastonia
443.75+@
444.15+@
444.55+
444.75+@
1292.82-@

Charlotte
224.40-@
443.95+
444.45+
444.60+

444.675+
444.85+@
444.95+
1253.25+

Lumberton
444.625+

Forest City
444.40+

Wilmington
224.20- 444.20+
224.50- 444.45+
442.50+ 444.65+
442.50+ 444.85+
443.95+

Raleigh	
224.64-	443.225+
442.15+	443.375+
442.45+	444.525+
442.45+	444.775+
443.125+	444.875+Ⓒ

222 Repeater Offset is 1.6 MH
440 Repeater Offset is 5 MH

NORTH CAROLINA FACTS

NUMBER OF HAMS: 15,326

CALL AREA: 4

STATE NICKNAME: TARHEEL STATE

HIGHEST POINT:
     MT. MITCHELL (6,684 FT.)

STATE CAPITAL: RALEIGH

NUMBER OF COUNTIES: 100

NUMBER OF 2M REPEATERS: 162

    222 REPEATERS: 35

    440 REPEATERS: 77

    900 MHz REPEATERS: 0

    1.2 GHz REPEATERS: 2

CTCSS TONES

A=67.0	Q=107.2	E=173.8
B=69.3	R=110.9	F=179.9
C=71.9	S=114.8	G=186.2
D=74.4	T=118.8	H=192.8
E=77.0	U=123.0	J=203.5
F=79.7	V=127.3	K=206.5
G=82.5	W=131.8	L=210.7
H=85.4	X=136.5	M=218.1
J=88.5	Y=141.3	N=225.7
K=91.5	Z=146.2	P=229.1
L=94.8	A=151.4	Q=233.6
M=97.4	B=156.7	R=241.8
N=100.0	C=162.2	S=250.3
P=103.5	D=167.9	T=254.1

North Carolina
2 METERS

2 Meter Repeater Offset is 600 KHz

Metro Area Listings

Raleigh Metro Area	
145.13-	146.88-
145.49-	147.015-
146.61-	147.15+
146.64-@	147.195+
146.73-	147.27+
146.775-	

Greensboro Metro Area	
145.25-	146.76-
145.29-	147.03+
145.31-@	147.21+
146.61-@	

Charlotte Metro Area	
145.23-	147.06+@
145.29-@	147.27+
145.35-	147.39+
146.94-@	

Winston-Salem Metro Area	
145.11-	146.64-@
145.47-	147.315+

Map Labels

Buxton 146.625-
Manteo 146.94-@
Nags Head 145.15- 146.835-@
Coinjock 145.29-
Elizabeth City 146.655-
Columbia 145.11-@
Anderson 145.17-
Trenton 145.21-
Williamston 147.345+@
Washington
Greenville 145.35-@ 147.375+
Newport 145.45-@
Swansboro 146.76-@
Ahoskie 145.13-@ 146.91-
Roanoke Rapids 147.03+
Macon 147.06+
Rocky Mount 146.805- 147.12+
Farmville 145.27-@
Goldsboro 146.85-
Grifton 146.685-
Kinston 145.47-@ 147.09+
New Bern 146.61-@
Beulaville 145.19-
Jacksonville 145.23- 147.00-@
Burgaw 146.94-
Wilmington 146.73- 146.82- 147.135+ 147.18+
Southport 146.67- 146.775-
Shallotte 145.37- 147.315+ 147.39+
Madison 146.895-
Hillsborough 147.225+@
Oxford 145.17- 145.37-
Eden 147.39+
Gibsonville 145.49-@
Burlington 146.67+@ 147.075+
Durham 145.23- 145.15- 147.36+@
Randleman
Selma 147.015+@
Clayton 145.29-
Dunn 146.70-
Broadway 147.105+
Clinton 146.79-
Fayetteville 146.805- 146.91- 147.045+ 147.33+ 147.165+
Spring Lake 146.715-
Lumberton 145.15- 147.165+ 147.36+ 147.21+
Whiteville 147.21+@
Leland 145.17-@
Tabor City 147.375+@
Red Springs 147.30+
Sanford 147.185+@
Carthage 147.24+ 147.255+
Aquadale 147.39+
Wadesboro 146.835-
Rockingham 146.955-
Laurinburg 146.625-
Greensboro 145.15- 145.45-@
Lexington 146.91-
Thomasville 147.00-@
Asheboro
Concord 146.655-
Albemarle 146.985-@
Monroe 146.805-@ 147.12+@
Gastonia 146.805+ 147.345+
Charlotte
Statesville 147.045+
Newton 145.17- 145.21-
Cherryville 145.11-
Forest City 146.67-
Shelby 146.88- 147.345+
Hendersonville 145.27-@ 146.64- 147.105+ 147.255+@
Lenoir 147.195+@ 147.33+
Morganton 147.15+
Hickory 145.21- 146.85-
Marion 146.985-@
Burnsville 146.955-@ 147.375+@
Bakersville 145.31-@
Banner Elk 146.625-
Boone 147.105+ 147.36+@
Jefferson 147.30+
Sparta 145.43-
N. Wilkesboro 145.37-@
Millers Creek 146.715-@
Mt. Airy 145.33-@ 146.94- 146.97-
High Point 145.41-@ 146.835- 147.165+
Winston-Salem 147.075+@
Mt Mitchell 145.19-
Asheville 146.76- 146.835- 146.91- 147.105+
Waynesville 147.27+@ 147.39+
Canton 146.805-
Franklin 145.49- 147.24+
Tuckasegee 147.30+
Murphy 146.865-
Andrews 147.045+
Brevard 147.135+

©NTJXN

Notes:
+ indicates + offset
- indicates - offset
@ indicates Autopatch

for information on use of Autopatch
be sure to check with repeater owner.

See UHF Map page
for CTCSS tone chart.

North Dakota

222 & UP

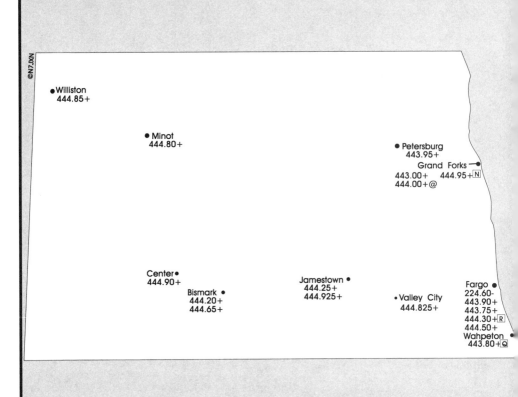

©N7JXN

Williston
444.85+

Minot
444.80+

Petersburg
443.95+

Grand Forks
443.00+   444.95+N
444.00+@

Center
444.90+

Jamestown
444.25+
444.925+

Fargo
224.60-
443.90+
443.75+
444.30+R
444.50+

Bismark
444.20+
444.65+

Valley City
444.825+

Wahpeton
443.80+Q

222 Repeater Offset is 1.6 MH:
440 Repeater Offset is 5 MH:

NORTH DAKOTA FACTS

NUMBER OF HAMS: 1,548

CALL AREA: 0

STATE NICKNAME: SIOUX STATE

HIGHEST POINT:
    WHITE BUTTE (3,506 FT.)

STATE CAPITAL: BISMARK

NUMBER OF COUNTIES: 53

NUMBER OF 2M REPEATERS: 29

    222 REPEATERS: 1

    440 REPEATERS: 17

    900 MHz REPEATERS: 0

    1.2 GHz REPEATERS: 0

CTCSS TONES

A=67.0	Q=107.2	E=173.8
B=69.3	R=110.9	F=179.9
C=71.9	S=114.8	G=186.2
D=74.4	T=118.8	H=192.8
E=77.0	U=123.0	J=203.5
F=79.7	V=127.3	K=206.5
G=82.5	W=131.8	L=210.7
H=85.4	X=136.5	M=218.1
J=88.5	Y=141.3	N=225.7
K=91.5	Z=146.2	P=229.1
L=94.8	A=151.4	Q=233.6
M=97.4	B=156.7	R=241.8
N=100.0	C=162.2	S=250.3
P=103.5	D=167.9	T=254.1

88

North Dakota
2 METERS

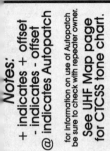

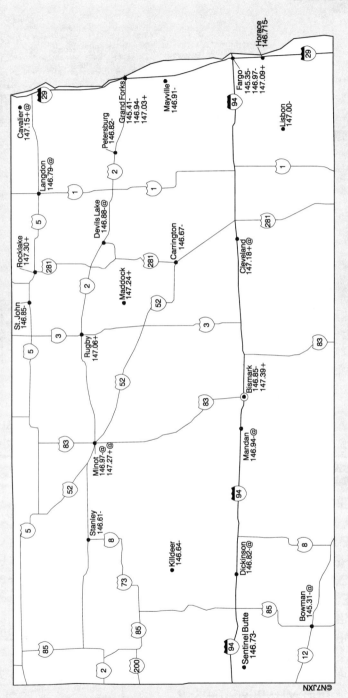

Cavalier ●
147.15+

Langdon
146.79-@

Rocklake
147.30+

St. John
146.85-

Petersburg
146.82-

Grand Forks
145.41-
146.94-
147.03+

Mayville ●
146.91-

Devils Lake
146.88-@

Carrington
146.67-

Cleveland
147.18-@

Fargo
145.35-
146.97-
147.09+

Horace
146.75-

Lisbon
147.00-

Maddock ●
147.24+

Rugby
147.06+

Bismark
146.85-
147.39+

Minot @
146.97-@
147.27+-@

Mandan
146.94-@

Stanley
146.61-

Killdeer ●
146.64-

Dickinson
146.82-@

Bowman
145.31-@

Sentinel Butte
146.73-

©N7JXN

Ohio

NORTH AMERICAN REPEATER ATL...

222 & UP

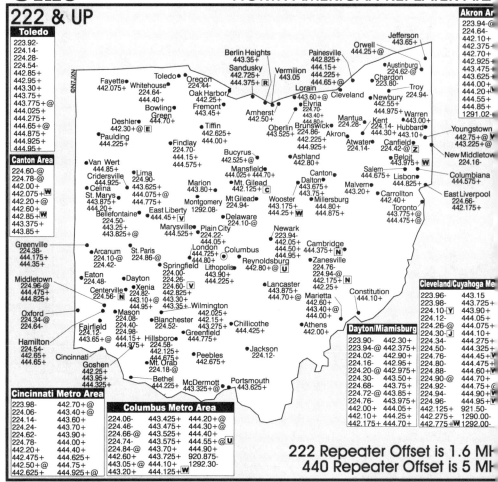

Akron Ar
223.94-@
224.64-
442.10+
442.375+
442.70+
442.925+
443.475+
443.625+
444.00+
444.20+
444.55+
444.85+
1291.02-

Toledo
223.92-
224.14-
224.28-
224.54-
442.85+
442.95+
443.30+
443.75+
443.775+@
444.025+
444.275+
444.65+@
444.875+
444.925+
444.95+

Canton Area
224.60-@
224.78-@
442.00+
442.075+W
442.20+@
442.60+
442.85+W
443.375+
443.85+

Greenville
224.38-
444.175+
444.35+

Middletown
224.96-@
444.475+
444.825+

Oxford
224.34-@
224.64-

Hamilton
224.54-
442.65+
444.65+

Cincinnati Metro Area

223.98-	442.70+@
224.06-	443.40+@
224.14-	443.60+
224.24-	443.70+
224.62-	443.90+
224.78-	444.00+
442.20+	444.40+
442.475+	444.625+
442.50+@	444.75+
442.625+	444.925+@

Columbus Metro Area

224.06-	443.425+	444.20+@
224.46-	443.475+	444.40+
224.66-@	443.525+	444.40+
224.74-	443.575+	444.55+@ [U]
224.84-@	443.70+	444.90+
442.60+	443.725+	920.875-
443.05+@	444.10+	1292.30-
443.20+	444.125+ [W]	

Cleveland/Cuyahoga Me

223.96-	443.15
223.98-	443.725+
224.10-[Y]	443.90+
224.12-	444.05+
224.26-@	444.075+
224.30-[J]	444.10+
224.34-	444.275+
224.50-	444.325+
224.76-	444.45+V
224.80-	444.475+V
224.88-	444.60+W
224.90-@	444.70+
224.92-	444.75+@
224.94-	444.90+V
224.96-	444.95+V
442.125+	921.50-
442.275+	1290.00-
442.775+W	1292.00-

Dayton/Miamisburg

223.90-	442.30+
223.94-@	442.375+
224.02-	442.90+
224.16-	442.95+
224.20-@	443.50+
224.30-	443.50+
224.68-	443.75+
224.72-@	443.85+
224.76-	443.975+
442.00+	444.05+
442.10+	444.25+
442.175+	444.70+

222 Repeater Offset is 1.6 MH
440 Repeater Offset is 5 MH

OHIO FACTS

NUMBER OF HAMS: 29,794

CALL AREA: 8

STATE NICKNAME: BUCKEYE STATE

HIGHEST POINT:
CAMPBELL HILL (1,550 FT.)

STATE CAPITAL: COLUMBUS

NUMBER OF COUNTIES: 88

NUMBER OF 2M REPEATERS: 242

222 REPEATERS: 81

440 REPEATERS: 192

900 MHz REPEATERS: 2

1.2 GHz REPEATERS: 3

CTCSS TONES

A=67.0	Q=107.2	E=173.8
B=69.3	R=110.9	F=179.9
C=71.9	S=114.8	G=186.2
D=74.4	T=118.8	H=192.8
E=77.0	U=123.0	J=203.5
F=79.7	V=127.3	K=206.5
G=82.5	W=131.8	L=210.7
H=85.4	X=136.5	M=218.1
J=88.5	Y=141.3	N=225.7
K=91.5	Z=146.2	P=229.1
L=94.8	A=151.4	Q=233.6
M=97.4	B=156.7	R=241.8
N=100.0	C=162.2	S=250.3
P=103.5	D=167.9	T=254.1

90

Akron Area

145.25-@
145.39-@
146.61-
146.64+@
146.895-
146.985-@
147.09+
147.135+
147.24+
147.27+@
147.30+

Canton Area

145.41-
145.49-
146.79-
146.955-@
147.12+@
147.18+

Toledo

146.61-
146.76-
146.94-
147.12+@
147.27+@

Cleveland/Cuyahoga Metro

145.15-	146.76-@
145.19-R	146.79-
145.21+R	146.82-@
145.29-@	146.85-
145.43+R	146.88-@
145.49-	147.06+
146.73-	147.195+
	147.36+@

Notes:
+ indicates + offset
- indicates - offset
@ indicates Autopatch

for information on use of Autopatch
be sure to check with repeater owner.

**See UHF Map page
for CTCSS tone chart.**

Map labels

Conneaut 145.25+@
Jefferson 147.39+@
Rock Creek 146.715-@
Troy 146.67-
[N] 145.23- 147.24+ 147.33+
Hubbard 145.11-@ 146.685- 146.835-
Warren 146.97-
Youngstown 145.275-@ 145.745- 146.91- 147.00+@
Austintown 147.375+
Beloit
Alliance 145.37-
Lisbon 146.805-
Carrollton 147.225+@ 147.315+@ 145.45-
Toronto 147.06+
East Palestine 146.775-
East Liverpool 146.70-
St. Clairsville 145.21-
Cadiz 146.655-@
Barnesville 146.64- 147.27+
Caldwell 147.285+
Constitution 146.745-@ 146.88-@ 146.97-

Madison 145.33-@
Chardon 146.94-
Newbury 147.015+
Cleveland 422
Mentor 147.165+ 147.255-
Painesville 147.091+@ 147.345+@
Vermillion 145.35-@ 145.47-R
Lorain
Elyria 145.23- 146.70-
Akron 147.105+@
Ashland 146.745- 147.105+@
Oberlin 147.285+ 147.15+@
Berlin 147.03+
Medina 147.21-
Nashville 145.13-
Millersburg 146.67-@
Mt Gilead 146.775-@
Coshocton 147.045+
Cambridge 146.85-
Zanesville 146.61- 146.82-
Logan 147.345+
Lancaster 146.70-
Newark 145.37- 146.88-
Columbus
Lithopolis 145.21- 145.39-
Circleville 147.18+ 146.85- 146.925-
Chillicothe
Athens 145.15- 146.625-@ 146.73- 147.15+
Gallipolis 147.06+
Chesapeake 146.715-

Mansfield 145.33-
Galion 146.85- 146.94-
Republic 146.685- 147.21-
Berlin Heights 146.805-
Sandusky 145.35-@ 146.655-R 146.91-
Oregon 147.375+@
Oak Harbor 147.075+
Amherst 146.625-
Fostoria 145.45- 147.255+
Delaware 145.17-@ 145.29-@

Van Wert 146.85- 147.12+@
Russells Point 145.37- 146.88-
Bowling Green 147.045+ 147.15-@
Findlay 147.045+ 147.15+@
Deshler 145.19-@
Ottawa 146.715-@
Lima 145.17-@ 146.61- 146.67-@ 146.94-
Wapakoneta 147.33+
Celina 146.61-
Bellefontaine 146.955-147.00+@
Marion 146.895- 147.30+ 147.03+
Kenton 146.625-
Marysville 145.35-@ 147.39+
London 147.285+
Springfield 145.31-145.45-
Xenia 147.165+
Wilmington 147.12+
Greenfield 146.745- 147.00+
Peebles 147.00+
Hillsboro 146.745- 147.21+
Blanchester 145.25-@
Bethel 147.225+@
Owensville 147.345+@
Cincinnati
Georgetown 146.73-@
Portsmouth 145.39- 147.36+

Wauseon 147.195+
Toledo
Whitehouse 147.345+
Napoleon 147.315+
Ridgeville Corners 145.41-
Bryan 146.82-
Defiance 147.09+ 147.225+@
Paulding 146.865
Greenville 146.79-@
Piqua 147.121+@
Arcanum 147.18+
Eaton 145.47-
Middletown 146.61-@ 147.315+
Oxford 145.39-
Hamilton 145.15- 146.97- 147.06+
Fairfield 147.33+ 145.19-145.21-@ 145.23-
Bellbrook 147.045+
Dayton
Urbana 147.375+

NXfZN@

Columbus Metro Area

145.11-	146.91-
145.13-@	146.97-
145.23-	147.06+
145.27-	147.09+
145.43-	147.12+
145.49+ [U]	147.15+
146.67-	147.21+
146.76-@	147.24+
146.805-	147.33+@

Dayton/Miamisburg Metro

145.11-	146.94-@
145.33-	146.985-
145.41-	147.015+
145.43-	147.075+
145.49-	147.105+
146.64-	147.135+
146.82-@	147.195+
146.85-	147.36+
146.91-	

Cincinnati Metro Area

145.19-@	146.85-
145.27-	146.88-@
145.31-@	146.925-
145.35-	147.00+
145.37-	147.03+
145.45-@	147.06+@
146.625-	147.09+
146.67-	147.15+
146.76-	147.30+

Meter Repeater Offset is 600 KHz

222 & UP

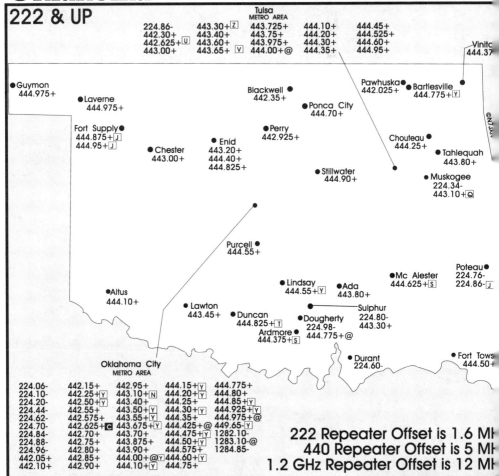

Tulsa METRO AREA

224.86-	443.30+ Z	443.725+	444.10+	444.45+
442.30+	443.40+	443.75+	444.20+	444.525+
442.625+ U	443.60+	443.975+	444.30+	444.60+
443.00+	443.65+ V	444.00+@	444.35+	444.95+

Vinit
444.37

● Guymon
444.975+

● Laverne
444.975+

Fort Supply ●
444.875+ J
444.95+ J

● Chester
443.00+

Blackwell ●
442.35+

● Enid
443.20+
444.40+
444.825+

● Perry
442.925+

● Ponca City
444.70+

Pawhuska ● ● Bartlesville
442.025+   444.775+ Y

Chouteau ●
444.25+

● Tahlequah
443.80+

● Stillwater
444.90+

● Muskogee
224.34-
443.10+ Q

Purcell ●
444.55+

● Altus
444.10+

● Lawton
443.45+

● Lindsay
444.55+ Y

● Ada
443.80+

● Mc Alester
444.625+ S

Poteau ●
224.76-
224.86- J

● Duncan
444.825+ T

● Dougherty
224.98-
444.775+@

Sulphur
224.80-
443.30+

Ardmore ●
444.375+ S

● Durant
224.60-

● Fort Tows
444.50+

Oklahoma City METRO AREA

224.06-	442.15+	442.95+	444.15+ Y	444.775+
224.10-	442.25+ Y	443.10+ N	444.20+ Y	444.80+
224.20-	442.50+ Y	443.40+	444.25+	444.85+ Y
224.44-	442.55+	443.50+ Y	444.30+ Y	444.925+ Y
224.62-	442.575+	443.55+ Y	444.35+	444.975+@
224.70-	442.625+ C	443.675+ Y	444.425+@	449.65+ Y
224.84-	442.70+	443.70+	444.475+ Y	1282.10-
224.88-	442.75+	443.875+	444.50+ Y	1283.10-@
224.96-	442.80+	443.90+	444.575+ Y	1284.85-
442.05+	442.85+	444.00+@ Y	444.60+ Y	
442.10+	442.90+	444.10+ Y	444.75+	

222 Repeater Offset is 1.6 MI
440 Repeater Offset is 5 MI
1.2 GHz Repeater Offset is 12 MI

OKLAHOMA FACTS

NUMBER OF HAMS: 8,303

CALL AREA: 5

STATE NICKNAME: SOONER STATE

HIGHEST POINT:
    BLACK MESA (4,973 FT.)

STATE CAPITAL: OKLAHOMA CITY

NUMBER OF COUNTIES: 77

NUMBER OF 2M REPEATERS: 141

    222 REPEATERS: 16

    440 REPEATERS: 90

    900 MHz REPEATERS: 0

    1.2 GHz REPEATERS: 1

CTCSS TONES

A=67.0	Q=107.2
B=69.3	R=110.9
C=71.9	S=114.8
D=74.4	T=118.8
E=77.0	U=123.0
F=79.7	V=127.3
G=82.5	W=131.8
H=85.4	X=136.5
J=88.5	Y=141.3
K=91.5	Z=146.2
L=94.8	A=151.4
M=97.4	B=156.7
N=100.0	C=162.2
P=103.5	D=167.9
E=173.8	
F=179.9	
G=186.2	
H=192.8	
J=203.5	
K=206.5	
L=210.7	
M=218.1	
N=225.7	
P=229.1	
Q=233.6	
R=241.8	
S=250.3	
T=254.1	

Oklahoma
2 METERS

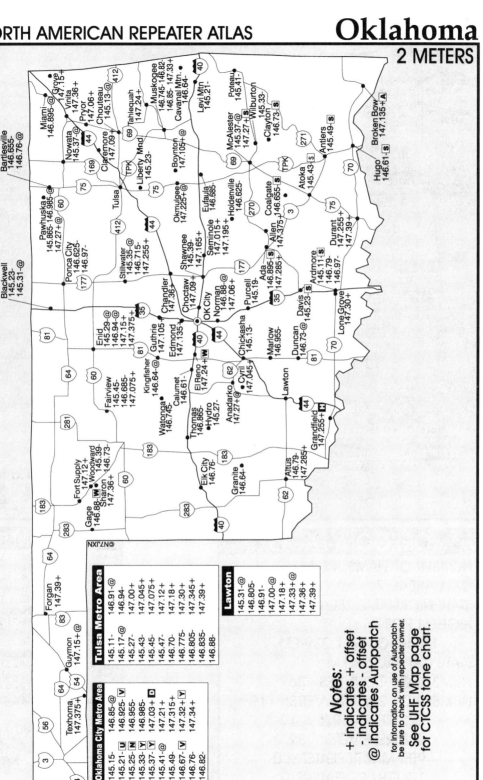

Oklahoma City Metro Area

145.15-	146.85-@
145.21-	146.925+
145.25-	146.955-
145.33-	146.985-
145.37-	147.03+
145.41-@	147.21+
145.49-	147.315+
145.67-	147.32+
146.76-	147.34+
146.82-	

Tulsa Metro Area

145.11-	146.91-@
145.17-@	146.94-
145.27-	147.00-
145.43-	147.045+
145.45-	147.075+
145.47-	147.18+
146.70-	147.30+
146.775+	147.345+
146.805-	147.39+
146.835-	
146.88-	

Lawton

145.31-@
146.805-
146.91-
147.00-@
147.18+
147.33+@
147.36+
147.39+

Notes:
+ indicates + offset
- indicates - offset
@ indicates Autopatch

for information on use of Autopatch
be sure to check with repeater owner.

See UHF Map page
for CTCSS tone chart.

2 Meter Repeater Offset is 600 KHz

93

222 & UP

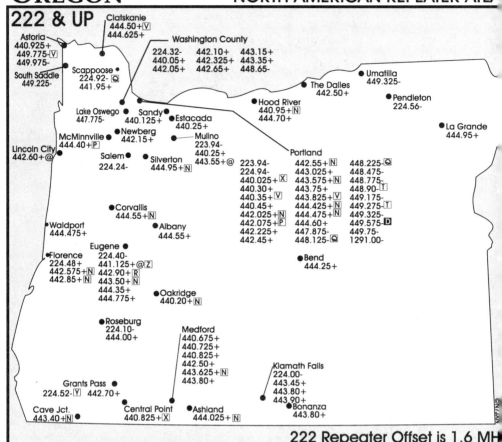

Clatskanie
444.50+ V
444.625+

Astoria
440.925+
449.775- V
449.975-

South Saddle
449.225-

Washington County
224.32-   442.10+   443.15+
440.05+   442.325+ 443.35+
442.05+   442.65+   448.65-

Scappoose •
224.92- Q
441.95+

Umatilla
449.325-

The Dalles
442.50+

Pendleton
224.56-

Lake Oswego •   Sandy •
447.775-   440.125+ • Estacada
McMinnville •   • Newberg   440.25+
444.40+ P   442.15+

Hood River
440.95+ N
444.70+

La Grande
444.95+

Lincoln City •
442.60+ @

Salem •   • Silverton
224.24-   444.95+ N

Mulino
223.94-
440.25+
443.55+ @

Portland
442.55+ N   448.225- Q
443.025+   448.475-
443.575+ N 448.775-
443.75+   448.90- T
443.825+ V 449.175-
444.425+ N 449.275- T
444.475+ N 449.325-
444.60+   449.575- D
447.875-   449.75-
448.125- Q 1291.00-

223.94-
224.94-
440.025+ X
440.30+
440.35+ V
440.45+
442.025+ N
442.075+ P
442.225+
442.45+

• Corvallis
444.55+ N

• Waldport
444.475+

• Albany
444.55+

Eugene •
224.40-
• Florence   441.125+ @ Z
224.48+   442.90+ R
442.575+ N 443.50+ N
442.85+ N   444.35+
444.775+

• Oakridge
440.20+ N

Bend
444.25+

• Roseburg
224.10-
444.00+

Medford
440.675+
440.725+
440.825+
442.50+
443.625+ N
443.80+

Klamath Falls
224.00-
443.45+
443.80+
443.90+

Grants Pass •
224.52- Y   442.70+

Cave Jct.
443.40+ N •

Central Point
440.825+ X

• Ashland
444.025+ N

• Bonanza
443.80+

222 Repeater Offset is 1.6 MH
440 Repeater Offset is 5 MH
1.2 GHz Repeater Offset is 12 MH

OREGON FACTS

NUMBER OF HAMS: 11,661

CALL AREA: 7

STATE NICKNAME: BEAVER STATE

HIGHEST POINT:
MT. HOOD (11,239 FT.)

STATE CAPITAL: SALEM

NUMBER OF COUNTIES: 36

NUMBER OF 2M REPEATERS: 119

222 REPEATERS: 12
440 REPEATERS: 82
900 MHz REPEATERS: 0
1.2 GHz REPEATERS: 1

CTCSS TONES

A=67.0	Q=107.2	E=173.8
B=69.3	R=110.9	F=179.9
C=71.9	S=114.8	G=186.2
D=74.4	T=118.8	H=192.8
E=77.0	U=123.0	J=203.5
F=79.7	V=127.3	K=206.5
G=82.5	W=131.8	L=210.7
H=85.4	X=136.5	M=218.1
J=88.5	Y=141.3	N=225.7
K=91.5	Z=146.2	P=229.1
L=94.8	A=151.4	Q=233.6
M=97.4	B=156.7	R=241.8
N=100.0	C=162.2	S=250.3
P=103.5	D=167.9	T=254.1

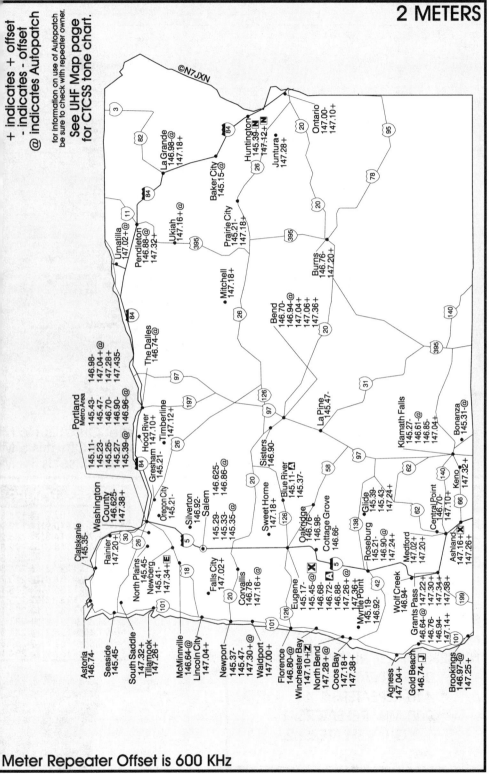

Meter Repeater Offset is 600 KHz

222 & UP

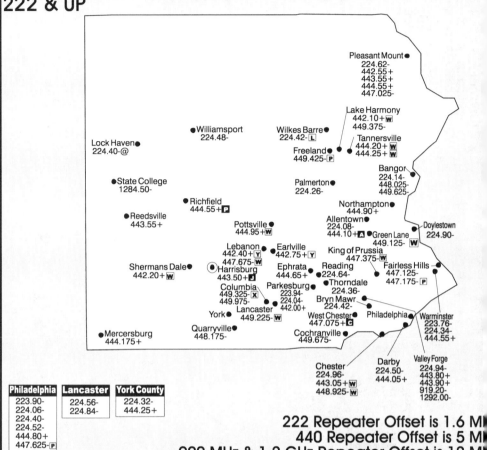

Pleasant Mount ●
224.62-
442.55 +
443.55 +
444.55 +
447.025-

Lake Harmony
442.10 + W
449.375-

● Williamsport
224.48-

Wilkes Barre ●
224.42- L

Tannersville
444.20 + W
444.25 + W

Lock Haven ●
224.40-@

Freeland ●
449.425- P

Bangor
224.14-
448.025-
449.625-

● State College
1284.50-

Palmerton ●
224.26-

Northampton ●
444.90 +

● Richfield
444.55 + P

Allentown ●
224.08-
444.10 + A ● Green Lane
449.125- W

Doylestown
224.90-

● Reedsville
443.55 +

Pottsville ●
444.95 + W

Lebanon ●
442.40 + Y
447.675- W

Earlville ●
442.75 + Y

King of Prussia
447.375- W

Shermans Dale ●
442.20 + W

● Harrisburg
443.50 + J

Ephrata ●
444.65 +

Reading ●
224.64-

Fairless Hills ●
447.125-
447.175- P

Columbia
449.325- X
449.975-

Parkesburg ●
223.94-
224.04-
442.00 +

● Thorndale
224.36-

York ●
Lancaster ●
449.225- W

Bryn Mawr ●
224.42-

West Chester ●
447.075 + C

Philadelphia ●

Warminster
223.76-
224.34-
444.55 +

Quarryville ●
448.175-

Cochranville ●
449.675-

● Mercersburg
444.175 +

Chester
224.96-
443.05 + W
448.925- W

Darby
224.50-
444.05 +

Valley Forge
224.94-
443.80 +
443.90 +
919.20-
1292.00-

Philadelphia	Lancaster	York County
223.90-	224.56-	224.32-
224.06-	224.84-	444.25 +
224.40-		
224.52-		
444.80 +		
447.625- P		
447.975- W		

222 Repeater Offset is 1.6 M
440 Repeater Offset is 5 M
900 MHz & 1.2 GHz Repeater Offset is 12 M

PENNSYLVANIA FACTS

NUMBER OF HAMS: 24,332

CALL AREA: 3

STATE NICKNAME: KEYSTONE STATE

HIGHEST POINT:
    MT. DAVIS (3,213 FT.)

STATE CAPITAL: HARRISBURG

NUMBER OF COUNTIES: 67

NUMBER OF 2M REPEATERS: 108

    222 REPEATERS: 25
    440 REPEATERS: 44
    900 MHz REPEATERS: 1
    1.2 GHz REPEATERS: 2

CTCSS TONES

A = 67.0	Q = 107.2	E = 173.8
B = 69.3	R = 110.9	F = 179.9
C = 71.9	S = 114.8	G = 186.2
D = 74.4	T = 118.8	H = 192.8
E = 77.0	U = 123.0	J = 203.5
F = 79.7	V = 127.3	K = 206.5
G = 82.5	W = 131.8	L = 210.7
H = 85.4	X = 136.5	M = 218.1
J = 88.5	Y = 141.3	N = 225.7
K = 91.5	Z = 146.2	P = 229.1
L = 94.8	A = 151.4	Q = 233.6
M = 97.4	B = 156.7	R = 241.8
N = 100.0	C = 162.2	S = 250.3
P = 103.5	D = 167.9	T = 254.1

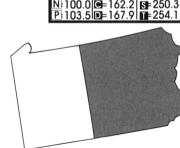

2 METERS

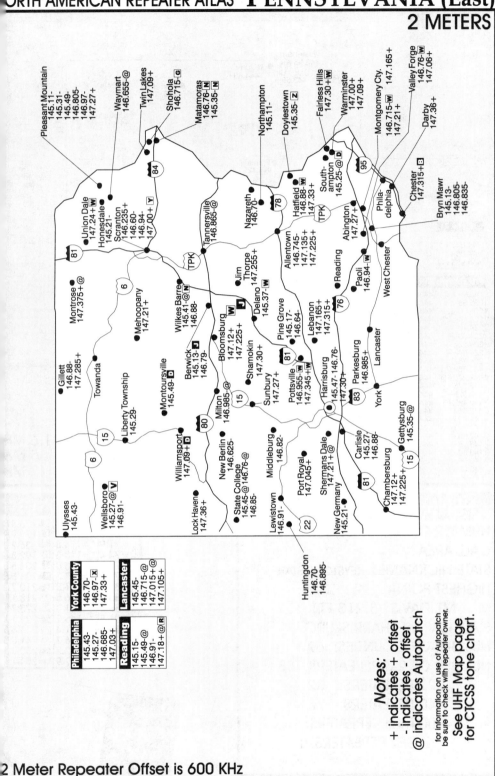

Pleasant Mountain
145.11-
145.31-
145.49-
146.805-
146.97-
147.27+

Waymart
146.655-@

Twin Lakes
147.09+

Shohola
146.715-G

Matamoras
146.76-N
145.35-N

Northampton
145.11-

Doylestown
145.35-Z

Fairless Hills
147.30+W

Warminster
147.00+
147.09+

Montgomery Cty.
146.715-W 147.165-+
147.21+

Valley Forge
146.76-W
147.06+

Darby
147.36+

Union Dale
147.24+W

Honesdale
145.21-

Scranton
146.235+
146.60-
146.94-
147.00+Y

Tannersville
146.865-@

Nazareth
146.70-

Hatfield
146.88-W
147.33+

South-
ampton
145.25+D

Chester
147.315+B

Bryn Mawr
145.13-
146.805-
146.835-

Phila-
delphia

Abington
147.27+

Montrose
147.375-@

Mehoopany
147.21+

Wilkes Barre
145.41-@N
146.88-

Jim
Thorpe
147.255+

Delano
145.37-W

Allentown
146.745-
147.135+
147.225+

Reading

Paoli
146.94-W

West Chester

Gillett
146.88-
147.285+

Towanda

Montoursville
145.49-D

Berwick
145.13-D
146.79-

Bloomsburg
147.12+
147.225+

Shamokin
147.30+

Pine Grove
145.17-
146.64-

Lebanon
147.165+
147.315+

Parkesburg
146.985+

Lancaster

Liberty Township
145.29-

Williamsport
147.09+D

New Berlin
146.625-

Milton
146.985-@

Middleburg
146.82-

Sunbury
147.27+

Pottsville
146.955-W
147.345+W

Harrisburg
145.47-146.76-
147.30+

York

Gettysburg
145.35-@

Ulysses
145.43-

Wellsboro
145.27-@V
146.91-

Lock Haven
147.36+

State College
145.45-@146.76-@
146.85-

Lewistown
146.91-

Port Royal
147.045+

Shermans Dale
147.21+@

New Germany
145.21-

Carlisle
145.27-
146.88-

Chambersburg
147.12+
147.225+

Huntingdon
146.70-
146.895-

Notes:
+ indicates + offset
- indicates - offset
@ indicates Autopatch

for information on use of Autopatch
be sure to check with repeater owner.

See UHF Map page
for CTCSS tone chart.

2 Meter Repeater Offset is 600 KHz

222 & UP

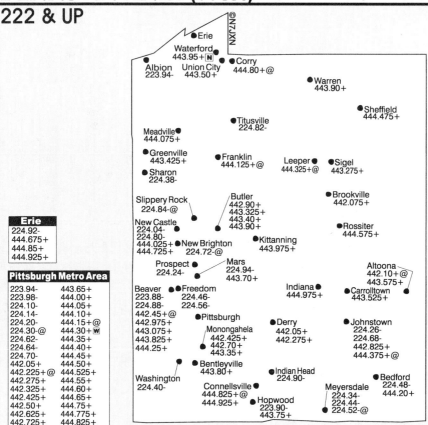

©N7YXN

Erie
Waterford
443.95+ N
Albion   Union City   Corry
223.94-   443.50+   444.80+@

Warren
443.90+

Sheffield
444.475+

Titusville
224.82-

Meadville●
444.075+

Greenville
443.425+   Franklin   Leeper ●   Sigel
Sharon   444.125+@   444.325+@ 443.275+
224.38-

Brookville
442.075+

Slippery Rock   Butler
224.84-@   442.90+
                       443.325+
New Castle   443.40+
224.04-   443.90+
224.80-
444.025+ ● New Brighton   Kittanning   Rossiter
444.725+   224.72-@   443.975+   444.575+

Prospect ●   Mars
224.24-   224.94-
                  443.70+   Altoona
                                                   442.10+@
Indiana ●   443.575+
Beaver ● ● Freedom   444.975+   Carrolltown
223.88-   224.46-   443.525+
224.88-   224.56-
442.45+@
442.975+ ● Pittsburgh
443.075+   Monongahela   Derry   Johnstown
443.825+   442.425+   442.05+   224.26-
444.25+   442.70+   442.275+   224.68-
            443.35+   442.825+
                                         444.375+@
         ● Bentleyville
           443.80+   Indian Head
Washington   224.90-   Bedford
224.40-   Connellsville   224.48-
          444.825+@   Meyersdale   444.20+
          444.925+   Hopwood   224.34-
                     223.90-   224.44-
                     443.75+   224.52-@

Erie

224.92-
444.675+
444.85+
444.925+

Pittsburgh Metro Area

223.94-	443.65+
223.98-	444.00+
224.10-	444.05+
224.14-	444.10+
224.20-	444.15+@
224.30-@	444.30+ W
224.62-	444.35+
224.64-	444.40+
224.70-	444.45+
442.05+	444.50+
442.225+@	444.525+
442.275+	444.55+
442.325+	444.60+
442.425+	444.65+
442.50+	444.75+
442.625+	444.775+
442.725+	444.825+
442.80+	444.90+@ W
443.15+	444.925+
443.50+	444.95+@
443.55+	920.50-
443.625+	1285.00-

222 Repeater Offset is 1.6 MH
440 Repeater Offset is 5 MH
900 MHz & 1.2 GHz Repeater Offset is 12 MH

PENNSYLVANIA FACTS

NUMBER OF HAMS: 24,332

CALL AREA: 3

STATE NICKNAME: KEYSTONE STATE

HIGHEST POINT:
      MT. DAVIS (3,213 FT.)

STATE CAPITAL: HARRISBURG

NUMBER OF COUNTIES: 67

NUMBER OF 2M REPEATERS: 88

      222 REPEATERS: 32

      440 REPEATERS: 76

      900 MHz REPEATERS: 1

      1.2 GHz REPEATERS: 1

CTCSS TONES

A=67.0	Q=107.2	E=173.8
B=69.3	R=110.9	F=179.9
C=71.9	S=114.8	G=186.2
D=74.4	T=118.8	H=192.8
E=77.0	U=123.0	J=203.5
F=79.7	V=127.3	K=206.5
G=82.5	W=131.8	L=210.7
H=85.4	X=136.5	M=218.1
J=88.5	Y=141.3	N=225.7
K=91.5	Z=146.2	P=229.1
L=94.8	A=151.4	Q=233.6
M=97.4	B=156.7	R=241.8
N=100.0	C=162.2	S=250.3
P=103.5	D=167.9	T=254.1

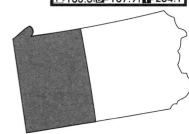

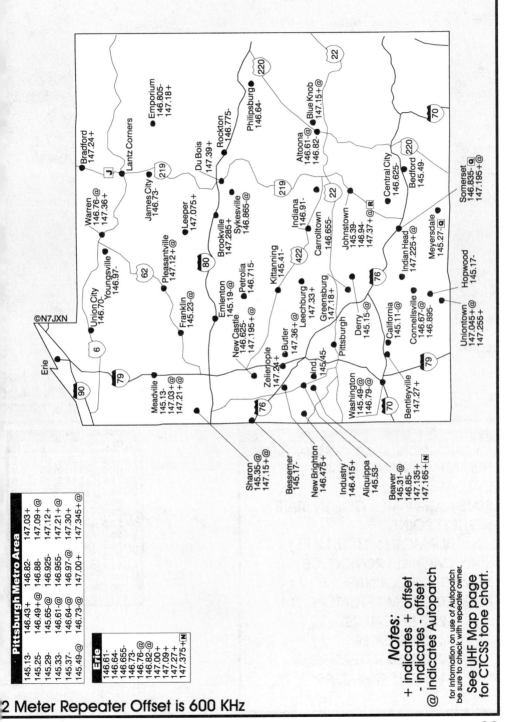

©N7JXN

Pittsburgh Metro Area

145.13-	146.82-	147.03+
145.25-	146.49+@	147.09+@
145.29-	145.65-@	147.12+
145.33-	146.61-@	147.21+@
145.37-	146.64-@	147.30+
145.49+@	146.73-@	147.00+	147.345+@

Erie

146.61-
146.64-
146.655-
146.73-
146.76-@
146.82-@
147.00+
147.09+
147.27+
147.375+N

Notes:
+ indicates + offset
− indicates − offset
@ indicates Autopatch

for information on use of Autopatch
be sure to check with repeater owner.

**See UHF Map page
for CTCSS tone chart.**

2 Meter Repeater Offset is 600 KHz

222 & UP

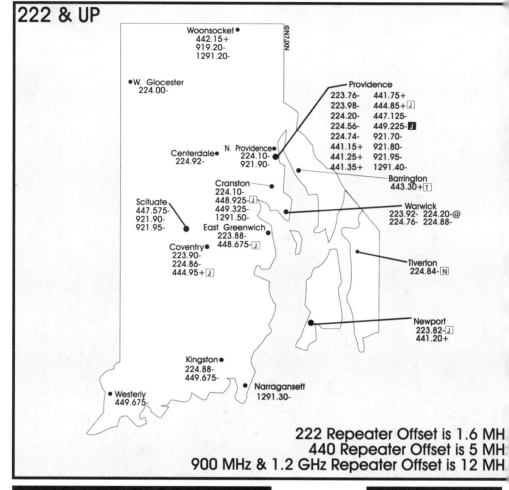

Woonsocket •
442.15+
919.20-
1291.20-

•W. Glocester
224.00-

Providence
223.76-   441.75+
223.98-   444.85+ J
224.20-   447.125-
224.56-   449.225- J
224.74-   921.70-
441.15+   921.80-
441.25+   921.95-
441.35+   1291.40-

Centerdale • N. Providence•
224.92-   224.10-
                   921.90-

Barrington
443.30+ T

Cranston
224.10-
448.925- J
449.325-
1291.50-

Scituate
447.575-
921.90-
921.95-

Warwick
223.92-   224.20-@
224.76-   224.88-

East Greenwich
223.88-
448.675- J

Coventry •
223.90-
224.86-
444.95+ J

Tiverton
224.84- N

Newport
223.82- J
441.20+

Kingston •
224.88-
449.675-

• Westerly
449.675-

• Narragansett
1291.30-

©N7JXN

222 Repeater Offset is 1.6 MH
440 Repeater Offset is 5 MH
900 MHz & 1.2 GHz Repeater Offset is 12 MH

RHODE ISLAND FACTS

NUMBER OF HAMS: 2,489
CALL AREA: 1
STATE NICKNAME: OCEAN STATE
HIGHEST POINT:
     JERIMOTH HILL (812 FT.)
STATE CAPITAL: PROVIDENCE
NUMBER OF COUNTIES: 5
NUMBER OF 2M REPEATERS: 14
      222 REPEATERS: 19
      440 REPEATERS: 17
      900 MHz REPEATERS: 7
      1.2 GHz REPEATERS: 4

CTCSS TONES

A=67.0	Q=107.2	E=173.8
B=69.3	R=110.9	F=179.9
C=71.9	S=114.8	G=186.2
D=74.4	T=118.8	H=192.8
E=77.0	U=123.0	J=203.5
F=79.7	V=127.3	K=206.5
G=82.5	W=131.8	L=210.7
H=85.4	X=136.5	M=218.1
J=88.5	Y=141.3	N=225.7
K=91.5	Z=146.2	P=229.1
L=94.8	A=151.4	Q=233.6
M=97.4	B=156.7	R=241.8
N=100.0	C=162.2	S=250.3
P=103.5	D=167.9	T=254.1

Rhode Island
2 METERS

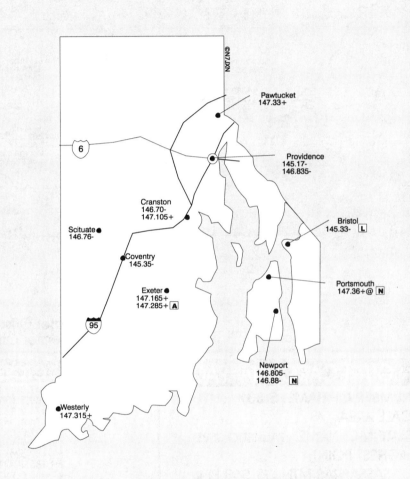

Pawtucket
147.33+

Providence
145.17-
146.835-

Cranston
146.70-
147.105+

Scituate ●
146.76-

Bristol
145.33- L

Coventry
145.35-

Exeter ●
147.165+
147.285+ A

Portsmouth
147.36+@ N

Newport
146.805-
146.88- N

●Westerly
147.315+

Notes:
+ indicates + offset
- indicates - offset
@ indicates Autopatch

for information on use of Autopatch
be sure to check with repeater owner.

See UHF Map page
for CTCSS tone chart.

Meter Repeater Offset is 600 KHz

South Carolina

222 & UP

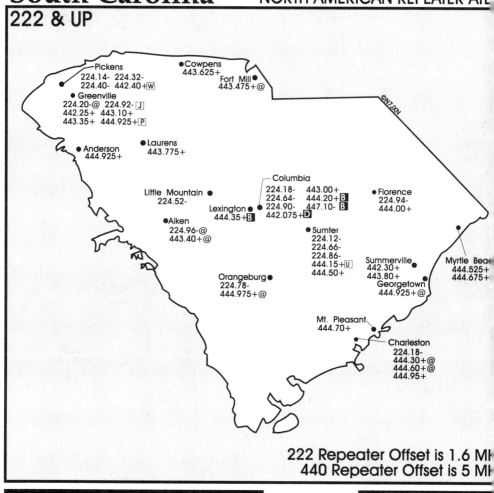

Pickens
224.14- 224.32-
224.40- 442.40+[W]

Cowpens
443.625+

Fort Mill
443.475+@

Greenville
224.20-@ 224.92-[J]
442.25+ 443.10+
443.35+ 444.925+[P]

Anderson
444.925+

Laurens
443.775+

Columbia
224.18- 443.00+
224.64- 444.20+[B]
224.90- 447.10-[B]
442.075+[D]

Little Mountain
224.52-

Florence
224.94-
444.00+

Lexington
444.35+[B]

Aiken
224.96-@
443.40+@

Sumter
224.12-
224.66-
224.86-
444.15+[U]
444.50+

Summerville
442.30+
443.80+

Myrtle Beac
444.525+
444.675+

Orangeburg
224.78-
444.975+@

Georgetown
444.925+@

Mt. Pleasant
444.70+

Charleston
224.18-
444.30+@
444.60+@
444.95+

222 Repeater Offset is 1.6 Mł
440 Repeater Offset is 5 Mł

SOUTH CAROLINA FACTS

NUMBER OF HAMS: 5,837

CALL AREA: 4

STATE NICKNAME: PALMETTO STATE

HIGHEST POINT:
   SASSAFRAS MTN. (3,560 FT.)

STATE CAPITAL: COLUMBIA

NUMBER OF COUNTIES: 46

NUMBER OF 2M REPEATERS: 81

   222 REPEATERS: 16

   440 REPEATERS: 28

   900 MHz REPEATERS: 0

   1.2 GHz REPEATERS: 0

CTCSS TONES

A=67.0	Q=107.2	E=173.8
B=69.3	R=110.9	F=179.9
C=71.9	S=114.8	G=186.2
D=74.4	T=118.8	H=192.8
E=77.0	U=123.0	J=203.5
F=79.7	V=127.3	K=206.5
G=82.5	W=131.8	L=210.7
H=85.4	X=136.5	M=218.1
J=88.5	Y=141.3	N=225.7
K=91.5	Z=146.2	P=229.1
L=94.8	A=151.4	Q=233.6
M=97.4	B=156.7	R=241.8
N=100.0	C=162.2	S=250.3
P=103.5	D=167.9	T=254.1

South Carolina
2 METERS

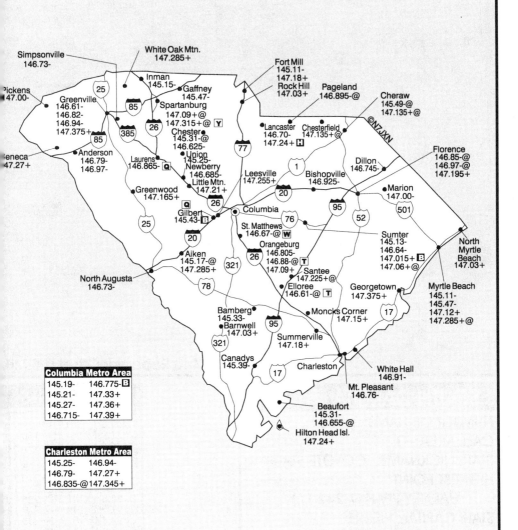

Simpsonville
146.73-

White Oak Mtn.
147.285+

Pickens
47.00-

Inman
145.15-

Gaffney
145.47-

Fort Mill
145.11-
147.18+
Rock Hill
147.03+

Pageland
146.895-@

Cheraw
145.49-@
147.135+@

Greenville
146.61-
146.82-
146.94-
147.375+

Spartanburg
147.09+@
147.315+@ Y

Chester
145.31-@
146.625-

Lancaster
146.70-

Chesterfield
147.135+@
147.24+ H

Florence
146.85-@
146.97-@
147.195+

Seneca
47.27+

Anderson
146.79-
146.97-

Laurens
146.865- Q

Union
145.25-
Newberry
146.685-
Little Mtn.
147.21+

Leesville
147.255+

Dillon
146.745-

Bishopville
146.925-

Marion
147.00-

Greenwood
147.165+

Gilbert
145.43- B

Columbia

St. Matthews
146.67-@ W

Sumter
145.13-
146.64-
147.015+ B
147.06+@

North
Myrtle
Beach
147.03+

Aiken
145.17-@
147.285+

Orangeburg
146.805-
146.88-@ T
147.09+

Santee
147.225+@

Georgetown
147.375+

Myrtle Beach
145.11-
145.47-
147.12+
147.285+@

North Augusta
146.73-

Elloree
146.61-@ T

Bamberg
145.33-
Barnwell
147.03+

Moncks Corner
147.15+

Summerville
147.18+

White Hall
146.91-

Canadys
145.39-

Charleston

Mt. Pleasant
146.76-

Beaufort
145.31-
146.655-@
Hilton Head Isl.
147.24+

Columbia Metro Area

145.19-	146.775- B
145.21-	147.33+
145.27-	147.36+
146.715-	147.39+

Charleston Metro Area

145.25-	146.94-
146.79-	147.27+
146.835-@	147.345+

Notes:
+ indicates + offset
- indicates - offset
@ indicates Autopatch

for information on use of Autopatch
be sure to check with repeater owner.

See UHF Map page
for CTCSS tone chart.

2 Meter Repeater Offset is 600 KHz

South Dakota

222 & UP

Aberdeen●
443.40+

Watertown●
444.65+

Huron ●
444.95-

Mitchell●
444.825+P

Sioux Falls●
444.20+J

©N7JXN

440 Repeater Offset is 5 MH:

SOUTH DAKOTA FACTS

NUMBER OF HAMS: 1,490
CALL AREA: 0
STATE NICKNAME: COYOTE STATE
HIGHEST POINT:
    HARNEY PEAK (7,242 FT.)
STATE CAPITAL: PIERRE
NUMBER OF COUNTIES: 66
NUMBER OF 2M REPEATERS: 40
    222 REPEATERS: 0
    440 REPEATERS: 5
    900 MHz REPEATERS: 0
    1.2 GHz REPEATERS: 0

CTCSS TONES

A=67.0	Q=107.2	E=173.8
B=69.3	R=110.9	F=179.9
C=71.9	S=114.8	G=186.2
D=74.4	T=118.8	H=192.8
E=77.0	U=123.0	J=203.5
F=79.7	V=127.3	K=206.5
G=82.5	W=131.8	L=210.7
H=85.4	X=136.5	M=218.1
J=88.5	Y=141.3	N=225.7
K=91.5	Z=146.2	P=229.1
L=94.8	A=151.4	Q=233.6
M=97.4	B=156.7	R=241.8
N=100.0	C=162.2	S=250.3
P=103.5	D=167.9	T=254.1

104

South Dakota
2 METERS

Clear Lake
145.43 [V]
147.18+

Gary
145.39-

Canton
145.35-
147.15+ @

14

29

90

18

Brookings
146.94 @

Humboldt
147.285+ [Z]

Sioux Falls
145.31-
146.895-

Beresford
147.24+

Yankton
146.85-

Vermillion
147.375+

Sisseton
146.88-

29

Watertown
145.39-
146.85-
147.39+

81

81

81

Britton
146.61-

12

Pierpont
147.33+

Garden City
146.67- [M]

212

Wessington Springs
147.09+
147.345+| [Z]

Mitchell
146.64-@ [Z]

Springfield
147.21+| [Z]

1

Aberdeen
146.91-

Redfield
147.15+

281

281

281

281

212

14

212

12

Reliance
146.94- [Z]

18

Bowdie
147.12+

183

83

83

Pierre
145.35-@
146.73-| [Z]

90

Murdo
147.30+ [Z]

Mobridge
147.21+

Ridgeview
147.06+ @

83

12

212

Eagle Butte
146.79-

14

Phillip
147.375+| [Z]

73

73

73

73

212

Rapid City
146.94-
147.84-@

385

18

385

212

Custer
146.85-
147.09+

Hot Springs
146.70-

385

85

90

Lead
146.76-

18

85

16

NXՐZNⒸ

Notes:
+ indicates + offset
- indicates - offset
@ indicates Autopatch

for information on use of Autopatch
be sure to check with repeater owner.

See UHF Map page
for CTCSS tone chart.

222 & UP

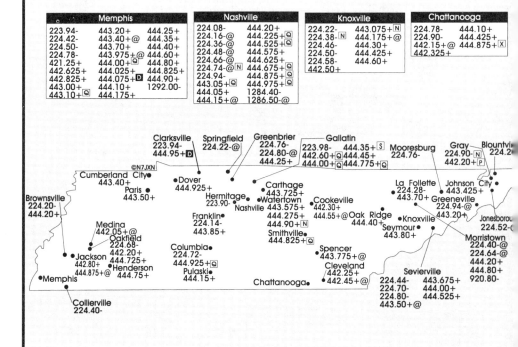

Memphis	
223.94-	443.20+
224.42-	443.40+@
224.50-	443.70+
224.78-	443.975+@
421.25+	444.00+
442.625+	444.025+
442.825+	444.075+ D
443.00+	444.10+
443.10+ Q	444.175+
	444.25+
	444.35+
	444.40+
	444.60+
	444.80+
	444.825+
	444.90+
	1292.00-

Nashville	
224.08-	444.20+
224.16-@	444.225+ Q
224.36-@	444.525+ Q
224.48-@	444.575+
224.66-@	444.625+
224.74-@ N	444.675+ Q
224.94-	444.875+ Q
443.05+ Q	444.975+ Q
444.05+	1284.40-
444.15+@	1286.50-@

Knoxville	
224.22-	443.075+ N
224.38- N	444.175+@
224.46-	444.30+
224.50-	444.425+
224.58-	444.60+
442.50+	

Chattanooga	
224.78-	444.10+
224.90-	444.425+
442.15+@	444.875+ X
442.325+	

Clarksville
223.94-
444.95+ D

Springfield
224.22-@

Greenbrier
224.76-
224.80-@
444.25+

Gallatin
223.98-   444.35+ S
442.60+ Q 444.45+
444.00+ Q 444.775+ Q

Mooresburg
224.76-

Gray
224.90- N

Blountvi
224.2

©N7JXN

Cumberland City
443.40+

Dover
444.925+

Carthage
443.725+

La Follette
224.28-
443.70+

Johnson City
443.425+

Brownsville
224.20-
444.20+

Paris
443.50+

Hermitage
223.90-

Watertown
Nashville 443.575+

Cookeville
442.30+

Greeneville
224.94-

Gray
443.20+

Jonesborou
224.52-0

Medina
442.05+@

Franklin
224.14-
443.85+

Oak Ridge
444.55+@ 444.40+

Knoxville
Seymour
443.80+

Morristown
224.40-@
224.64-@
444.20+
444.80+
920.80-

Oakfield
224.68-
442.20+

Jackson
442.80+
444.725+

Henderson
444.75+

Columbia
224.72-
444.925+ Q

Smithville
444.825+ Q

Spencer
443.775+@

Memphis
444.875+@

Pulaski
444.15+

Chattanooga

Cleveland
442.25+
442.45+@

Sevierville
224.44-   443.675+
224.70-   444.00+
224.80-   444.525+
443.50+@

Collierville
224.40-

222 Repeater Offset is 1.6 MH
440 Repeater Offset is 5 MH

TENNESSEE FACTS

NUMBER OF HAMS: 12,626

CALL AREA: 4

STATE NICKNAME: VOLUNTEER STATE

HIGHEST POINT:
   CLINGMANS DOME (6,643 FT.)

STATE CAPITAL: NASHVILLE

NUMBER OF COUNTIES: 95

NUMBER OF 2M REPEATERS: 168

    222 REPEATERS: 40

    440 REPEATERS: 84

    900 MHz REPEATERS: 1

    1.2 GHz REPEATERS: 3

CTCSS TONES

A=67.0	Q=107.2	E=173.8	
B=69.3	R=110.9	F=179.9	
C=71.9	S=114.8	G=186.2	
D=74.4	T=118.8	H=192.8	
E=77.0	U=123.0	J=203.5	
F=79.7	V=127.3	K=206.5	
G=82.5	W=131.8	L=210.7	
H=85.4	X=136.5	M=218.1	
J=88.5	Y=141.3	N=225.7	
K=91.5	Z=146.2	P=229.1	
L=94.8	A=151.4	Q=233.6	
M=97.4	B=156.7	R=241.8	
N=100.0	C=162.2	S=250.3	
P=103.5	D=167.9	T=254.1	

Tennessee
2 METERS

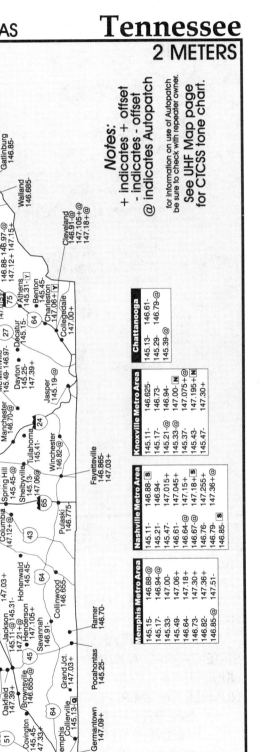

Notes:
+ indicates + offset
- indicates - offset
@ indicates Autopatch

for information on use of Autopatch
be sure to check with repeater owner.

See UHF Map page
for CTCSS tone chart.

Memphis Metro Area

145.15-	146.88-@
145.17-	146.94-@
145.33-	147.00-
145.49-	147.06-@
146.64-	147.18+
146.73-	147.30+
146.82-	147.36+
146.85-@	147.51-

Nashville Metro Area

145.11-	146.88-[S]
145.21-	146.94-
145.47-	147.015+
146.61-	147.045+
146.64-@	147.15+
146.67-@	147.18+[S]
146.76-	147.255+
146.79-	147.36+@
146.85-[S]	

Knoxville Metro Area

145.11-	146.625-
145.17-	146.73-
145.21-@	146.94-
145.33-@	147.00-[N]
145.37-	147.075+@
145.43-	147.195+[N]
145.47-	147.30+

Chattanooga

145.13-	146.61-
145.29-	146.79-@
145.39-@	

Bristol 146.67-@ 146.76- 146.88-
Blountville 147.00+
Johnson City 145.29- 146.79-
Mtn. City 145.47-
Erwin 145.25-@ 147.165+
Mtn. City 147.27+
[81]
[181]
Kingsport 146.97- Gray 145.11-[P]
Rogersville 147.315+ 145.13-@
Morristown 145.45-147.03+ 147.225+@
[32]
[40]
Gatlinburg 146.85-
La Follette 145.13-@ 146.67- 147.36+
Maynardville 145.23-
Walland 146.685-
[75]
Lake City 146.82-@
Knoxville
Oliver Spg. 146.745-
Alcoa 146.655- 146.82-@
Oak Ridge 146.88-146.97-@ 147.12+ 147.15+
Cleveland 146.91-@ 147.105+ 147.18+@
[441]
Petros
Crossville 147.21+@ 147.255+
Rockwood 147.015-
Athens 145.31-[Y]
Charleston 147.06+[Y]
Collegedale 147.00-
[27]
[75]
Benton 145.45-
[64]
Jamestown 147.09+[N]
Cookeville 145.11-145.43-@ 147.21+@
Smithville 145.37-@
Pikeville 147.285+
McMinnville 145.49-146.97-
Dayton 145.25- 147.39+
Decatur 145.15-
Jasper 145.19-
[27]
Carthage 145.19-
Lebanon 145.31-[N]
Manchester 146.70-@
Tullahoma 145.41-
Winchester 146.82-@
[24]
Fayetteville 146.865- 147.03+
Lebanon 145.39- 147.015+ 147.105+
Lafayette 145.31-[A]
Hendersonville
Spawille 145.27- 147.345+ 147.015+
Smyrna 145.23-
Franklin 145.15-
Spring Hill 145.45-@
Shelbyville 145.13- 147.06
Murfreesboro 145.17-147.315+
[231]
Pulaski 146.775-
[65]
Gallatin 145.13-[Q] 147.24+[S] 147.27+[S] 147.30+[S]
[31]
[65]
Goodlettsville 146.985-
Greenbrier 147.075+
Nashville
Dickson 147.375+
Columbia 147.12+@
[PKY]
[43]
Clarksville 147.00+ 147.39+@
Cumberland City 145.33-
Nolensville 145.35-
[40]
Lexington 147.03+
Hohenwald 145.45-
[64]
Collinwood 146.655
Ramer 146.70-
Dover 145.41-
Paris 147.36+@
Martin 146.625-@
[79]
Bruceton 145.17-[Q]
Jackson 145.11@145.31-
Humboldt 145.35-@
Henderson 147.21+ 147.105+
Savannah 146.91-
Grand Jct. 147.03+
[45]
Pochahontas 145.25-
Union City 146.70-@ 147.015+@
[N7JXN]
Puryear 147.165+@
Dyersburg 146.745-
Brownsville 146.655-@
Oakfield 147.39+
[51]
Covington 145.45- 147.33+
[64]
Collierville 145.13-[Q]
Germantown 147.09+
Trenton 146.865-@
[422]
Alamo 147.135+
Medina 146.97-@
[51]
Memphis
Grand Jct. 147.03+

222 & UP

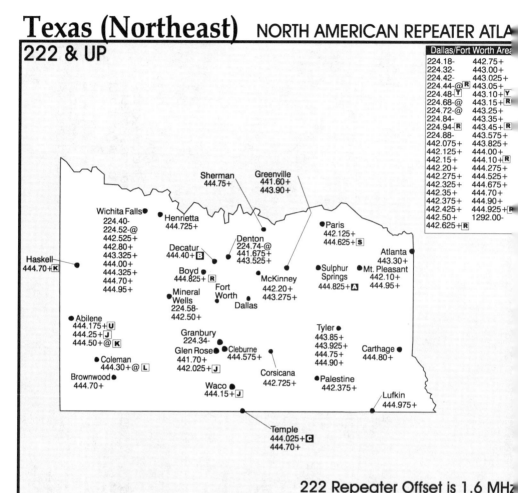

Dallas/Fort Worth Area

224.18-	442.75+
224.32-	443.00+
224.42-	443.025+
224.44-@ R	443.05+
224.48- T	443.10+ Y
224.68-@	443.15+ R
224.72-@	443.25+
224.84-	443.35+
224.94- R	443.45+ R
224.88-	443.575+
442.075+	443.825+
442.125+	444.00+
442.15+	444.10+ R
442.20+	444.275+
442.275+	444.525+
442.325+	444.675+
442.35+	444.70+
442.375+	444.90+
442.425+	444.925+ R
442.50+	1292.00-
442.625+ R	

Sherman
444.75+

Greenville
441.60+
443.90+

Wichita Falls●
224.40-
224.52-@
442.525+
442.80+
443.325+
444.00+
444.325+
444.70+
444.95+

Henrietta
444.725+

Paris
442.125+
444.625+ S

Denton
224.74-@
441.675+
443.525+

Decatur
444.40+ B

Atlanta ●
443.30+

Haskell
444.70+ K

Boyd ●
444.825+ R

McKinney
442.20+
443.275+

Sulphur
Springs
444.825+ A

Mt. Pleasant
442.10+
444.95+

Mineral
Wells
224.58-
442.50+

Fort
Worth

Dallas

● Abilene
444.175+ U
444.25+ J
444.50+@ K

Granbury
224.34-

Tyler ●
443.85+
443.925+
444.75+
444.90+

Carthage ●
444.80+

● Coleman
444.30+@ L

Glen Rose● ●Cleburne
441.70+   444.575+
442.025+ J

Corsicana
442.725+

Palestine
442.375+

Brownwood ●
444.70+

Waco ●
444.15+ J

Lufkin
444.975+

Temple
444.025+ C
444.70+

222 Repeater Offset is 1.6 MHz
440 Repeater Offset is 5 MHz

TEXAS FACTS

NUMBER OF HAMS: 38,158

CALL AREA: 5

STATE NICKNAME: LONE STAR STATE

HIGHEST POINT:
    GUADALUPE PEAK (8,749 FT.)

STATE CAPITAL: AUSTIN

NUMBER OF COUNTIES: 254

NUMBER OF 2M REPEATERS: 164

    222 REPEATERS: 14

    440 REPEATERS: 74

    900 MHz REPEATERS: 0

    1.2 GHz REPEATERS: 1

CTCSS TONES

A=67.0	Q=107.2	E=173.8
B=69.3	R=110.9	F=179.9
C=71.9	S=114.8	G=186.2
D=74.4	T=118.8	H=192.8
E=77.0	U=123.0	J=203.5
F=79.7	V=127.3	K=206.5
G=82.5	W=131.8	L=210.7
H=85.4	X=136.5	M=218.1
J=88.5	Y=141.3	N=225.7
K=91.5	Z=146.2	P=229.1
L=94.8	A=151.4	Q=233.6
M=97.4	B=156.7	R=241.8
N=100.0	C=162.2	S=250.3
P=103.5	D=167.9	T=254.1

Longview
146.64-@
146.92-
147.10+
147.30+@ Q

Jacksonville
145.49-
146.80-
147.02+
147.38+ @

Daingerfield
145.23-
145.31-@
145.47-

Atlanta
146.98-@

Greenville
146.78-@ 147.02+
147.16+@

Naples
145.41-@
146.84-

Mt. Pleasant
146.88-146.94-

Pittsburg
147.26+

Tyler
145.21-146.96-@
147.00- J 147.10+

Carthage
147.18+@

Nacogdoches
146.66-@ P
146.84

Texarkana
145.45-
146.62-
147.12+

Mt. Pleasant
146.94-
147.32+ S

Clarksville
147.20+

Marshall
146.86-@

Lufkin
145.37-
146.94-@
147.26+

Gainesville
145.29-@
147.34+@

Sherman
145.49-
147.00+
147.08+

Bonham
145.47-@

Paris
146.76-@
147.34+

Sulphur Springs
147.36+

Kilgore
145.45-

Athens
147.22+

Rusk
147.04+

Alto
145.33-
147.34+ X

Palestine
146.74-
147.08+
147.14+@

Temple
145.49-
146.82-
147.34+

Wichita Falls
146.66-
146.70-
146.94-
147.06+
147.14+
147.32+

Nocona
147.36+

Denton
146.92-@ 146.74-@

McKinney

Emory
146.92-

Mabank
147.28+

Corsicana
145.29-

Malakoff
145.47-@

Crockett
145.21-

Killeen
145.15-
145.19-@
145.43-
146.76-
147.02+@ N
147.12+@ N
147.24+@
147.32+@

Henrietta
146.68-
147.32+

Bowie
145.41-
147.22+

Decatur
145.39-

Boyd
146.98-@

Mineral Wells
146.64-

Cleburne
145.49-
146.78-

Fairfield
145.11-

Eddy
146.72- J

Vernon
147.02+
147.08+

Electra
147.12+ H

Olney
147.24+@

Graham
147.24+
147.34+

Breckenridge
147.38+

Granbury
147.08+

Glen Rose
145.27-
147.02+

Hamilton
147.20+

Waco
146.66-@
146.88-
146.98-@
147.16+

Seymour
147.10+

Archer City
146.84-

Haskell
146.74-

Cisco
145.35-
147.06+

Bangs
147.00+

Gatesville
146.96-

Lampasas
146.86- J

Abilene
146.70-
146.76+ Z
146.88-
146.96-

Albany
147.22-

Baird
147.30+ L

Coleman
146.98- L

Brownwood
146.82-
146.94- L

Circled/boxed route markers: 82, 59, 96, 271, 30, 20, 75, 45, 35E, 79, 35W, 82, 287, 281, 281, 67, 281, 44, 70, 277, 20, R, R, J, J

Notes:
+ indicates + offset
- indicates - offset
@ indicates Autopatch

for information on use of Autopatch
be sure to check with repeater owner.

See UHF Map page
for CTCSS tone chart.

2 Meter Repeater Offset is 600 KHz

222 & UP

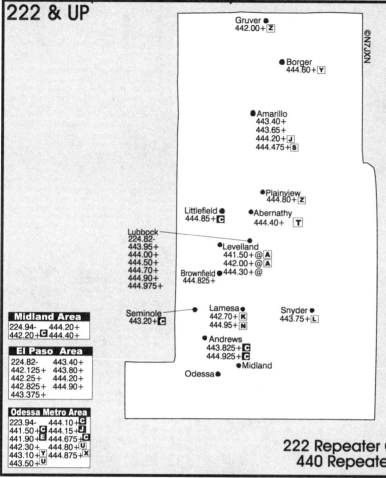

Gruver ●
442.00+ Z

●Borger
444.60+ Y

●Amarillo
443.40+
443.65+
444.20+ J
444.475+ S

●Plainview
444.80+ Z

Littlefield ●
444.85+ C

●Abernathy
444.40+ T

Lubbock
224.82-
443.95+
444.00+
444.50+
444.70+
444.90+
444.975+

●Levelland
441.50+@ A
442.00+@ A
Brownfield ●444.30+@
444.825+

Seminole ●
443.20+ C

Lamesa ●
442.70+ K
444.95+ N

Snyder ●
443.75+ L

●Andrews
443.825+ C
444.925+ C

●Midland

Odessa ●

@NZJXN

Midland Area
224.94-	444.20+
442.20+ C	444.40+

El Paso Area
224.82-	443.40+
442.125+	443.80+
442.25+	444.20+
442.825+	444.90+
443.375+	

Odessa Metro Area
223.94-	444.10+ C
441.50+ C	444.15+ J
441.90+ E	444.675+ C
442.30+	444.80+ U
443.10+ Y	444.875+ X
443.50+ U	

222 Repeater Offset is 1.6 MH
440 Repeater Offset is 5 MH

TEXAS FACTS

NUMBER OF HAMS: 38,158

CALL AREA: 5

STATE NICKNAME: LONE STAR STATE

HIGHEST POINT:
   GUADALUPE PEAK (8,749 FT.)

STATE CAPITAL: AUSTIN

NUMBER OF COUNTIES: 254

NUMBER OF 2M REPEATERS: 67

   222 REPEATERS: 4

   440 REPEATERS: 46

   900 MHz REPEATERS: 0

   1.2 GHz REPEATERS: 0

CTCSS TONES
A=67.0	Q=107.2	E=173.8
B=69.3	R=110.9	F=179.9
C=71.9	S=114.8	G=186.2
D=74.4	T=118.8	H=192.8
E=77.0	U=123.0	J=203.5
F=79.7	V=127.3	K=206.5
G=82.5	W=131.8	L=210.7
H=85.4	X=136.5	M=218.1
J=88.5	Y=141.3	N=225.7
K=91.5	Z=146.2	P=229.1
L=94.8	A=151.4	Q=233.6
M=97.4	B=156.7	R=241.8
N=100.0	C=162.2	S=250.3
P=103.5	D=167.9	T=254.1

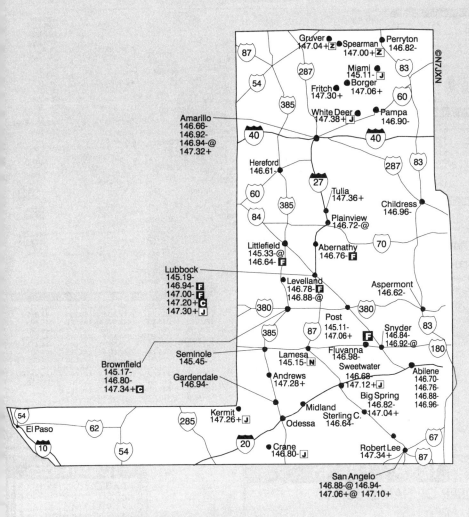

@N7JXN

Gruver ●
147.04+ **Z** ● Spearman
147.00+ **Z**

Perryton
146.82-

87

287

Miami ●
145.11- **J**

83

54

Fritch ●
147.30+

Borger
147.06+

60

385

White Deer ●
147.38+ **J**

● Pampa
146.90-

Amarillo
146.66-
146.92-
146.94-@
147.32+

40

40

Hereford
146.61-

287

83

27

60

Tulia
147.36+

385

84

Childress
146.96-

Plainview
146.72-@

Littlefield
145.33-@
146.64- **F**

Abernathy
146.76- **F**

70

Lubbock
145.19-
146.94- **F**
147.00- **F**
147.20+ **C**
147.30+ **J**

Levelland
146.78- **F**
146.88-@

Aspermont
146.62-

380

380

Post
145.11-
147.06+ **F**

Snyder
146.84-
146.92-@

83

180

Seminole
145.45-

385

87

Fluvanna
146.98-

Lamesa
145.15- **N**

Brownfield
145.17-
146.80-
147.34+ **C**

Gardendale
146.94-

Andrews
147.28+

Sweetwater
146.68-
147.12+ **J**

Abilene
146.70-
146.76-
146.88-
146.96-

Big Spring
146.82-

147.04+

Midland
Sterling C. 146.64-

54

El Paso

62

Kermit ●
147.26+ **J**

285

Odessa

10

54

20

Crane
146.80- **J**

Robert Lee
147.34+

67

87

San Angelo
146.88-@ 146.94-
147.06+@ 147.10+

El Paso Area		Odessa Metro Area		Midland Area	
145.33-	147.16+@	145.47-	146.88-	145.13- **J**	147.22+ **J**
146.62-	147.24+	146.66-	147.14+ **J**	145.39-	147.30+
146.70-@ **C**	147.28+ **C**	146.70- **J**		146.76-	147.38+
146.88-					

2 Meter Repeater Offset is 600 KHz

222 & UP

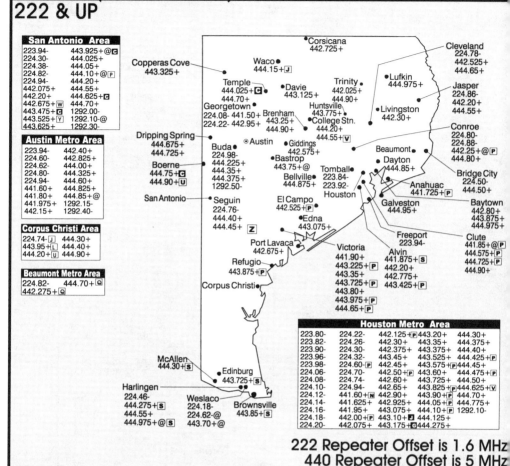

San Antonio Area

223.94-	443.925+@🄲
224.30-	444.025+
224.38-	444.05+
224.82-	444.10+@🄿
224.94-	444.20+
442.075+	444.55+
442.20+	444.625+🄲
442.675+🅆	444.70+
443.475+🄲	1292.00-
443.525+🅈	1292.10-@
443.625+	1292.30-

Austin Metro Area

223.94-	442.40+
224.60-	442.825+
224.62-	444.00+
224.80-	444.325+
224.94-	444.60+
441.60+	444.825+
441.80+	444.85+@
441.975+	1292.15-
442.15+	1292.40-

Corpus Christi Area

224.74+🄹	444.30+
443.95+🄻	444.40+
444.20+🅄	444.90+

Beaumont Metro Area

224.82-	444.70+🅀
442.275+🅀	

Corsicana 442.725+
Cleveland 224.78- 442.525+ 444.65+
Copperas Cove 443.325+
Waco ● 444.15+🄹
Temple 444.025+🄲 444.70+
Davie 443.125+
Trinity 442.025+ 444.90+
Lufkin 444.975+
Jasper 224.86- 442.20+ 444.55+
Georgetown ● 224.08- 441.50+ 224.22- 442.95+
Brenham 443.25+ 444.90+
Huntsville 443.775+
College Stn. 444.55+🅅
Livingston 442.30+
Conroe 224.80- 224.88- 442.25+@🄿 444.80+
Dripping Spring ● 444.675+ 444.725+
Austin ⊙
Giddings 442.575+
Beaumont ●
Dayton 444.85+
Bridge City 224.50- 444.50+
Buda ● 224.98- 444.225+ 444.35+ 444.375+ 1292.50-
Bastrop 443.75+@
Tomball ● 223.84- 223.92-
Anahuac 441.725+🄿
Baytown 442.80+ 443.875+ 444.975+
Boerne 444.75+🄲 444.90+🅄
Bellville 444.875+
San Antonio ● Seguin 224.76- 444.40+ 444.45+ 🅉
El Campo 442.525+🄿
Houston 444.20+
Galveston 444.95+
Clute 441.85+@🄿 444.575+🄿 444.725+🄿 444.90+
Edna 443.075+
Port Lavaca 442.675+
Victoria 441.90+ 443.225+🄿 443.35+ 443.725+🄿 443.80+ 443.975+🄿 444.65+🄿
Freeport 223.94-
Refugio 443.875+🄿
Corpus Christi ●
Alvin 441.875+🅂 442.20+ 442.775+ 443.425+🄿
McAllen 444.30+🅂
Edinburg 443.725+🅂
Harlingen 224.46- 444.275+🅂 444.55+ 444.975+@🅂
Weslaco 224.18- 224.62-@ 443.70+@
Brownsville 443.85+🅂

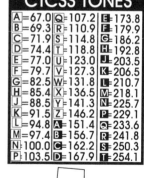

Houston Metro Area

223.80-	224.22-	442.125+🄿	443.20+	444.30+
223.82-	224.26-	442.30+	443.35+	444.375+
223.90-	224.30-	442.375+	443.375+	444.40+
223.96-	224.32-	443.45+	443.525+	444.425+🄿
223.98-	224.60-🄿	442.45+	443.575+🄿	444.45+
224.06-	224.70-	442.50+🄿	443.60+	444.475+🄿
224.08-	224.74-	442.60+	443.725+	444.50+
224.10-	224.94-	442.65+	443.825+🄿	444.625+🅅
224.12-	441.60+🄽	442.90+	443.90+🄿	444.70+
224.14-	441.625+	442.925+	444.05+🄿	444.775+
224.16-	441.95+	443.075+	444.10+🄿	1292.10-
224.18-	442.00+🄿	443.10+🄹	444.125+	
224.20-	442.075+	443.175+🄲	444.275+	

222 Repeater Offset is 1.6 MHz
440 Repeater Offset is 5 MHz

TEXAS FACTS

NUMBER OF HAMS: 38,158

CALL AREA: 5

STATE NICKNAME: LONE STAR STATE

HIGHEST POINT:
GUADALUPE PEAK (8,749 FT.)

STATE CAPITAL: AUSTIN

NUMBER OF COUNTIES: 254

NUMBER OF 2M REPEATERS: 176

222 REPEATERS: 46

440 REPEATERS: 114

900 MHz REPEATERS: 0

1.2 GHz REPEATERS: 0

CTCSS TONES

A=67.0	Q=107.2	E=173.8	
B=69.3	R=110.9	F=179.9	
C=71.9	S=114.8	G=186.2	
D=74.4	T=118.8	H=192.8	
E=77.0	U=123.0	J=203.5	
F=79.7	V=127.3	K=206.5	
G=82.5	W=131.8	L=210.7	
H=85.4	X=136.5	M=218.1	
J=88.5	Y=141.3	N=225.7	
K=91.5	Z=146.2	P=229.1	
L=94.8	A=151.4	Q=233.6	
M=97.4	B=156.7	R=241.8	
N=100.0	C=162.2	S=250.3	
P=103.5	D=167.9	T=254.1	

112

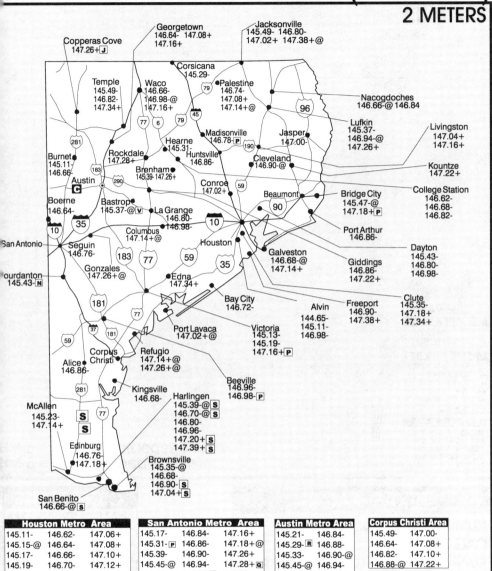

Copperas Cove 147.26+ J

Georgetown 146.64- 147.08+ 147.16+

Jacksonville 145.49- 146.80- 147.02+ 147.38+ @

Corsicana 145.29-

Temple 145.49- 146.82- 147.34+

Waco 146.66- 146.98- 147.16+

Palestine 146.74- 147.08+ 147.14+ @

79

96

Nacogdoches 146.66-@ 146.84

Lufkin 145.37- 146.94-@ 147.26+

Livingston 147.04+ 147.16+

77 6 79 45

Hearne 145.31-

Madisonville 146.78- P

Jasper 147.00-

281

Burnet 145.11- 146.66

Rockdale 147.28+

Huntsville 146.86-

Cleveland 146.90-@

190

Kountze 147.22+

183

Brenham 145.39-147.26+

Austin C

290

Conroe 147.02+

59

Beaumont 145.47-@ 147.18+ P

Bridge City

College Station 146.62- 146.68- 146.82-

Boerne 146.64-

Bastrop 145.37-@ V

La Grange 146.80- 146.98-

10

Port Arthur 146.86-

San Antonio

35

Columbus 147.14+ @

Port Arthur 146.86-

Dayton 145.43-

10

Seguin 146.76-

183 77

Houston

59

35

Galveston 146.68-@ 147.14+

Giddings 146.86- 147.22+

146.80- 146.98-

ourdanton 145.43- N

Gonzales 147.26+ @

Edna 147.34+

Clute 145.35- 147.18+ 147.34+

181

Bay City 146.72-

Alvin 144.65- 145.11- 146.98-

Freeport 146.90- 147.38+

77

37 181

Port Lavaca 147.02+ @

Victoria 145.13- 145.19- 147.16+ P

59

Corpus Christi

Refugio 147.14+ @ 147.26+ @

Alice 146.86-

281

Beeville 146.96- 146.98- P

Kingsville 146.68-

Harlingen 145.39-@ S 146.70-@ S 146.80- 146.96- 147.20+ S 147.39+ S

McAllen 145.23- 147.14+

S S

77

Edinburg 146.76- 147.18+

Brownsville 145.35-@ 146.68- 146.90- S 147.04+ S

San Benito 146.66-@ S

Houston Metro Area		
145.11-	146.62-	147.06+
145.15-@	146.64-	147.08+
145.17-	146.66-	147.10+
145.19-	146.70-	147.12+
145.23-	146.74-	147.16+
145.29-@	146.76-	147.20+
145.31-	146.78-	147.22+
145.33-	146.82-	147.26+
145.37-	146.84-	147.28+
145.39-	146.88-	147.30+ B
145.41-	146.92-	147.32+ @
145.45-	146.94- D	147.36+
145.47-	146.96-	
145.49- P	147.00+	

San Antonio Metro Area		
145.17-	146.84-	147.16+
145.31- P	146.86-	147.18+ @
145.39-	146.90-	147.26+
145.45-@	146.94-	147.28+ Q
145.62-	146.96- J	147.30+ J
146.66-	146.98-	147.32+ C
146.70-	147.00-	147.34+ C
146.72- C	147.02+@	147.36+@
146.78-	147.06+	147.38+
146.80-	147.08+ @	
146.82-	147.12+	

Austin Metro Area		
145.21-	146.84-	
145.29- R	146.88-	
145.33-	146.90-@	
145.45-@	146.94-	
145.47-	147.06+	
146.61-	147.12+	
146.70-@	147.18+	
146.78-@	147.36+	

Killeen Metro Area	
145.19-	147.02+ N
145.43-	147.24+
146.76-	147.32+

Corpus Christi Area	
145.49-	147.00-
146.64-	147.08+
146.82-	147.10+
146.88-@	147.22+

Beaumont Metro Area	
145.27-	147.20+
146.70-@	147.30+
146.76-	147.34+

Notes:
+ indicates + offset
- indicates - offset
@ indicates Autopatch

for information on use of Autopatch
be sure to check with repeater owner.

See UHF Map page
for CTCSS tone chart.

2 Meter Repeater Offset is 600 KHz

222 & UP

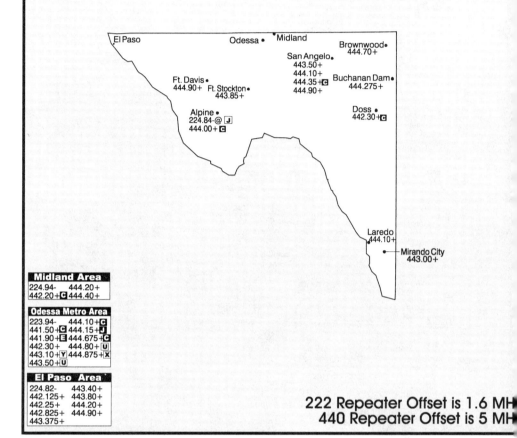

Midland Area

224.94-	444.20+
442.20+■	444.40+

Odessa Metro Area

223.94-	444.10+■
441.50+■	444.15+■
441.90+■	444.675+■
442.30+	444.80+■
443.10+■	444.875+■
443.50+■	

El Paso Area

224.82-	443.40+
442.125+	443.80+
442.25+	444.20+
442.825+	444.90+
443.375+	

222 Repeater Offset is 1.6 MH
440 Repeater Offset is 5 MH

TEXAS FACTS

NUMBER OF HAMS: 38,158

CALL AREA: 5

STATE NICKNAME: LONE STAR STATE

HIGHEST POINT:
    GUADALUPE PEAK (8,749 FT.)

STATE CAPITAL: AUSTIN

NUMBER OF COUNTIES: 254

NUMBER OF 2M REPEATERS: 55

    222 REPEATERS: 6
    440 REPEATERS: 60
    900 MHz REPEATERS: 0
    1.2 GHz REPEATERS: 0

CTCSS TONES

A=67.0	Q=107.2	E=173.8
B=69.3	R=110.9	F=179.9
C=71.9	S=114.8	G=186.2
D=74.4	T=118.8	H=192.8
E=77.0	U=123.0	J=203.5
F=79.7	V=127.3	K=206.5
G=82.5	W=131.8	L=210.7
H=85.4	X=136.5	M=218.1
J=88.5	Y=141.3	N=225.7
K=91.5	Z=146.2	P=229.1
L=94.8	A=151.4	Q=233.6
M=97.4	B=156.7	R=241.8
N=100.0	C=162.2	S=250.3
P=103.5	D=167.9	T=254.1

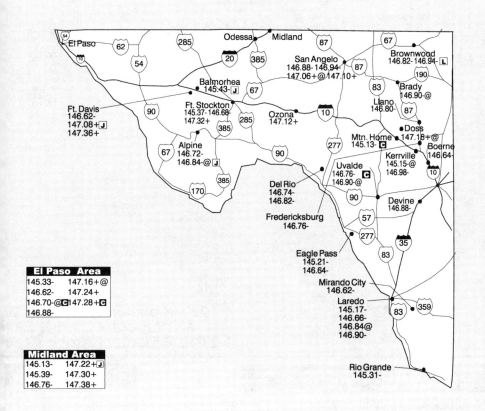

El Paso

62

285

Odessa

Midland

87

67

20

385

Brownwood
146.82-146.94- L

54

San Angelo
146.88-146.94-
147.06+@147.10+

87

190

Balmorhea
145.43- J

67

83

Brady
146.90-@

Ft. Davis
146.62-
147.08+ J
147.36+

90

Ft. Stockton
145.37-146.68-
147.32+

285

Ozona
147.12+

10

Llano
146.80-

87

385

Doss
147.18+@

Alpine
146.72-
146.84-@ J

67

90

277

Mtn. Home 145.13- C

Boerne
146.64-

Kerrville
145.15-@
146.98-

385

Del Rio
146.74-
146.82-

Uvalde
146.76- C
146.90-@

10

170

Devine
146.88-

90

Fredericksburg
146.76-

57

277

Eagle Pass
145.21-
146.64-

83

35

Mirando City
146.62-

Laredo
145.17-
146.66-
146.84@
146.90-

83

359

Rio Grande
145.31-

El Paso Area

145.33-	147.16+@
146.62-	147.24+
146.70-@C	147.28+C
146.88-	

Midland Area

145.13-	147.22+ J
145.39-	147.30+
146.76-	147.38+

Notes:
+ indicates + offset
- indicates - offset
@ indicates Autopatch

for information on use of Autopatch
be sure to check with repeater owner.

**See UHF Map page
for CTCSS tone chart.**

2 Meter Repeater Offset is 600 KHz

Utah

222 & UP

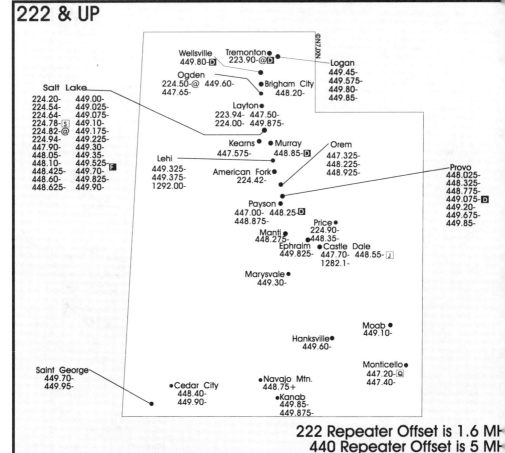

Wellsville
449.80-☒

Tremonton●
223.90-@☒

Logan
449.45-
449.575-
449.80-
449.85-

Ogden
224.50-@ 449.60-
447.65-

Brigham City
448.20-

©N7JXN

Salt Lake
224.20-   449.00-
224.54-   449.025-
224.64-   449.075-
224.78-☒   449.10-
224.82-@   449.175-
224.94-   449.225-
447.90-   449.30-
448.05-   449.35-
448.10-   449.525-
448.425-   449.70-
448.60-   449.825-
448.625-   449.90-
              449.70-☒

Layton●
223.94- 447.50-
224.00- 449.875-

Kearns ● ● Murray
447.575-   448.85-☒

Orem
447.325-
448.225-
448.925-

Lehi
449.325-
449.375-
1292.00-

American Fork●
224.42-

Provo
448.025-
448.325-
448.775-
449.075-☒
449.20-
449.675-
449.85-

Payson ● 448.25-☒
447.00-
448.875-

Price ●
224.90-
448.35-

Manti ●
448.275-

Ephraim ● Castle Dale
449.825- 447.70- 448.55- ☒
          1282.1-

Marysvale ●
449.30-

Moab ●
449.10-

Hanksville●
449.60-

Monticello ●
447.20-☒
447.40-

Saint George●
449.70-
449.95-

●Cedar City
448.40-
449.90-

●Navajo Mtn.
448.75+

●Kanab
449.85-
449.875-

222 Repeater Offset is 1.6 MH
440 Repeater Offset is 5 MH
1.2 GHz Repeater Offset is 12 MH

UTAH FACTS

NUMBER OF HAMS: 5,984

CALL AREA: 7

STATE NICKNAME: BEEHIVE STATE

HIGHEST POINT:
KINGS PEAK (13,528 FT.)

STATE CAPITAL: SALT LAKE CITY

NUMBER OF COUNTIES: 29

NUMBER OF 2M REPEATERS: 91

222 REPEATERS: 12

440 REPEATERS: 62

900 MHz REPEATERS: 0

1.2 GHz REPEATERS: 2

CTCSS TONES

A=67.0	Q=107.2	E=173.8
B=69.3	R=110.9	F=179.9
C=71.9	S=114.8	G=186.2
D=74.4	T=118.8	H=192.8
E=77.0	U=123.0	J=203.5
F=79.7	V=127.3	K=206.5
G=82.5	W=131.8	L=210.7
H=85.4	X=136.5	M=218.1
J=88.5	Y=141.3	N=225.7
K=91.5	Z=146.2	P=229.1
L=94.8	A=151.4	Q=233.6
M=97.4	B=156.7	R=241.8
N=100.0	C=162.2	S=250.3
P=103.5	D=167.9	T=254.1

Utah
2 METERS

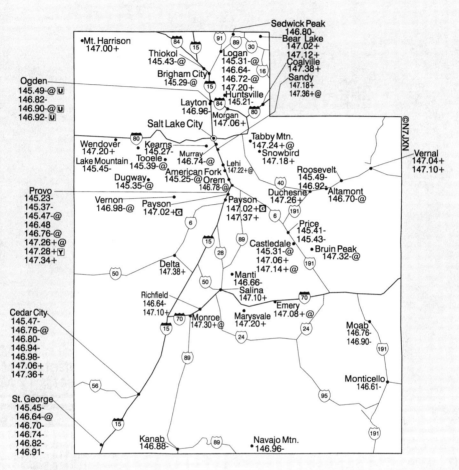

- •Mt. Harrison
  147.00+
- Thiokol
  145.43-@
- Brigham City
  145.29-@
- Sedwick Peak
  146.80-
- Bear Lake
  147.02+
  147.12+
- Logan
  145.31-@
  146.64-
  146.72-@
  147.20+
- Coalville
  147.38+
- Sandy
  147.18+
  147.36+@
- Ogden
  145.49-@ U
  146.82-
  146.90-@ U
  146.92- U
- Huntsville
- Layton 84 145.21-
  146.96-
- Morgan
  147.06+
- Salt Lake City
- Wendover
  147.20+
- Kearns
  145.27-
- Tabby Mtn.
  147.24+@
- •Snowbird
  147.18+
- Vernal
  147.04+
  147.10+
- Lake Mountain
  145.45-
- Tooele
- Murray
  146.74-@
- Lehi
  147.22+@
- Dugway
  145.35-@
- American Fork
  145.25-@ Orem
  146.78-
- Roosevelt
  145.49-
  146.92-
- Altamont
  146.70-@
- Provo
  145.23-
  145.37-
  145.47-@
  146.48
  146.76-@
  147.26+@
  147.28+ Y
  147.34+
- Vernon
  146.98-@
- Payson
  147.02+ C
- Payson
  147.02+ C
  147.37+
- Duchesne
  147.26+
- Price
  145.41-
  145.43-
- Castledale
  145.31-@
  147.06+
  147.14+@
- Bruin Peak
  147.32-@
- Delta
  147.38+
- Manti
  146.66-
- Salina
  147.10+
- Emery
  147.08+@
- Moab
  146.76-
  146.90-
- Cedar City
  145.47-
  146.76-@
  146.80-
  146.94-
  146.98-
  147.06+
  147.36+
- Richfield
  146.64-
  147.10+
- Monroe
  147.30+@
- Marysvale
  147.20+
- Monticello
  146.61-
- St. George
  145.45-
  146.64-@
  146.70-
  146.74-
  146.82-
  146.91-
- Kanab
  146.88-
- Navajo Mtn.
  •146.96-

@N7XJN

Salt Lake City
Metro Area
145.21-@
145.45-
146.62-
146.70-
146.74-
146.84-
146.88-@
146.94-
147.04+
147.12+@
147.14+
147.16+@
147.30+@
147.38+
147.60

Notes:
+ indicates + offset
- indicates - offset
@ indicates Autopatch

for information on use of Autopatch
be sure to check with repeater owner.

See UHF Map page
for CTCSS tone chart.

2 Meter Repeater Offset is 600 KHz

222 & UP

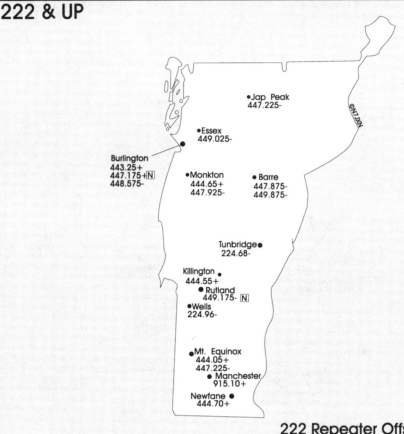

- Jap Peak
  447.225-
- Essex
  449.025-

Burlington
443.25+
447.175+
448.575-

- Monkton
  444.65+
  447.925-
- Barre
  447.875-
  449.875-

Tunbridge●
224.68-

Killington ●
444.55+
● Rutland
449.175-
●Wells
224.96-

● Mt. Equinox
444.05+
447.225-
● Manchester
915.10+

Newfane ●
444.70+

©N7JXN

222 Repeater Offset is 1.6 MHz
440 Repeater Offset is 5 MHz
900 MHz Repeater Offset is 12 MHz

VERMONT FACTS

NUMBER OF HAMS: 1,922

CALL AREA: 1

STATE NICKNAME: GREEN MOUNTAIN STATE

HIGHEST POINT:
    MT. MANSFIELD (4,393 FT.)

STATE CAPITAL: MONTPELIER

NUMBER OF COUNTIES: 14

NUMBER OF 2M REPEATERS: 23

    222 REPEATERS: 2
    440 REPEATERS: 14
    900 MHz REPEATERS: 1
    1.2 GHz REPEATERS: 0

CTCSS TONES

A=67.0	Q=107.2	E=173.8
B=69.3	R=110.9	F=179.9
C=71.9	S=114.8	G=186.2
D=74.4	T=118.8	H=192.8
E=77.0	U=123.0	J=203.5
F=79.7	V=127.3	K=206.5
G=82.5	W=131.8	L=210.7
H=85.4	X=136.5	M=218.1
J=88.5	Y=141.3	N=225.7
K=91.5	Z=146.2	P=229.1
L=94.8	A=151.4	Q=233.6
M=97.4	B=156.7	R=241.8
N=100.0	C=162.2	S=250.3
P=103.5	D=167.9	T=254.1

Vermont
2 METERS

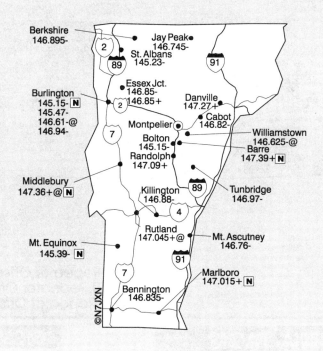

Berkshire
146.895-

Jay Peak●
146.745-
St. Albans
145.23-

Essex Jct.
146.85-
146.85+

Danville
147.27+●

Burlington
145.15- **N**
145.47-
146.61-@
146.94-

Cabot
146.82-

Montpelier ●

Williamstown
146.625-@

Bolton
145.15-

Barre
147.39+ **N**

Randolph●
147.09+

Middlebury
147.36+@ **N**

Killington
146.88-

Tunbridge
146.97-

Rutland
147.045+@

Mt. Ascutney
146.76-

Mt. Equinox
145.39- **N**

Marlboro
147.015+ **N**

Bennington
146.835-

©N7JXN

Notes:
+ indicates + offset
- indicates - offset
@ indicates Autopatch

for information on use of Autopatch
be sure to check with repeater owner.

See UHF Map page
for CTCSS tone chart.

Meter Repeater Offset is 600 KHz

119

222 & UP

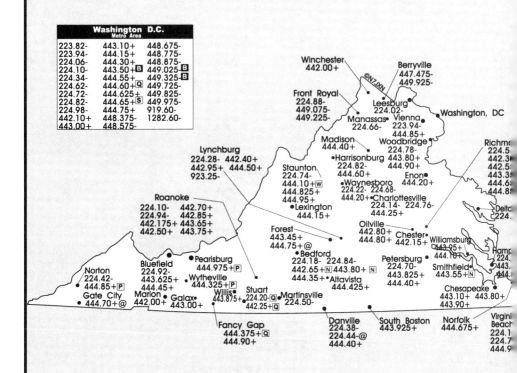

Washington D.C. Metro Area

223.82-	443.10+	448.675-
223.94-	444.15+	448.775-
224.06-	444.30+	448.875-
224.10-	443.50+B	449.025-B
224.34-	444.55+	449.325-B
224.62-	444.60+Q	449.725-
224.72-	444.625+	449.825-
224.82-	444.65+S	449.975-
224.98-	444.75+	919.60-
442.10+	448.375-	1282.60-
443.00+	448.575-	

Winchester
442.00+

Berryville
447.475-
449.925-

@N7JXN

Front Royal
224.88-
449.075-
449.225-

Leesburg
224.02-

Washington, DC

Manassas
224.66-

Vienna
223.94-
444.85+

Madison
444.40+

Woodbridge
224.78-

Richm
224.5
442.3
442.5
443.3
444.6
444.8

Lynchburg
224.28- 442.40+
442.95+ 444.50+
923.25-

Harrisonburg 443.80+
224.82-
444.60+

443.80+
444.90+

Enon
444.20+

Staunton
224.74-
444.10+W
444.825+
444.95+

Waynesboro
224.22- 224.68-
444.20+

Charlottesville
224.14- 224.76-
444.25+

Deltc
C224.

Lexington
444.15+

Oilville
442.80+
444.80+

Chester
442.15+

Williamsburg
443.95+

Hamp
224.
443.
444.

Roanoke
224.10- 442.70+
224.94- 442.85+
442.175+ 443.65+
442.50+ 443.75+

Forest
443.45+
444.75+@

Bedford
224.18- 224.84-
442.65+N 443.80+ N
444.35+ Altavista
444.425+

Petersburg
224.70-
443.825+
444.40+

Smithfield
443.55+N

Bluefield
224.92-
443.625+
444.45+

Pearisburg
444.975+P

Wytheville
444.325+P

Norton
224.42-
444.85+P

Marion
442.00+

Galax
443.00+

Willis
443.875+

Stuart
224.20-Q
442.25+Q

Martinsville
224.50-

Chesapeake
443.10+ 443.80+
443.90+

Gate City
444.70+@

Fancy Gap
444.375+Q
444.90+

Danville
224.38-
224.44-@
444.40+

South Boston
443.925+

Norfolk
444.675+

Virgini
Beach
224.1
224.7
444.9

222 Repeater Offset is 1.6 MH
440 Repeater Offset is 5 MH
900 MHz Repeater Offset is 12 MH

VIRGINIA FACTS

NUMBER OF HAMS: 15,519

CALL AREA: 4

STATE NICKNAME: OLD DOMINION

HIGHEST POINT:
MT. ROGERS (5,729 FT.)

STATE CAPITAL: RICHMOND

NUMBER OF COUNTIES: 95

NUMBER OF 2M REPEATERS: 154

222 REPEATERS: 37

440 REPEATERS: 87

900 MHz REPEATERS: 2

1.2 GHz REPEATERS: 1

CTCSS TONES

A=67.0	Q=107.2	E=173.8
B=69.3	R=110.9	F=179.9
C=71.9	S=114.8	G=186.2
D=74.4	T=118.8	H=192.8
E=77.0	U=123.0	J=203.5
F=79.7	V=127.3	K=206.5
G=82.5	W=131.8	L=210.7
H=85.4	X=136.5	M=218.1
J=88.5	Y=141.3	N=225.7
K=91.5	Z=146.2	P=229.1
L=94.8	A=151.4	Q=233.6
M=97.4	B=156.7	R=241.8
N=100.0	C=162.2	S=250.3
P=103.5	D=167.9	T=254.1

2 METERS

Notes:
+ indicates + offset
- indicates - offset
@ indicates Autopatch

for information on use of Autopatch
be sure to check with repeater owner.

See UHF Map page
for CTCSS tone chart.

Williamsburg Ⓥ
145.41-@
146.67-@
146.76-@

Charlottesville Ⓦ
146.76-
146.895-
146.925-

Roanoke Ⓠ
145.21-
145.39-
146.745-
146.94-@
146.985-

Richmond
145.11-@
145.19-
145.43-
146.64-
146.88-
146.94-
147.03-
147.135+ Ⓠ

Washington Metro Area
145.11-@	146.655-	146.97-
145.15-	146.685-	147.045+
145.19-	146.715-	147.21+
145.31-	146.76-	147.24+
145.47-	146.79-	147.315+
146.625-	146.91-	147.36+

Harrisonburg
145.13-
145.47-
146.895-
147.225+ Ⓦ
147.255+ Ⓦ
147.315+

2 Meter Repeater Offset is 600 KHz

121

Hampton
146.73-
146.94-
147.225+

Newport News
145.49-@
147.165+

VA Beach
146.895-
146.97-
147.045+
147.375+

Accomac
147.255+

Saluda
145.45-@

Yorktown
147.345+

Norfolk Ⓧ
145.11-Ⓧ
145.33-
146.61-@
146.79-@

Chesapeake
145.29-
146.61-@
146.79-@

Kilmarnock
145.21-@

Smithfield Ⓝ
147.195+@

Portsmouth
146.85-@

Suffolk
147.00-

Franklin
147.30+

Warsaw
147.33+

Gloucester
145.37-

Walkerton
146.715-

Richmond
Chester 295
145.31-

Williamsburg
Colonial Hts
145.39-

Bluemont
147.30+

Alexandria

Enon
147.06+

Beaverdam

Culpeper
147.12+

Fredericksburg
147.015+

Troy
145.29-

Gum Spg.
147.27+

Chesterfield
147.09+

Petersburg
147.39+

Greenbay
145.15-

Emporia

Winchester
145.21-
145.35-
146.82-

Warrenton
145.35-
147.165+

New Market
146.625-

Harrisonburg

Amelia CH
147.18+

Farmville
146.91-

Lunenburg
147.24+

Chase City
146.91-

Waynesboro
147.075+

Char-
lottes-
ville

Lynchburg
146.61-
147.015+
147.195+

Gladys
147.375+

Altavista
146.655-

Rustburg
146.835-

South Boston
147.06+

Danville
146.70-
146.925-

Stuarts Draft
147.36+

Forest
145.37-
147.165+

Bedford
145.23-
146.685-

Salem
146.88-

Martinsville
147.285+ Ⓠ

Collinsville
147.12+ Ⓟ

Stuarts Draft
147.36+

New Market
146.625-

Staunton
146.70-
146.85- Ⓦ
146.97-
147.045+ Ⓦ

Lexington
147.30+@
147.33+

Covington
146.805-

Fincastle
146.64-@

Roanoke

Blacksburg
146.715-

Pearisburg
147.135+

Pulaski
147.18+

Dublin
146.67-

Galax
145.13- Ⓟ
147.09+@

Bluefield
145.49-
146.955-
147.15+

Bald Knob
146.865-
146.91-

Bland
145.35-
146.775-@
146.895- Ⓟ

Wytheville
145.27-
146.64-@

Elk Creek
147.24+@

Jewell Ridge
147.15+

Richlands
147.15+

Marion
147.15+

Dante
147.255+

Gate City
146.82-@

Abingdon
146.61-147.345+

Bristol
146.88-

Grundy
146.835-
147.315+@

Coeburn
145.43-@

Wise
146.865-@

Norton
147.015+

Pennington Gap
146.70-

222 & UP

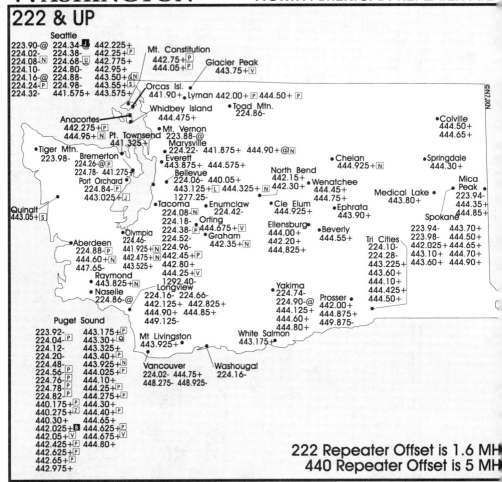

Seattle
223.90-@ 224.34- 442.225+
224.02- 224.38- 442.25+[P]
224.08-[N] 224.68-[U] 442.775+
224.10- 224.80- 442.95+
224.16-@ 224.88- 443.50+[N]
224.24-[P] 224.98- 443.55+[S]
224.32- 441.575+ 443.575+

Mt. Constitution
442.75+[P]
444.05+[P] Glacier Peak
443.75+[V]

Orcas Isl.
441.90+ Lyman 442.00+ [P] 444.50+ [P]

Whidbey Island
444.475+ Toad Mtn.
224.86-

Anacortes
442.275+[P] Mt. Vernon
444.95+[N] Pt. Townsend 223.88-@
441.325+ Marysville
224.22- 441.875+ 444.90+@[N]

Colville
444.50+
444.65+

Tiger Mtn.
223.98- Bremerton
224.26-@[P]
224.78- 441.275+ Everett
443.875+ 444.575+

Chelan
444.925+[N] Springdale
444.30+

Port Orchard
224.84-[P]
443.025+[J] Bellevue
224.06- 440.05+
443.125+[L] 444.325+ [N] 442.30+ [P]
1277.25-

North Bend
442.15+
444.45+ Wenatchee
444.45+
444.75+

Mica
Peak
223.94-
444.35+
444.85+

Medical Lake
443.80+

Quinalt
443.05+[S] Tacoma
224.08-[N]
224.18-
224.38-[P] Enumclaw
224.42-
Orting
444.675+[V] Cle Elum
444.925+ Ephrata
443.90+

Spokane
223.94- 443.70+
223.98- 444.50+
442.025+ 444.65+
443.10+ 444.70+
443.60+ 444.90+

Aberdeen
224.88-[P]
444.60+[N]
447.65- Olympia
224.46-
441.925+[N]
442.475+[N]
443.525+ 224.52-
224.96-
442.45+[P]
442.80+
444.25+[V] Graham
442.35+[N]

Ellensburg
444.00+
442.20+
444.825+ Beverly
444.55+

Tri Cities
224.10-
224.28-
443.225+
443.60+
444.10+
444.425+
444.50+

Raymond
443.825+[N] Longview
1292.40-
224.16- 224.66-
442.125+ 442.825+
444.90+ 444.85+
449.125-

Yakima
224.74-
224.90-@
444.125+
444.60+
444.80+ Prosser
442.00+
444.875+
449.875-

Naselle
224.86-@

Puget Sound
223.92- 443.175+[P]
224.04-[P] 443.30+[Q]
224.12- 443.325+
224.20- 443.40+[P]
224.48-[P] 443.925+[N]
224.56-[P] 444.025+[P]
224.76-[P] 444.10+
224.78-[P] 444.25+[P]
224.82-[P] 444.275+[P]
440.175+[P] 444.30+
440.275+[Z] 444.40+[P]
440.30+ 444.65+
442.025+[B] 444.625+[P]
442.05+[V] 444.675+[V]
442.425+[P] 444.80+
442.625+[P]
442.65+[P]
442.975+

Mt Livingston
443.925+ White Salmon
443.175+

Vancouver
224.02- 444.75+
448.275- 448.925- Washougal
224.16-

222 Repeater Offset is 1.6 MH▶
440 Repeater Offset is 5 MH▶

WASHINGTON FACTS

NUMBER OF HAMS: 21,779

CALL AREA: 7

STATE NICKNAME: EVERGREEN STATE

HIGHEST POINT:
   MT. RAINIER (14,410 FT.)

STATE CAPITAL: OLYMPIA

NUMBER OF COUNTIES: 39

NUMBER OF 2M REPEATERS: 147

   222 REPEATERS: 50

   440 REPEATERS: 109

   900 MHz REPEATERS: 0

   1.2 GHz REPEATERS: 3

CTCSS TONES.

A=67.0	Q=107.2	E=173.8
B=69.3	R=110.9	F=179.9
C=71.9	S=114.8	G=186.2
D=74.4	T=118.8	H=192.8
E=77.0	U=123.0	J=203.5
F=79.7	V=127.3	K=206.5
G=82.5	W=131.8	L=210.7
H=85.4	X=136.5	M=218.1
J=88.5	Y=141.3	N=225.7
K=91.5	Z=146.2	P=229.1
L=94.8	A=151.4	Q=233.6
M=97.4	B=156.7	R=241.8
N=100.0	C=162.2	S=250.3
P=103.5	D=167.9	T=254.1

WASHINGTON
2 METERS

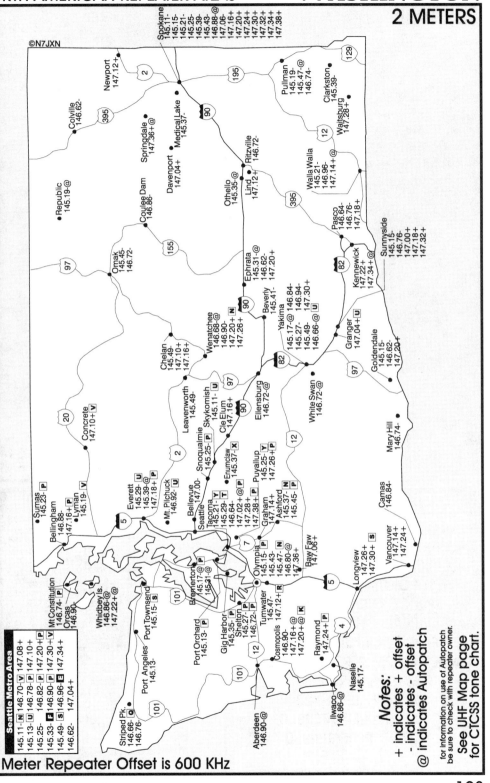

©N7JXN

Spokane
145.11-
145.15-
145.21-
145.25-
145.39-
145.43-
146.88-@
147.06-
147.16-
147.20+
147.24+
147.30+
147.32+
147.34+
147.38+

Newport 147.12 +

Colville 146.62-

Republic 145.19-@

Springdale 147.36+@

Medical Lake 145.37-

Davenport 147.04+

Coulee Dam 146.86-

Pullman
145.19-
145.47-@
146.74-

Clarkston 145.39-

Waitsburg 147.28+

Ritzville 146.72-

Lind 147.12+

Othello 145.35-@

Walla Walla
145.21-
146.96-
147.14+@

Pasco
146.64-
146.76-
147.18+

Omak 145.45- 146.72-

Ephrata
145.31-@
146.62-
147.20+

Kennewick
147.22+
147.34+@

Sunnyside
145.15-
146.76-
147.00+
147.18+
147.32+

Beverly 145.41-

Chelan
145.49-
147.10+
147.16+

Wenatchee
146.68-@
146.90-
147.20+ N
147.26+

Yakima
145.17-@ 146.84-
145.27- 146.94-
145.49- 147.30+
146.66+ U

Granger 147.04+ U

Goldendale
145.15-
146.62-
147.20+

Leavenworth 145.49-

Skykomish 145.11- U

Ellensburg 146.72-@

White Swan 146.72-@

Mary Hill 146.74-

Concrete 147.10+ V

Everett
145.29-
145.39- U
147.18+ P

Mt. Pilchuck 146.92- U

Bellevue 147.00-

Snoqualmie 145.25- P

Cle Elum 145.27- P

Enumclaw 145.37- X

Puyallup 147.26+ P

Sumas 145.23- P

Bellingham 146.88-
147.16+ P

Lyman 145.19- V

Seattle 147.38+ P

Tacoma
145.21- Y
145.29- T
146.64-
147.02+@ P
147.28+

Graham 145.25- Y

Ashford 145.37- N 145.45-

Camas 146.84-

Vancouver 147.14+ 147.24+

Longview 147.26+ 147.30+ S

Baw Faw 147.06+

Olympia
145.15- P
145.43-
145.47- N
147.36+

Bremerton 145.17-@ P 145.21-@

Whidbey Is. 146.86-@ 147.22+@

Mt Constitution 146.74- P

Orcas 146.90

Port Townsend 145.15- S

Port Angeles 145.13-

Port Orchard 145.13- P

Gig Harbor 145.35- P

Shelton 145.27- P

Tumwater 147.12+ R

Cosmopolis
146.90-
147.16+@ P
147.20+@ K

Raymond 147.24+ P

Naselle 145.17-

Aberdeen 146.90-@

Ilwaco 146.86-@

Striped Pk. 146.66- Q 146.76-

Notes:
+ indicates + offset
- indicates - offset
@ indicates Autopatch

for information on use of Autopatch
be sure to check with repeater owner.

See UHF Map page for CTCSS tone chart.

Seattle Metro Area

145.11- N	146.70- V	147.08 +	
145.13- U	146.78- P	147.10+	
145.25-	146.82- P	147.20+ P	
145.33- F	146.90- P	147.30+ V	
145.49- S	146.96- E	147.34+	
146.62-	147.04+		

Meter Repeater Offset is 600 KHz

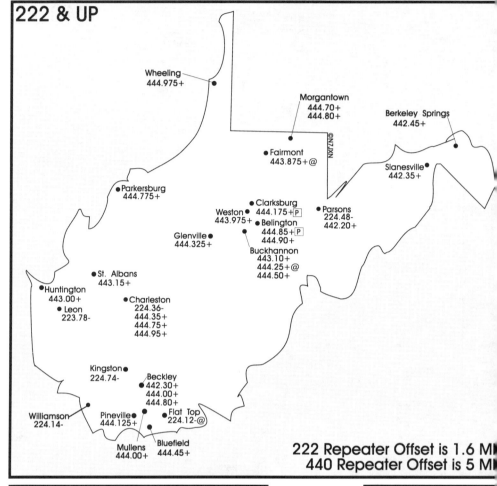

222 & UP

Wheeling
444.975+

Morgantown
444.70+
444.80+

Berkeley Springs
442.45+

©N7XN

Fairmont
443.875+@

Slanesville
442.35+

Parkersburg
444.775+

Clarksburg
Weston ● 444.175+ P
443.975+ ● Belington
444.85+ P
444.90+

Parsons
224.48-
442.20+

Glenville ●
444.325+

Buckhannon
443.10+
444.25+@
444.50+

St. Albans
443.15+

Huntington
443.00+
Leon
223.78-

Charleston
224.36-
444.35+
444.75+
444.95+

Kingston ●
224.74-

Beckley
442.30+
444.00+
444.80+

Williamson
224.14-

Pineville ●
444.125+

Flat Top
224.12-@

Mullens
444.00+

Bluefield
444.45+

222 Repeater Offset is 1.6 M
440 Repeater Offset is 5 M

WEST VIRGINIA FACTS

NUMBER OF HAMS: 5,429

CALL AREA: 8

STATE NICKNAME: MOUNTAIN STATE

HIGHEST POINT:
    SPRUCE KNOB (4,863 FT.)

STATE CAPITAL: CHARLESTON

NUMBER OF COUNTIES: 55

NUMBER OF 2M REPEATERS: 92

    222 REPEATERS: 6
    440 REPEATERS: 28
    900 MHz REPEATERS: 0
    1.2 GHz REPEATERS: 0

CTCSS TONES

A=67.0	Q=107.2	E=173.8
B=69.3	R=110.9	F=179.9
C=71.9	S=114.8	G=186.2
D=74.4	T=118.8	H=192.8
E=77.0	U=123.0	J=203.5
F=79.7	V=127.3	K=206.5
G=82.5	W=131.8	L=210.7
H=85.4	X=136.5	M=218.1
J=88.5	Y=141.3	N=225.7
K=91.5	Z=146.2	P=229.1
L=94.8	A=151.4	Q=233.6
M=97.4	B=156.7	R=241.8
N=100.0	C=162.2	S=250.3
P=103.5	D=167.9	T=254.1

WEST VIRGINIA
2 METERS

Notes:
+ indicates + offset
- indicates - offset
@ indicates Autopatch

for information on use of Autopatch
be sure to check with repeater owner.

See UHF Map page
for CTCSS tone chart.

Martinsburg
145.15- 147.255+
147.345+
Harpers Ferry
145.35-
Charles Town
146.985-

Berkeley Springs
146.745-

Moorefield
145.19- T

Romney
147.39+
50

Spruce Knob
147.285+ P
Upper Tract
146.655-

Franklin
147.345+

Terra Alta
147.00+ @
220 P

Davis
147.135+ T
Parsons
145.37-

Bartow
145.11-

Morgantown
145.43-@
146.76-
147.075+@

68

Grafton
147.375+

Elkins
146.775-

Buckhannon
147.12+
145.13-
145.41-@ 146.85-
147.06+ @ U

219

Union
145.41-
146.685-

Weirton
146.94-@

250

Fairmont
145.35-@ U

©N7JXN

Bridgeport
147.12+

Weston
145.39-
147.165+

Glenville
145.29-@ 146.85-
146.835-
Gassaway
146.61-

Craigsville
145.27- P
Richwood
145.19-
145.47-
147.33+

Hinton
147.255+ @

Flat Top
146.625-@

Wheeling
145.19-
146.715-
146.76-

Mc Mechen
146.91-

New Martinsville
146.985-@

St. Marys
147.03+

50

Clarksburg
146.685- P

Harrisville
147.30+

Elizabeth
147.00+ @
Grantsville
145.45-

79

Flatwoods
146.655-

Spencer
147.105+

Amber Ridge
147.21+

Fenwick
146.94-

64

Oak Hill
146.79-

Lewisburg
146.73-
147.39+

219

Princeton
146.925-@ 147.06+
147.225+

Parkersburg
145.49-@ T
146.97-
147.255+@
147.39+

Ravenswood
146.67-
146.70-

Leon
147.18+

Liberty
145.41-

Charleston

Madison
147.12+

77

Logan
146.97-
147.11-
147.345+

Mullens
147.03+
Welch
145.45-

Scott
Depot
147.27+

35

64

Salt Rock
145.11-

Huntington
145.21-
146.64-
146.76-

St. Albans
147.00-
147.15+
147.375+

Williamson
145.33-@

Beckley
145.17-@
145.23-@
145.31-@
145.37-@
146.85-

Bluefield
145.49-

Charleston Metro Area
145.25- 146.82-@
145.35-@ 146.88-

Meter Repeater Offset is 600 KHz

125

222 & UP

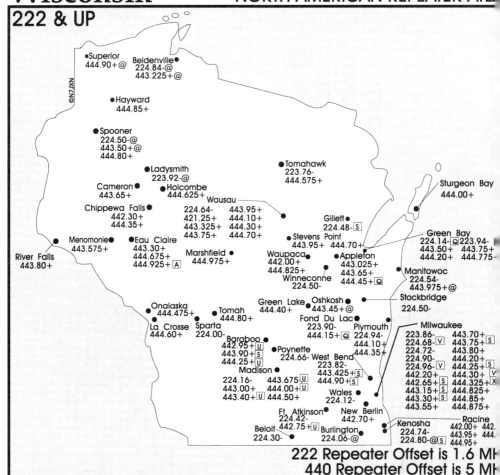

•Superior
444.90+@
Beidenville•
224.84-@
443.225+@

©N7JXN

•Hayward
444.85+

•Spooner
224.50-@
443.50+@
444.80+

•Ladysmith
223.92-@

•Tomahawk
223.76-
444.575+

Cameron •
443.65+

•Holcombe
444.625+ Wausau

Sturgeon Bay
444.00+

Chippewa Falls •
442.30+
444.35+

224.64- 443.95+
421.25+ 444.10+
443.325+ 444.30+
443.75+ 444.70+

Gillett •
224.48- S

Green Bay
224.14-Q 223.94-
443.50+ 443.75+
444.20+ 444.775+

Menomonie•
443.575+

•Eau Claire
443.30+
444.675+
444.925+ A

Marshfield •
444.975+

• Stevens Point
443.95+ 444.70+

River Falls
443.80+

Waupaca•
442.00+
444.825+

•Appleton
443.025+
443.65+

Manitowoc
224.54-
443.975+@

Winneconne
224.50-

444.45+Q

Stockbridge
224.50-

Onalaska
444.475+

•Tomah
444.80+

Green Lake
444.40+

Oshkosh •
443.45+@

Milwaukee

La Crosse Sparta
444.60+ 224.00-

Fond Du Lac•
223.90-
444.15+Q

223.86- 443.70+
224.68-V 443.75+S
224.72- 443.80+
224.90- 444.20+
224.96-V 444.25+S
442.20+ 444.30+ V
442.65+S 444.325+X
443.15+S 444.825+
443.30+S 444.85+
443.55+ 444.875+

Baraboo •
442.95+U
443.90+S
444.25+U

•Poynette
224.66-

Plymouth
224.94-
444.10+
444.35+

West Bend
223.82-
443.425+S
444.90+S

Madison •

224.16- 443.675+U
443.00+ 444.00+U
443.40+ U 444.50+

Wales
224.12-

Ft. Atkinson•
224.42-
442.75+U

New Berlin
442.70+

Kenosha
224.74-
224.80-@S

Racine
442.00+ 442.
443.95+ 444.
444.95+

Beloit
224.30-

Burlington
224.06-@

222 Repeater Offset is 1.6 Mi
440 Repeater Offset is 5 Mi

CTCSS TONES

A=67.0	Q=107.2	E=173.8
B=69.3	R=110.9	F=179.9
C=71.9	S=114.8	G=186.2
D=74.4	T=118.8	H=192.8
E=77.0	U=123.0	J=203.5
F=79.7	V=127.3	K=206.5
G=82.5	W=131.8	L=210.7
H=85.4	X=136.5	M=218.1
J=88.5	Y=141.3	N=225.7
K=91.5	Z=146.2	P=229.1
L=94.8	A=151.4	Q=233.6
M=97.4	B=156.7	R=241.8
N=100.0	C=162.2	S=250.3
P=103.5	D=167.9	T=254.1

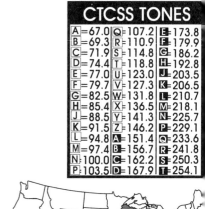

Wisconsin
2 METERS

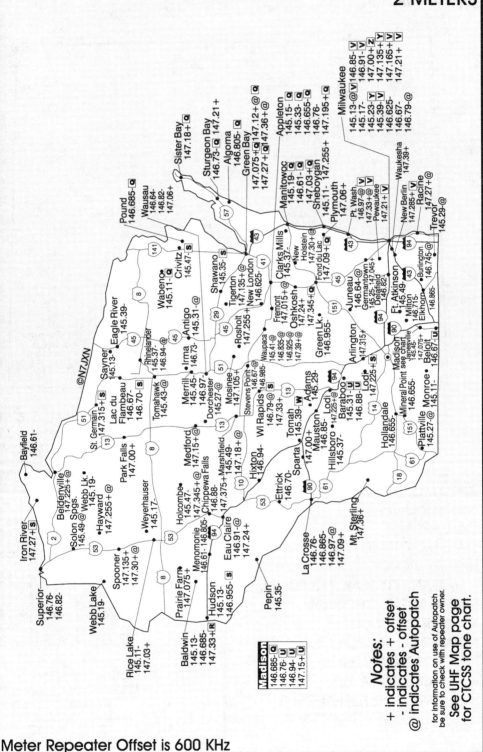

Milwaukee
145.13-@ V 146.85-V
145.17- 146.91-V
145.23+Y 147.00+Z
145.39+V 147.135+Y
146.625- 147.165+V
146.67- 147.21+
146.79-@

Appleton
145.15-Q
145.33-Q
146.655-
146.76-

New Berlin V
147.285+V
Racine
Waukesha 147.27+@
147.39+ Trevor
147.21+ 145.29-@

Pt. Wash.
146.97-@ V
147.33+@ V
Pewaukee
147.21+ V

Sister Bay
147.18+ Q

Sturgeon Bay
146.73-Q 147.21+

Algoma
146.805-Q
Green Bay
147.075+Q 147.12+@ Q
147.27+Q 147.36+@

Manitowoc
145.19-Q
146.61-Q
147.03+Q
Sheboygan
145.11- 147.255+
Plymouth
147.06+

Pound
146.685-Q

Wausau
146.64-
146.82-
147.06+

Clarks Mills
145.35-@

New
Holstein
147.30+Q
Fond du Lac
147.09+Q

Ft. Atkinson
145.49-
Milton
146.715-
Elkhorn
146.865

Burlington
146.745-@

Wabeno
145.11-Q
Crivitz
145.47-S

Shawano
145.35-S

Tigerton
147.135+
New London
146.625-

Fremont
147.015+@
Oshkosh
146.835@ 147.24+
146.925@ 147.345+@
147.39+@

Juneau
146.64-@
Germantown
146.25-@ 146.045-@
Delafield
146.82-

Delafield

Eagle River
145.39-

Rhinelander
145.37-
146.94-@

Antigo
145.31-@

Irma
146.73-

Rosholt
147.255+

Waupaca
145.41-@
146.67@

Green Lk.
146.955-

Arlington
147.315+

Madison
see chart,
Janesville
146.715-
147.075+
146.67-U

©N7JXN

Sayner
145.13-

Tomahawk
145.43-@

Merrill
145.45-
146.97-
Dorchester
145.27-@

Mosinee
147.105+

Stevens Point
146.985-

Adams
145.29-

Lodi
146.79@ 145.31-U
147.33+ Baraboo
145.31-U
146.88-U
Lodi
S

Madison
146.655-

Eau Claire

Lac du
Flambeau
146.67-
146.70-S

St. Germain
147.315+S

Park Falls
147.00+

Holcombe
145.47-
147.345+@ 147.15+@
Chippewa Falls
145.49-
147.375+Marshfield
147.18+@

Hixton
146.94-

WI Rapids 146.985-

Tomah
145.39-W

Sparta

Mauston
147.00+
146.85-
Hillsboro
145.37-

Monroe
145.11-

Plattville
145.27-@

Beldenville
147.225+@
Solon Spgs.
145.49-@ Webb Lk.
•Hayward 145.19-
147.255+@

Weyerhauser
145.17-

Medford
145.47-
146.88-

Menomonie
146.61-146.805-

Prairie Farm
147.075+

Hudson
145.13-
146.955-S

Baldwin
145.13-
146.685-
147.33+R

Pepin
145.35-

La Crosse
146.76-
146.865-
146.97-@
147.09+

Mt. Sterling
147.36+

Hollandale
146.655-

Bayfield
146.61-

Iron River
147.27+S

Superior
146.76-
146.82-

Webb Lake
145.19-

Spooner
147.135+
147.30+@

Rice Lake
145.11-
147.03+

Notes:
+ indicates + offset
- indicates - offset
@ indicates Autopatch

Madison
146.685-Q
146.76-U
146.94-U
147.15+U

See UHF Map page
for CTCSS tone chart.

for information on use of Autopatch
be sure to check with repeater owner.

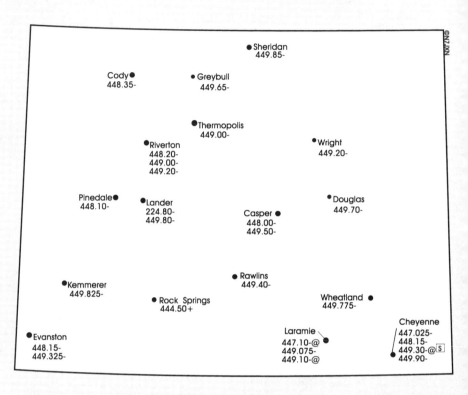

©N7JXN

Sheridan
449.85-

Cody●
448.35-

● Greybull
449.65-

●Thermopolis
449.00-

●Riverton
448.20-
449.00-
449.20-

● Wright
449.20-

Pinedale●
448.10-

●Lander
224.80-
449.80-

Casper ●
448.00-
449.50-

● Douglas
449.70-

● Rawlins
449.40-

●Kemmerer
449.825-

● Rock Springs
444.50+

Wheatland ●
449.775-

Cheyenne
447.025-
448.15-
449.30-@ S
449.90-

●Evanston
448.15-
449.325-

Laramie
447.10-@
449.075-
449.10-@

222 Repeater Offset is 1.6 MI
440 Repeater Offset is 5 MI
900 MHz Repeater Offset is 12 MI

WYOMING FACTS

NUMBER OF HAMS: 1,462
CALL AREA: 7
STATE NICKNAME: EQUALITY STATE
HIGHEST POINT:
    GANNETT PEAK (13,804 FT.)
STATE CAPITAL: CHEYENNE
NUMBER OF COUNTIES: 23
NUMBER OF 2M REPEATERS: 43
    222 REPEATERS: 1
    440 REPEATERS: 26
    900 MHz REPEATERS: 0
    1.2 GHz REPEATERS: 0

CTCSS TONES

A=67.0	Q=107.2	E=173.8
B=69.3	R=110.9	F=179.9
C=71.9	S=114.8	G=186.2
D=74.4	T=118.8	H=192.8
E=77.0	U=123.0	J=203.5
F=79.7	V=127.3	K=206.5
G=82.5	W=131.8	L=210.7
H=85.4	X=136.5	M=218.1
J=88.5	Y=141.3	N=225.7
K=91.5	Z=146.2	P=229.1
L=94.8	A=151.4	Q=233.6
M=97.4	B=156.7	R=241.8
N=100.0	C=162.2	S=250.3
P=103.5	D=167.9	T=254.1

WYOMING
2 METERS

Notes:
+ indicates + offset
- indicates - offset
@ indicates Autopatch

for information on use of Autopatch
be sure to check with repeater owner.

See UHF Map, page
for CTCSS tone chart.

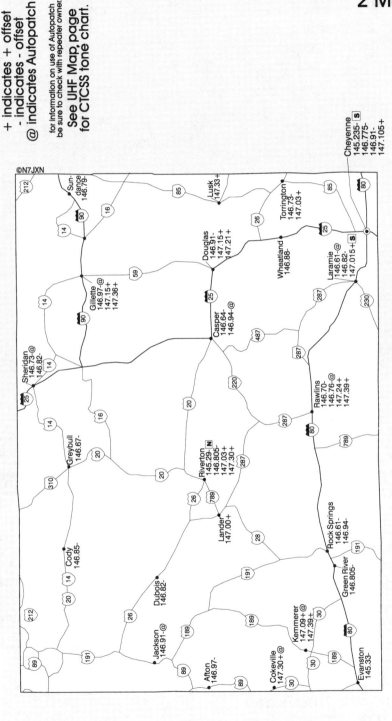

©N7JXN

Cheyenne
145.235- S
146.775-
146.91-
147.105+

Sun-
dance
146.79-

Lusk
147.33+

Torrington
146.73-
147.03+

Douglas
146.91-
147.15+
147.21+

Wheatland
146.88-

Laramie
146.61-@
146.82-
147.015+ S

Gillette
146.97-@
147.15+
147.36+

Casper
146.64-
146.94-@

Sheridan
146.73-@
146.82-

Rawlins
146.70-
146.76-@
147.24+
147.39+

Greybull
146.67-

Riverton
145.29- N
146.805-
147.03+
147.30+

Rock Springs
146.61-
146.94-

Cody
146.85-

Lander
147.00+

Green River
146.805-

Dubois
146.82-

Kemmerer
147.09+@
147.39±

Jackson
146.91-@

Atton
146.97-

Cokeville
147.30+@

Evanston
145.33-

2 Meter Repeater Offset is 600 KHz

Alberta

222 & UP

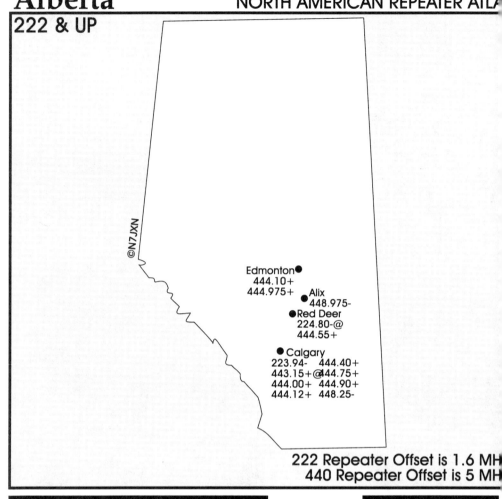

©N7JXN

Edmonton●
444.10+
444.975+
●Alix
448.975-
●Red Deer
224.80-@
444.55+

● Calgary
223.94-   444.40+
443.15+@444.75+
444.00+   444.90+
444.12+ 448.25-

222 Repeater Offset is 1.6 MH
440 Repeater Offset is 5 MH

ALBERTA FACTS

NUMBER OF HAMS: 3,340

CALL AREA: VE6

LARGEST CITY: EDMONTON

HIGHEST POINT:
    MT. COLUMBIA (12,294 FT.)

STATE CAPITAL: EDMONTON

AREA: 255,285 SQ. MILES

NUMBER OF 2M REPEATERS: 47

    222 REPEATERS: 2

    440 REPEATERS: 11

    900 MHz REPEATERS: 0

    1.2 GHz REPEATERS: 0

CTCSS TONES

A=67.0	Q=107.2	E=173.8
B=69.3	R=110.9	F=179.9
C=71.9	S=114.8	G=186.2
D=74.4	T=118.8	H=192.8
E=77.0	U=123.0	J=203.5
F=79.7	V=127.3	K=206.5
G=82.5	W=131.8	L=210.7
H=85.4	X=136.5	M=218.1
J=88.5	Y=141.3	N=225.7
K=91.5	Z=146.2	P=229.1
L=94.8	A=151.4	Q=233.6
M=97.4	B=156.7	R=241.8
N=100.0	C=162.2	S=250.3
P=103.5	D=167.9	T=254.1

Alberta
2 METERS

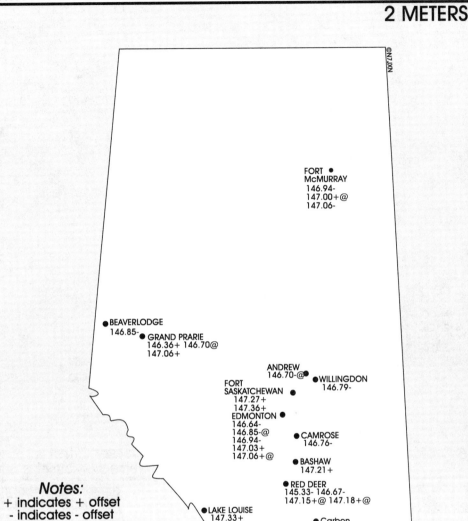

FORT ● McMURRAY
146.94-
147.00+@
147.06-

●BEAVERLODGE
146.85-
●GRAND PRARIE
146.36+ 146.70@
147.06+

ANDREW
146.70-@
FORT SASKATCHEWAN ●
147.27+
147.36+
EDMONTON ●
146.64-
146.85-@
146.94-
147.03+
147.06+@

●WILLINGDON
146.79-

●CAMROSE
146.76-

●BASHAW
147.21+

●RED DEER
145.33- 146.67-
147.15+@ 147.18+@

Notes:
+ indicates + offset
- indicates - offset
@ indicates Autopatch

for information on use of Autopatch
be sure to check with repeater owner.

See UHF Map page
for CTCSS tone chart.

●LAKE LOUISE
147.33+

● Carbon
146.715-

● BANFF
147.03+

●AIRDRIE
147.15+

HIGH
RIVER ●
147.00+@

●BROOKS
147.12+
147.27+

MEDICINE ●
HAT 146.70-
147.06+@

CALGARY
145.15-   147.06+
146.61-   147.09+
146.64-   147.24+
146.73-@   147.27+@
146.76-@   147.36+
146.85-@   147.39+@
146.94-

Warner ●
146.67-

Milk River ●
146.76-@

2 Meter Repeater Offset is 600 KHz

British Columbia

222 & UP

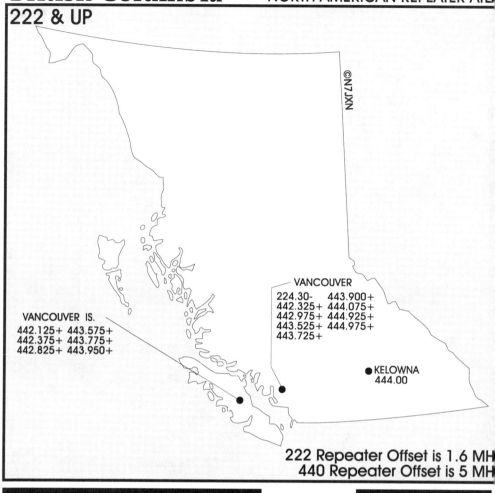

©N7JXN

VANCOUVER
224.30-	443.900+
442.325+	444.075+
442.975+	444.925+
443.525+	444.975+
443.725+	

VANCOUVER IS.
442.125+	443.575+
442.375+	443.775+
442.825+	443.950+

● KELOWNA
444.00

222 Repeater Offset is 1.6 MH
440 Repeater Offset is 5 MH

BRITISH COLUMBIA FACTS

NUMBER OF HAMS: 7,184

CALL AREA: VE7

LARGEST CITY: VANCOUVER

HIGHEST POINT:
   MT. FAIRWEATHER (15,300 FT.)

STATE CAPITAL: VICTORIA

AREA: 366,253 SQ. MILES

NUMBER OF 2M REPEATERS: 75

   222 REPEATERS: 1
   440 REPEATERS: 15
   900 MHz REPEATERS: 0
   1.2 GHz REPEATERS: 0

CTCSS TONES

A=67.0	Q=107.2	E=173.8
B=69.3	R=110.9	F=179.9
C=71.9	S=114.8	G=186.2
D=74.4	T=118.8	H=192.8
E=77.0	U=123.0	J=203.5
F=79.7	V=127.3	K=206.5
G=82.5	W=131.8	L=210.7
H=85.4	X=136.5	M=218.1
J=88.5	Y=141.3	N=225.7
K=91.5	Z=146.2	P=229.1
L=94.8	A=151.4	Q=233.6
M=97.4	B=156.7	R=241.8
N=100.0	C=162.2	S=250.3
P=103.5	D=167.9	T=254.1

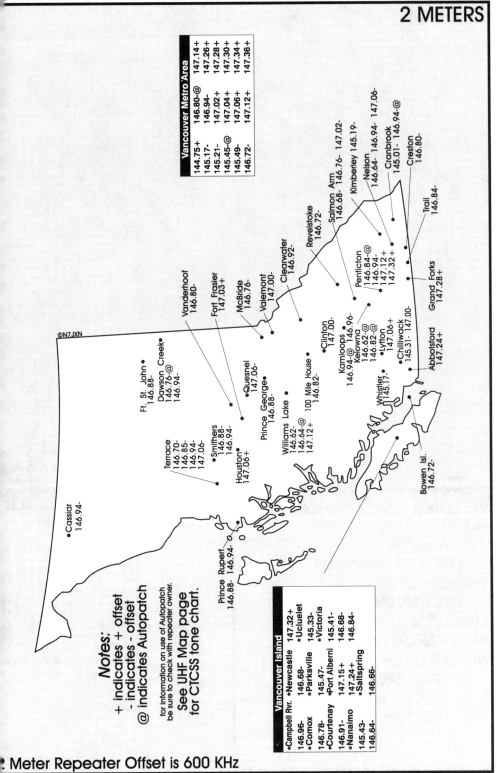

Vancouver Metro Area

144.75+	146.80-@	147.14+
145.17-	146.94-	147.26+
145.21-	147.02+	147.28+
145.45-@	147.04+	147.30+
145.49-	147.06+	147.34+
146.72-	147.12+	147.36+

Cranbrook
145.01- 146.94-@

Creston
146.80-

Nelson
146.64- 146.94- 147.06-

Kimberley 145.19-

Salmon Arm
146.88- 146.76- 147.02-

Trail
146.84-

Revelstoke
146.72-

Penticton
146.84-@
146.94-
147.12+
147.32+

Grand Forks
147.28+

Clearwater
146.92-

Vanderhoof
146.80-

Fort Frasier
147.03+

McBride
146.76-

Valemont
147.00-

Clinton
147.00-

Kelowna
146.62-@
146.82-@

Kamloops
146.94-@ 146.96-

Chilliwack
145.31- 147.00-

Abbotsford
147.24+

Lytton
147.06+

Ft. St. John •
146.88-

Dawson Creek•
146.76-@
146.94-

Quesnel•
147.06-

Prince George•
146.88-

Williams Lake •
146.62-
146.64-@
147.12+

100 Mile House •
146.82-

Whistler
145.17-

Smithers •
146.88-
146.94-

Houston•
147.06+

Terrace
146.70-
146.85-
146.94-
147.06-

Bowen Isl.
146.72-

©N7JXN

Cassiar
146.94-

Prince Rupert
146.88- 146.94- ○

Notes:

+ indicates + offset
- indicates - offset
@ indicates Autopatch

for information on use of Autopatch
be sure to check with repeater owner.

See UHF Map page
for CTCSS tone chart.

Vancouver Island

*Campbell Rvr.	*Newcastle 147.32+	
146.96-	146.68-	*Ucluelet
*Comox	*Parksville	145.33-
146.78-	145.47-	*Victoria
*Courtenay	*Port Alberni	145.41-
146.91-	147.15+	146.68-
*Nanaimo	147.24+	146.84-
145.43-	*Saltspring	
146.64-	146.66-	

Meter Repeater Offset is 600 KHz

133

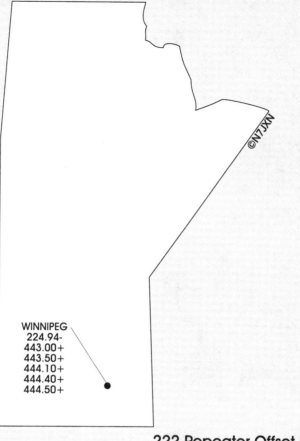

222 & UP

WINNIPEG
224.94-
443.00+
443.50+
444.10+
444.40+
444.50+

222 Repeater Offset is 1.6 MH
440 Repeater Offset is 5 MH

MANITOBA FACTS

NUMBER OF HAMS: 1,405

CALL AREA: VE4

LARGEST CITY: WINNIPEG

HIGHEST POINT:
   BALDY MOUNTAIN (2,729 FT.)

STATE CAPITAL: WINNIPEG

AREA: 250,999 SQ. MILES

NUMBER OF 2M REPEATERS: 34

   222 REPEATERS: 1

   440 REPEATERS: 5

   900 MHz REPEATERS: 0

   1.2 GHz REPEATERS: 0

CTCSS TONES

A=67.0	Q=107.2	E=173.8
B=69.3	R=110.9	F=179.9
C=71.9	S=114.8	G=186.2
D=74.4	T=118.8	H=192.8
E=77.0	U=123.0	J=203.5
F=79.7	V=127.3	K=206.5
G=82.5	W=131.8	L=210.7
H=85.4	X=136.5	M=218.1
J=88.5	Y=141.3	N=225.7
K=91.5	Z=146.2	P=229.1
L=94.8	A=151.4	Q=233.6
M=97.4	B=156.7	R=241.8
N=100.0	C=162.2	S=250.3
P=103.5	D=167.9	T=254.1

Manitoba
2 METERS

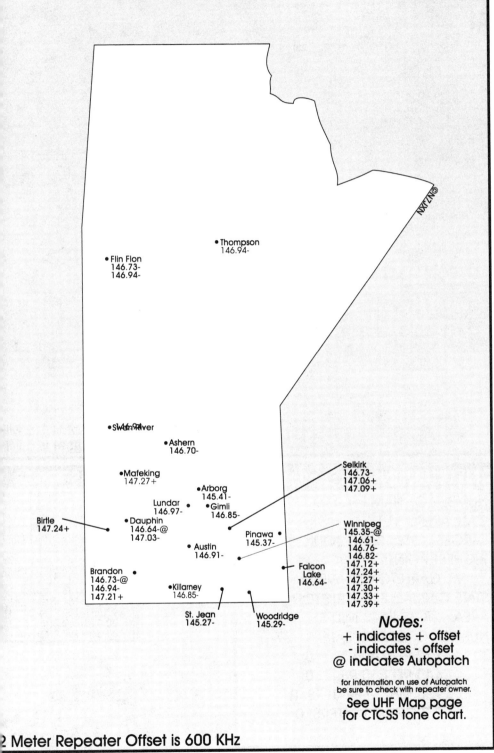

• Thompson
146.94-

• Flin Flon
146.73-
146.94-

•Swan River

•Ashern
146.70-

•Mafeking
147.27+

Selkirk
146.73-
147.06+
147.09+

• Arborg
145.41-

Lundar
146.97-

•Gimli
146.85-

Birtle
147.24+

• Dauphin
146.64-@
147.03-

Winnipeg
145.35-@
146.61-
146.76-
146.82-
147.12+
147.24+
147.27+
147.30+
147.33+
147.39+

Pinawa •
145.37-

• Austin
146.91-

Brandon •
146.73-@
146.94-
147.21+

Falcon
Lake
146.64-

•Killarney
146.85-

St. Jean
145.27-

Woodridge
145.29-

Notes:
+ indicates + offset
- indicates - offset
@ indicates Autopatch

for information on use of Autopatch
be sure to check with repeater owner.

See UHF Map page
for CTCSS tone chart.

2 Meter Repeater Offset is 600 KHz

222 & UP

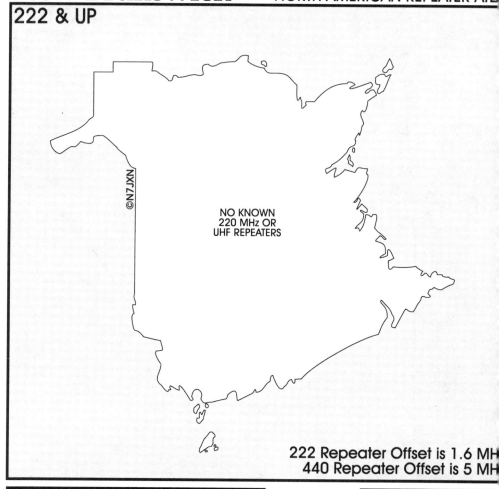

©N7JXN

NO KNOWN
220 MHz OR
UHF REPEATERS

222 Repeater Offset is 1.6 MH
440 Repeater Offset is 5 MH

NEW BRUNSWICK FACTS

NUMBER OF HAMS: 1,199

CALL AREA: VE1

LARGEST CITY: SAINT JOHN

HIGHEST POINT:
    MT. CARLETON (2,690 FT.)

STATE CAPITAL: FREDERICTON

AREA: 28,354 SQ. MILES

NUMBER OF 2M REPEATERS: 27

    222 REPEATERS: 0

    440 REPEATERS: 0

    900 MHz REPEATERS: 0

    1.2 GHz REPEATERS: 0

CTCSS TONES

A=67.0	Q=107.2	E=173.8
B=69.3	R=110.9	F=179.9
C=71.9	S=114.8	G=186.2
D=74.4	T=118.8	H=192.8
E=77.0	U=123.0	J=203.5
F=79.7	V=127.3	K=206.5
G=82.5	W=131.8	L=210.7
H=85.4	X=136.5	M=218.1
J=88.5	Y=141.3	N=225.7
K=91.5	Z=146.2	P=229.1
L=94.8	A=151.4	Q=233.6
M=97.4	B=156.7	R=241.8
N=100.0	C=162.2	S=250.3
P=103.5	D=167.9	T=254.1

New Brunswick
2 METERS

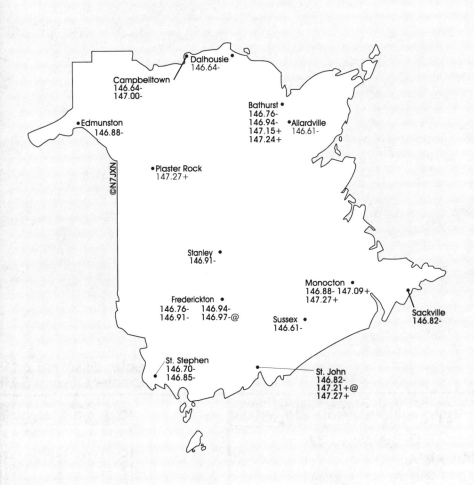

Dalhousie •
146.64-

Campbelltown
146.64-
147.00-

Bathurst •
146.76-
146.94-
147.15+
147.24+

•Allardville
146.61-

•Edmunston
146.88-

•Plaster Rock
147.27+

©N7JXN

Stanley •
146.91-

Monocton •
146.88- 147.09+
147.27+

Sackville
146.82-

Frederickton •
146.76-   146.94-
146.91-   146.97-@

Sussex •
146.61-

St. Stephen
146.70-
146.85-

St. John
146.82-
147.21+@
147.27+

Notes:
+ indicates + offset
- indicates - offset
@ indicates Autopatch

for information on use of Autopatch
be sure to check with repeater owner.

See UHF Map page
for CTCSS tone chart.

2 Meter Repeater Offset is 600 KHz

137

222 & UP

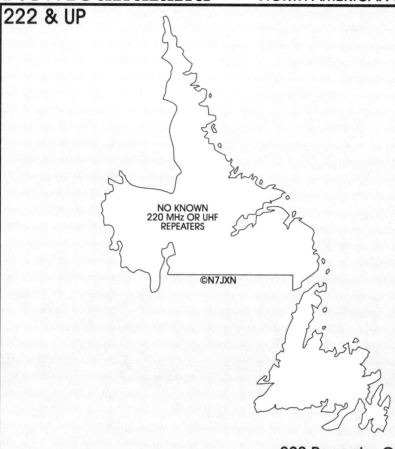

NO KNOWN
220 MHz OR UHF
REPEATERS

©N7JXN

222 Repeater Offset is 1.6 MH
440 Repeater Offset is 5 MH

NEWFOUNDLAND FACTS

NUMBER OF HAMS: 1,037

CALL AREA: VO1

LARGEST CITY: ST. JOHNS

HIGHEST POINT:
TORNGAT MOUNTAINS (5,420 FT.)

STATE CAPITAL: ST. JOHNS

AREA: 156,184 SQ. MILES

NUMBER OF 2M REPEATERS: 18

222 REPEATERS: 0

440 REPEATERS: 0

900 MHz REPEATERS: 0

1.2 GHz REPEATERS: 0

CTCSS TONES

A=67.0	Q=107.2	E=173.8
B=69.3	R=110.9	F=179.9
C=71.9	S=114.8	G=186.2
D=74.4	T=118.8	H=192.8
E=77.0	U=123.0	J=203.5
F=79.7	V=127.3	K=206.5
G=82.5	W=131.8	L=210.7
H=85.4	X=136.5	M=218.1
J=88.5	Y=141.3	N=225.7
K=91.5	Z=146.2	P=229.1
L=94.8	A=151.4	Q=233.6
M=97.4	B=156.7	R=241.8
N=100.0	C=162.2	S=250.3
P=103.5	D=167.9	T=254.1

Newfoundland
2 METERS

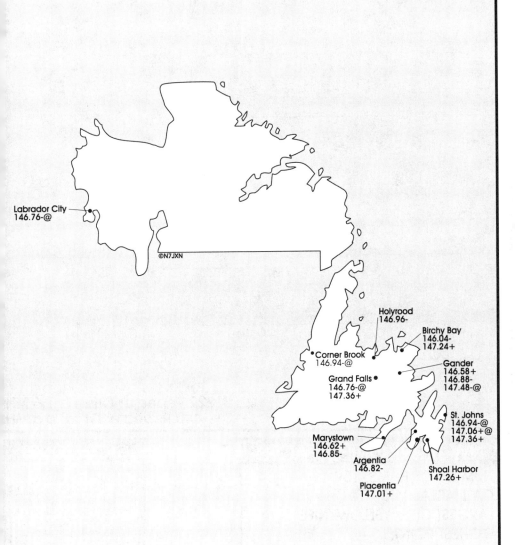

Labrador City
146.76-@

©N7JXN

Holyrood
146.96-

Birchy Bay
146.04-
147.24+

•Corner Brook
146.94-@

Gander
146.58+
146.88-
147.48-@

Grand Falls •
146.76-@
147.36+

St. Johns
146.94-@
147.06+@
147.36+

Marystown
146.62+
146.85-

Argentia
146.82-

Shoal Harbor
147.26+

Placentia
147.01+

Notes:
+ indicates + offset
- indicates - offset
@ indicates Autopatch

for information on use of Autopatch
be sure to check with repeater owner.
See UHF Map page
for CTCSS tone chart.

2 Meter Repeater Offset is 600 KHz

222 & UP

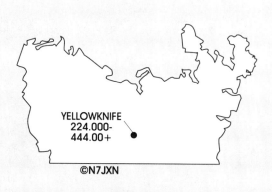

YELLOWKNIFE
224.000-
444.00+

©N7JXN

222 Repeater Offset is 1.6 MH₂
440 Repeater Offset is 5 MH₂

NW TERRITORIES FACTS

NUMBER OF HAMS: 109

CALL AREA: VE8

LARGEST CITY: YELLOWKNIFE

HIGHEST POINT:
   MT. MACBRIEN (9,062 FT.)

STATE CAPITAL: YELLOWKNIFE

AREA: 1,304,896 SQ. MILES

NUMBER OF 2M REPEATERS: 7

   222 REPEATERS: 1
   440 REPEATERS: 1
   900 MHz REPEATERS: 0
   1.2 GHz REPEATERS: 0

CTCSS TONES

A=67.0	Q=107.2	E=173.8
B=69.3	R=110.9	F=179.9
C=71.9	S=114.8	G=186.2
D=74.4	T=118.8	H=192.8
E=77.0	U=123.0	J=203.5
F=79.7	V=127.3	K=206.5
G=82.5	W=131.8	L=210.7
H=85.4	X=136.5	M=218.1
J=88.5	Y=141.3	N=225.7
K=91.5	Z=146.2	P=229.1
L=94.8	A=151.4	Q=233.6
M=97.4	B=156.7	R=241.8
N=100.0	C=162.2	S=250.3
P=103.5	D=167.9	T=254.1

Northwest Territories

2 METERS

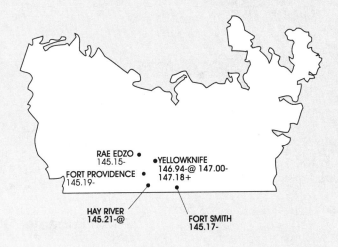

RAE EDZO •
145.15-

•YELLOWKNIFE
146.94-@ 147.00-
147.18+

FORT PROVIDENCE •
145.19-

HAY RIVER
145.21-@

FORT SMITH
145.17-

Notes:
+ indicates + offset
- indicates - offset
@ indicates Autopatch

for information on use of Autopatch
be sure to check with repeater owner.

See UHF Map page
for CTCSS tone chart.

2 Meter Repeater Offset is 600 KHz

222 & UP

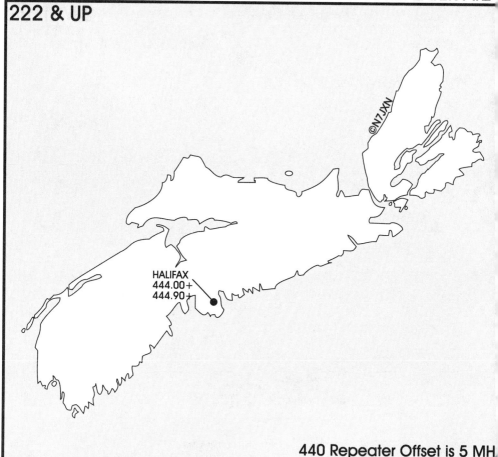

HALIFAX
444.00+
444.90+

©N7JXN

440 Repeater Offset is 5 MH

NOVA SCOTIA FACTS

NUMBER OF HAMS: 1,774

CALL AREA: VE1

LARGEST CITY: HALIFAX

HIGHEST POINT:
CAPE BRETON HIGHLANDS (1,747 FT.)

STATE CAPITAL: HALIFAX

AREA: 21,425 SQ. MILES

NUMBER OF 2M REPEATERS: 25

222 REPEATERS: 0
440 REPEATERS: 2
900 MHz REPEATERS: 0
1.2 GHz REPEATERS: 0

CTCSS TONES

A=67.0	Q=107.2	E=173.8
B=69.3	R=110.9	F=179.9
C=71.9	S=114.8	G=186.2
D=74.4	T=118.8	H=192.8
E=77.0	U=123.0	J=203.5
F=79.7	V=127.3	K=206.5
G=82.5	W=131.8	L=210.7
H=85.4	X=136.5	M=218.1
J=88.5	Y=141.3	N=225.7
K=91.5	Z=146.2	P=229.1
L=94.8	A=151.4	Q=233.6
M=97.4	B=156.7	R=241.8
N=100.0	C=162.2	S=250.3
P=103.5	D=167.9	T=254.1

Nova Scotia
2 METERS

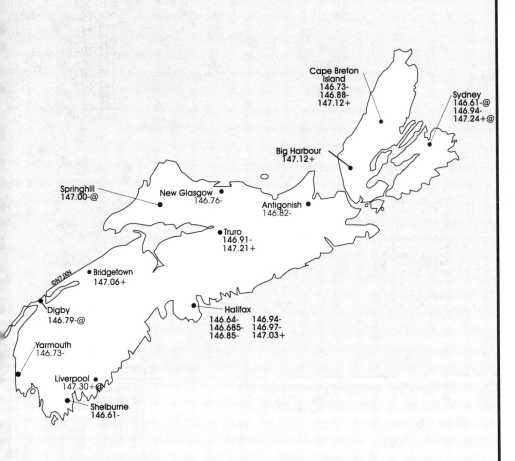

Cape Breton Island
146.73-
146.88-
147.12+

Sydney
146.61-@
146.94-
147.24+@

Big Harbour
147.12+

Springhill
147.00-@

New Glasgow
146.76-

Antigonish
146.82-

Truro
146.91-
147.21+

Bridgetown
147.06+

©N7JXN

Digby
146.79-@

Halifax
146.64-   146.94-
146.685- 146.97-
146.85-   147.03+

Yarmouth
146.73-

Liverpool
147.30+@

Shelburne
146.61-

Notes:
+ indicates + offset
- indicates - offset
@ indicates Autopatch

for information on use of Autopatch
be sure to check with repeater owner.

See UHF Map page
for CTCSS tone chart.

2 Meter Repeater Offset is 600 KHz

Ontario

222 & UP

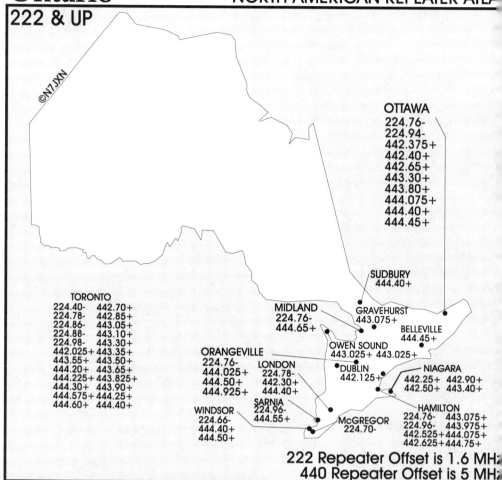

©N7JXN

OTTAWA
224.76-
224.94-
442.375+
442.40+
442.65+
443.30+
443.80+
444.075+
444.40+
444.45+

SUDBURY
444.40+

TORONTO
224.40- 442.70+
224.78- 442.85+
224.86- 443.05+
224.88- 443.10+
224.98- 443.30+
442.025+ 443.35+
443.55+ 443.50+
444.20+ 443.65+
444.225+ 443.825+
444.30+ 443.90+
444.575+ 444.25+
444.60+ 444.40+

MIDLAND
224.76-
444.65+

GRAVEHURST
443.075+

BELLEVILLE
444.45+

OWEN SOUND
443.025+ 443.025+

ORANGEVILLE
224.76-
444.025+
444.50+
444.925+

LONDON
224.78-
442.30+
444.40+

DUBLIN
442.125+

NIAGARA
442.25+ 442.90+
442.50+ 443.40+

SARNIA
224.96-
444.55+

WINDSOR
224.66-
444.40+
444.50+

McGREGOR
224.70-

HAMILTON
224.76- 443.075+
224.96- 443.975+
442.525+444.075+
442.625+444.75+

222 Repeater Offset is 1.6 MH;
440 Repeater Offset is 5 MH;

ONTARIO FACTS

NUMBER OF HAMS: 14,621

CALL AREA: VE3

LARGEST CITY: TORONTO

HIGHEST POINT:
   TIMISKAMING (2,275 FT.)

STATE CAPITAL: TORONTO

AREA: 412,580 SQ. MILES

NUMBER OF 2M REPEATERS: 75

      222 REPEATERS: 15

      440 REPEATERS: 54

      900 MHz REPEATERS: 0

      1.2 GHz REPEATERS: 0

CTCSS TONES

A=67.0	Q=107.2	E=173.8
B=69.3	R=110.9	F=179.9
C=71.9	S=114.8	G=186.2
D=74.4	T=118.8	H=192.8
E=77.0	U=123.0	J=203.5
F=79.7	V=127.3	K=206.5
G=82.5	W=131.8	L=210.7
H=85.4	X=136.5	M=218.1
J=88.5	Y=141.3	N=225.7
K=91.5	Z=146.2	P=229.1
L=94.8	A=151.4	Q=233.6
M=97.4	B=156.7	R=241.8
N=100.0	C=162.2	S=250.3
P=103.5	D=167.9	T=254.1

Ontario
2 METERS

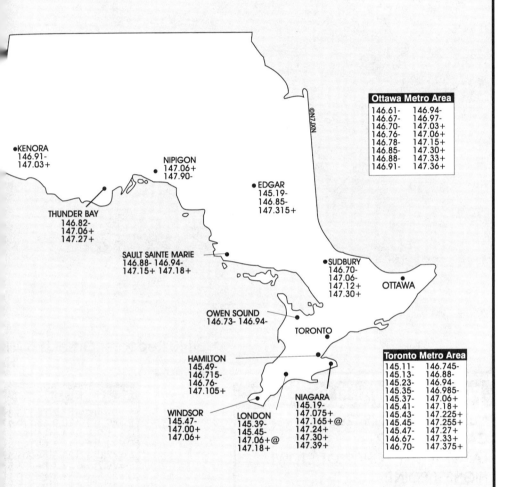

KENORA
146.91-
147.03+

NIPIGON
147.06+
147.90-

THUNDER BAY
146.82-
147.06+
147.27+

EDGAR
145.19-
146.85-
147.315+

Ottawa Metro Area

146.61-	146.94-
146.67-	146.97-
146.70-	147.03+
146.76-	147.06+
146.78-	147.15+
146.85-	147.30+
146.88-	147.33+
146.91-	147.36+

SAULT SAINTE MARIE
146.88- 146.94-
147.15+ 147.18+

SUDBURY
146.70-
147.06-
147.12+
147.30+

OTTAWA

OWEN SOUND
146.73- 146.94-

TORONTO

HAMILTON
145.49-
146.715-
146.76-
147.105+

WINDSOR
145.47-
147.00+
147.06+

LONDON
145.39-
145.45-
147.06+@
147.18+

NIAGARA
145.19-
147.075+
147.165+@
147.24+
147.30+
147.39+

Toronto Metro Area

145.11-	146.745-
145.13-	146.88-
145.23-	146.94-
145.35-	146.985-
145.37-	147.06+
145.41-	147.18+
145.43-	147.225+
145.45-	147.255+
145.47-	147.27+
146.67-	147.33+
146.70-	147.375+

Notes:
+ indicates + offset
- indicates - offset
@ indicates Autopatch

for information on use of Autopatch
be sure to check with repeater owner.
See UHF Map page
for CTCSS tone chart.

2 Meter Repeater Offset is 600 KHz

222 & UP

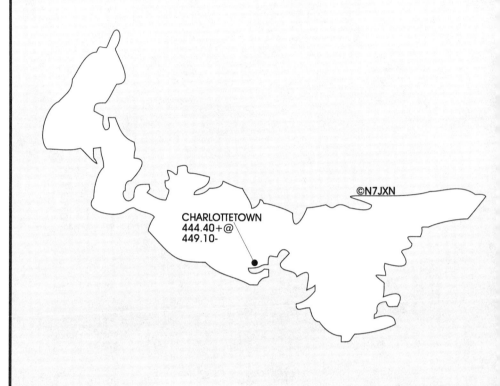

CHARLOTTETOWN
444.40+@
449.10-

©N7JXN

440 Repeater Offset is 5 MH

PRINCE EDWARD IS. FACTS

NUMBER OF HAMS: 290
CALL AREA: VY2
LARGEST CITY: CHARLOTTETOWN
HIGHEST POINT:
    PRINCE EDWARD IS. (465 FT.)
STATE CAPITAL: CHARLOTTETOWN
AREA: 2,184 SQ. MILES
NUMBER OF 2M REPEATERS: 4
        222 REPEATERS: 0
        440 REPEATERS: 2
        900 MHz REPEATERS: 0
        1.2 GHz REPEATERS: 0

CTCSS TONES

A=67.0	Q=107.2	E=173.8
B=69.3	R=110.9	F=179.9
C=71.9	S=114.8	G=186.2
D=74.4	T=118.8	H=192.8
E=77.0	U=123.0	J=203.5
F=79.7	V=127.3	K=206.5
G=82.5	W=131.8	L=210.7
H=85.4	X=136.5	M=218.1
J=88.5	Y=141.3	N=225.7
K=91.5	Z=146.2	P=229.1
L=94.8	A=151.4	Q=233.6
M=97.4	B=156.7	R=241.8
N=100.0	C=162.2	S=250.3
P=103.5	D=167.9	T=254.1

Prince Edward Is.
2 METERS

- O'Leary
  147.12+

- Summerside
  146.85-@

Charlottetown
146.67-@ 146.94-@

©N7JXN

Meter Repeater Offset is 600 KHz

222 & UP

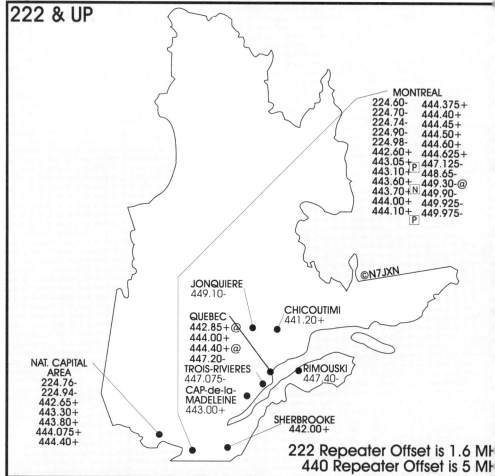

MONTREAL
224.60-	444.375+
224.70-	444.40+
224.74-	444.45+
224.90-	444.50+
224.98-	444.60+
442.60+	444.625+
443.05+ P	447.125-
443.10+	448.65-
443.60+	449.30-@
443.70+ N	449.90-
444.00+	449.925-
444.10+ P	449.975-

©N7JXN

JONQUIERE
449.10-

CHICOUTIMI
441.20+

QUEBEC
442.85+@
444.00+
444.40+@
447.20-

NAT. CAPITAL
AREA
224.76-
224.94-
442.65+
443.30+
443.80+
444.075+
444.40+

TROIS-RIVIERES
447.075-

RIMOUSKI
447.40-

CAP-de-la-
MADELEINE
443.00+

SHERBROOKE
442.00+

222 Repeater Offset is 1.6 MH
440 Repeater Offset is 5 MH

QUEBEC FACTS

NUMBER OF HAMS: 9,178

CALL AREA: VE2

LARGEST CITY: MONTREAL

HIGHEST POINT:
   MONT D'IBERVILLE (5,420 FT.)

STATE CAPITAL: QUEBEC

AREA: 594,857 SQ. MILES

NUMBER OF 2M REPEATERS: 109

   222 REPEATERS: 7
   440 REPEATERS: 35
   900 MHz REPEATERS: 0
   1.2 GHz REPEATERS: 0

CTCSS TONES

A=67.0	Q=107.2	E=173.8
B=69.3	R=110.9	F=179.9
C=71.9	S=114.8	G=186.2
D=74.4	T=118.8	H=192.8
E=77.0	U=123.0	J=203.5
F=79.7	V=127.3	K=206.5
G=82.5	W=131.8	L=210.7
H=85.4	X=136.5	M=218.1
J=88.5	Y=141.3	N=225.7
K=91.5	Z=146.2	P=229.1
L=94.8	A=151.4	Q=233.6
M=97.4	B=156.7	R=241.8
N=100.0	C=162.2	S=250.3
P=103.5	D=167.9	T=254.1

Quebec
2 METERS

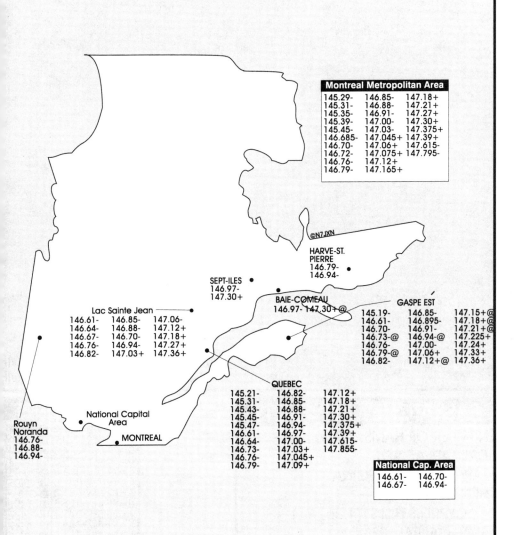

Montreal Metropolitan Area		
145.29-	146.85-	147.18+
145.31-	146.88-	147.21+
145.35-	146.91-	147.27+
145.39-	147.00-	147.30+
145.45-	147.03-	147.375+
146.685-	147.045+	147.39+
146.70-	147.06+	147.615-
146.72-	147.075+	147.795-
146.76-	147.12+	
146.79-	147.165+	

©N7JXN

HARVE-ST. PIERRE
146.79-
146.94-

SEPT-ILES
146.97-
147.30+

BAIE-COMEAU
146.97- 147.30+@

GASPE EST		
145.19-	146.85-	147.15+@
146.61-	146.895-	147.18+@
146.70-	146.91-	147.21+@
146.73-@	146.94-@	147.225+
146.76-	147.00-	147.24+
146.79-@	147.06+	147.33+
146.82-	147.12+@	147.36+

Lac Sainte Jean
146.61-	146.85-	147.06-
146.64-	146.88-	147.12+
146.67-	146.70-	147.18+
146.76-	146.94-	147.27+
146.82-	147.03+	147.36+

QUEBEC
145.21-	146.82-	147.12+
145.31-	146.85-	147.18+
145.43-	146.88-	147.21+
145.45-	146.91-	147.30+
145.47-	146.94-	147.375+
146.61-	146.97-	147.39+
146.64-	147.00-	147.615-
146.73-	147.03+	147.855-
146.76-	147.045+	
146.79-	147.09+	

National Capital Area

MONTREAL

Rouyn Noranda
146.76-
146.88-
146.94-

National Cap. Area	
146.61-	146.70-
146.67-	146.94-

Notes:
+ indicates + offset
- indicates - offset
@ indicates Autopatch

for information on use of Autopatch
be sure to check with repeater owner.

See UHF Map page
for CTCSS tone chart.

2 Meter Repeater Offset is 600 KHz

Saskatchewan

222 & UP

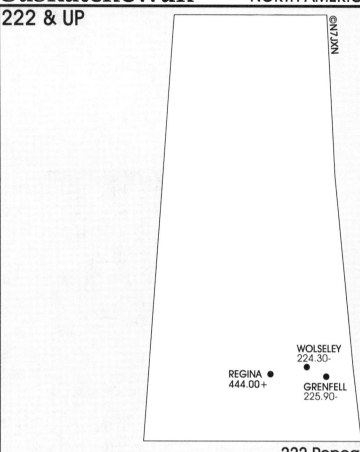

©N7JXN

WOLSELEY
224.30-

REGINA ●
444.00+

●

● GRENFELL
225.90-

222 Repeater Offset is 1.6 MH
440 Repeater Offset is 5 MH

SASKATCHEWAN FACTS

NUMBER OF HAMS: 1,166

CALL AREA: VE5

LARGEST CITY: REGINA

HIGHEST POINT:
   CYPRESS HILLS (4,567 FT.)

STATE CAPITAL: REGINA

AREA: 251,699 SQ. MILES

NUMBER OF 2M REPEATERS: 29

   222 REPEATERS: 2
   440 REPEATERS: 1
   900 MHz REPEATERS: 0
   1.2 GHz REPEATERS: 0

CTCSS TONES

A=67.0	Q=107.2	E=173.8
B=69.3	R=110.9	F=179.9
C=71.9	S=114.8	G=186.2
D=74.4	T=118.8	H=192.8
E=77.0	U=123.0	J=203.5
F=79.7	V=127.3	K=206.5
G=82.5	W=131.8	L=210.7
H=85.4	X=136.5	M=218.1
J=88.5	Y=141.3	N=225.7
K=91.5	Z=146.2	P=229.1
L=94.8	A=151.4	Q=233.6
M=97.4	B=156.7	R=241.8
N=100.0	C=162.2	S=250.3
P=103.5	D=167.9	T=254.1

Saskatchewan

2 METERS

Notes:
+ indicates + offset
- indicates - offset
@ indicates Autopatch

for information on use of Autopatch
be sure to check with repeater owner.

See UHF Map page
for CTCSS tone chart.

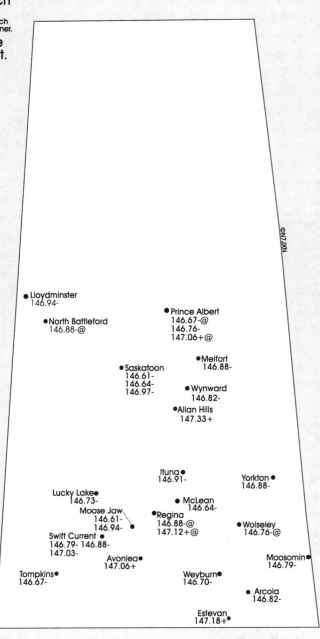

• Lloydminster
146.94-

• Prince Albert
146.67-@
146.76-
147.06+@

• North Battleford
146.88-@

• Melfort
146.88-

• Saskatoon
146.61-
146.64-
146.97-

• Wynward
146.82-

• Allan Hills
147.33+

Ituna •
146.91-

Yorkton •
146.88-

Lucky Lake•
146.73-

• McLean
146.64-

Moose Jaw
146.61-
146.94-

•Regina
146.88-@
147.12+@

•Wolseley
146.76-@

Swift Current •
146.79- 146.88-
147.03-

Avonlea•
147.06+

Moosomin•
146.79-

Tompkins•
146.67-

Weyburn•
146.70-

• Arcola
146.82-

Estevan•
147.18+•

Meter Repeater Offset is 600 KHz

Yukon
222 & UP

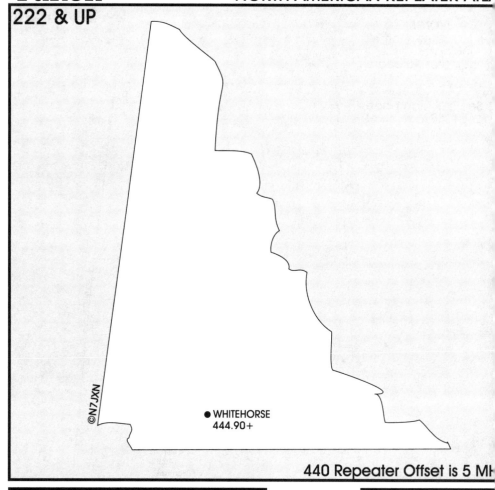

● WHITEHORSE
444.90+

©NXΓ∠N

440 Repeater Offset is 5 MI

YUKON FACTS

NUMBER OF HAMS: 85
CALL AREA: VY1
LARGEST CITY: WHITEHORSE
HIGHEST POINT:
   MT. LOGAN (19,524 FT.)
STATE CAPITAL: WHITEHORSE
AREA: 207,075 SQ. MILES
NUMBER OF 2M REPEATERS: 4
     222 REPEATERS: 0
     440 REPEATERS: 1
     900 MHz REPEATERS: 0
     1.2 GHz REPEATERS: 0

CTCSS TONES

A=67.0	Q=107.2	E=173.8
B=69.3	R=110.9	F=179.9
C=71.9	S=114.8	G=186.2
D=74.4	T=118.8	H=192.8
E=77.0	U=123.0	J=203.5
F=79.7	V=127.3	K=206.5
G=82.5	W=131.8	L=210.7
H=85.4	X=136.5	M=218.1
J=88.5	Y=141.3	N=225.7
K=91.5	Z=146.2	P=229.1
L=94.8	A=151.4	Q=233.6
M=97.4	B=156.7	R=241.8
N=100.0	C=162.2	S=250.3
P=103.5	D=167.9	T=254.1

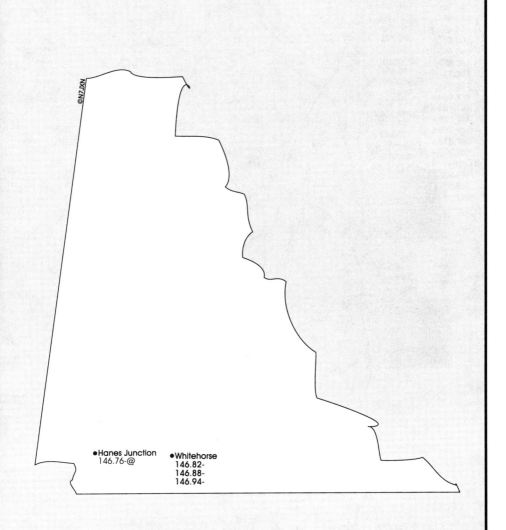

●Hanes Junction
146.76-@

●Whitehorse
146.82-
146.88-
146.94-

Notes:
+ indicates + offset
- indicates - offset
@ indicates Autopatch

for information on use of Autopatch
be sure to check with repeater owner.

See UHF Map page
for CTCSS tone chart.

Meter Repeater Offset is 600 KHz

Atlanta

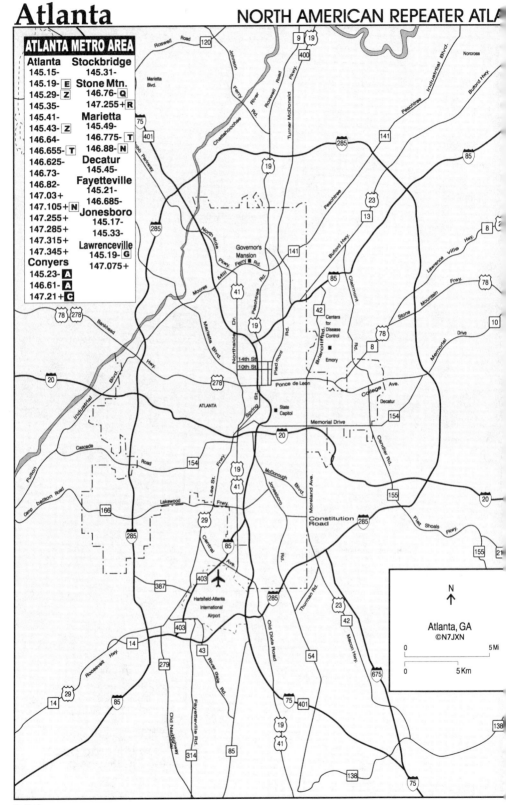

ATLANTA METRO AREA

Atlanta	Stockbridge
145.15-	145.31-
145.19- E	**Stone Mtn.**
145.29- Z	146.76- Q
145.35-	147.255+ R
145.41-	**Marietta**
145.43- Z	145.49-
146.64-	146.775- T
146.655- T	146.88- N
146.625-	**Decatur**
146.73-	145.45-
146.82-	**Fayetteville**
147.03+	145.21-
147.105+ N	146.685-
147.255+	**Jonesboro**
147.285+	145.17-
147.315+	145.33-
147.345+	**Lawrenceville**
Conyers	145.19- G
145.23- A	147.075+
146.61- A	
147.21+ C	

Atlanta, GA
©N7JXN

N
↑

0   5 Mi

0   5 Km

Boston

Boston Metropolitan Area		
5.11-	146.67-	147.03+
5.21-@	146.715-	147.075+ A
5.23-J	146.79-	147.195+ N
5.27-	146.82-	147.21+ N
5.31-	146.88-@	147.33+
5.33-	146.91-	147.36+
5.43-	146.985-	147.39+
6.64-	147.015+	

Lynn Woods Reservation

Walden Reservoir

107

Lexington

Middlesex Falls Reservation

Saugus

3

2

93 28

99

1A

Cambridge Reservoir

Concord Tpke.

Massachusetts Ave.

16

1

Waltham

3

95

128

20

Radcliffe College

Harvard University

Cambridge

Bunker Hill Mon.

Mass. Ave.

Main House

Logan International Airport

Brandeis University

Charles River

Memorial Drive

Mass. Inst. of Tech.

State House

Massachusetts Tpke.

90

wealth Ave.

Beacon St.

Boston Harbor

Commonwealth Ave.

Boston College

Common

Brookline

Huntington

Beacon St.

9

Columbia Rd.

Wash. St.

Mass. Ave.

Boston Commons

93

Boston-Worcester Tpke.

Hammond Pond Pkwy.

JFK Library and Museum

Boston Harbour Islands State Park

9

Wellesley

Franklin Park Zoo

Franklin Park

BOSTON

VFW Pkwy.

Washington St.

Stony Brook Reservation

93

Quincy

95

28

1

128

Dedham

3

N
↑

Boston, MA
©N7JXN

0   3 Mi

0   3 Km

Blue Hills Reservaton

1

128

93

3

Pilgrims Highway

95

Chicago Metro Area		
145.11-Q	146.67-Q	147.015+
145.15-Q	146.70-N	147.06
145.19-	146.715-Q	147.09+
145.21-	146.73-Q	147.135+
145.23-Q	146.76-Q	147.15+
145.25-	146.79-Q	147.195+
145.27-	146.805-Q	147.225+
145.31-	146.85-	147.285+
145.33-	146.88-Q	147.315+
145.37-	146.925-Q	147.33+
145.39-Q	146.955-S	147.345+
145.49-Q	146.97-Q	147.36+
146.64-	146.985-@Q	

N
↑

Chicago, IL
©N7JXN

0   5 Mi

0   5 Km

Dallas/Ft. Worth

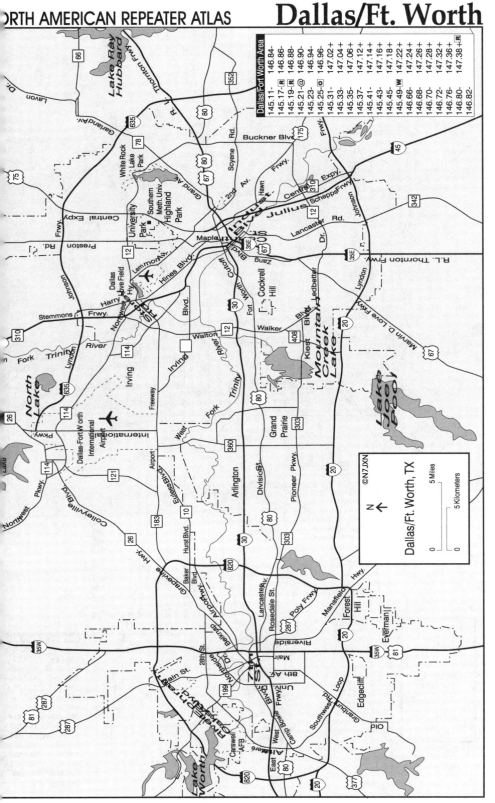

Dallas/Fort Worth Area	
145.11-	146.84-
145.17-.R	146.86-
145.19-.R	146.88-
145.21-@	146.90-
145.23-	146.94-
145.25-.O	146.96-
145.31-	147.02+
145.33-	147.04+
145.35-	147.06+
145.37-	147.12+
145.41-	147.14+
145.43-	147.16+
145.45-	147.18+
145.49-.W	147.22+
146.66-	147.24+
146.68-	147.26+
146.70-	147.28+
146.72-	147.32+
146.76-	147.36+
146.80-	147.38-+R
146.82-	

Dallas/Ft. Worth, TX

©N7JXN

N ←

0 — 5 Miles
0 — 5 Kilometers

Denver

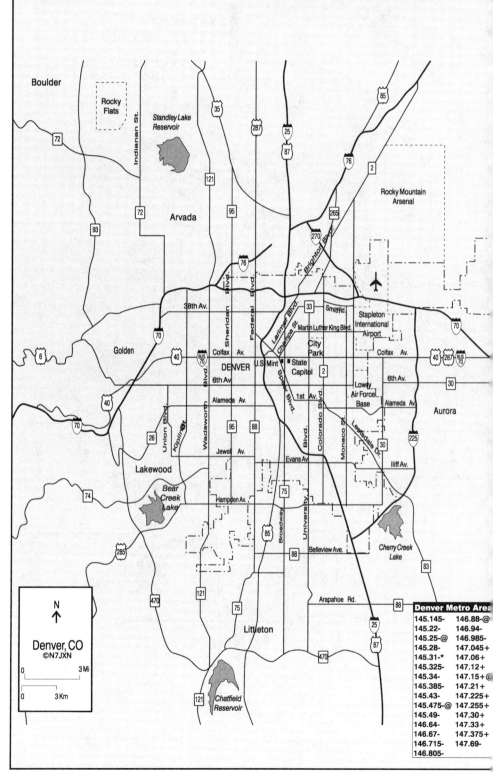

Boulder

Rocky Flats

Standley Lake Reservoir

85

35

287

25

72

87

76

2

121

Rocky Mountain Arsenal

72

Arvada

95

265

93

270

76

Brighton Blvd.

76

38th Av.

33

Smith Rd.

Stapleton International Airport

70

Golden

70

40

Colfax Av.

Martin Luther King Blvd.

Colfax Av.

40

287

70

6

BUS 70

DENVER

U.S Mint

City Park

Lowry Air Force Base

6th Av.

30

40

6th Av

State Capitol

2

Alameda Av.

1st Av.

Alameda Av.

Aurora

70

26

95

88

Jewel Av.

30

225

Lakewood

Evans Av

Iliff Av.

74

Bear Creek Lake

Hampden Av.

75

285

85

Belleview Ave.

Cherry Creek Lake

83

121

Arapahoe Rd.

88

470

75

N

↑

Denver, CO
©N7JXN

Littleton

25

87

0   3 Mi

470

0   3 Km

121

Chatfield Reservoir

Denver Metro Area	
145.145-	146.88-@
145.22-	146.94-
145.25-@	146.985-
145.28-	147.045+
145.31-*	147.06+
145.325-	147.12+
145.34-	147.15+@
145.385-	147.21+
145.43-	147.225+
145.475-@	147.255+
145.49-	147.30+
146.64-	147.33+
146.67-	147.375+
146.715-	147.69-
146.805-	

Detroit

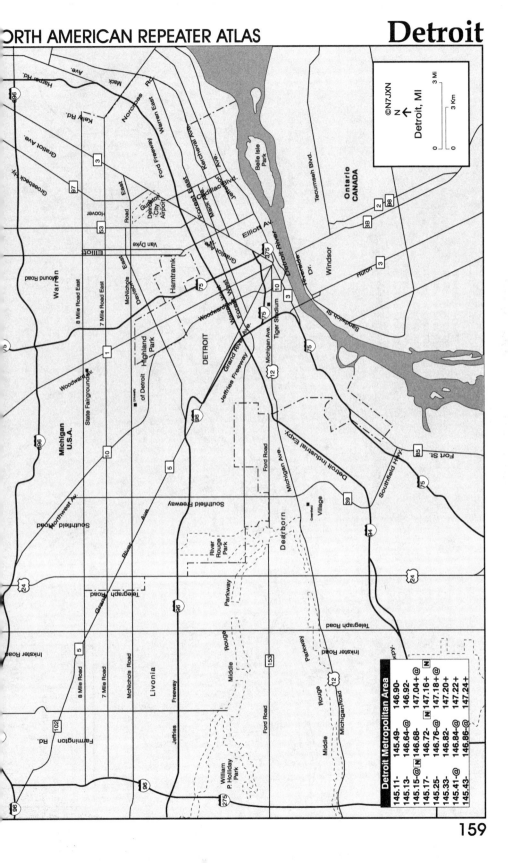

©N7JXN
Detroit, MI

3 Mi
3 Km

Belle Isle Park

Ontario
CANADA

Windsor

Michigan
U.S.A.

DETROIT

Highland Park

Hamtramk

Dearborn

Livonia

Detroit Metropolitan Area	
145.11-	146.90-
145.13-	146.92-
145.15-@ N	146.68-	147.04+@
145.17-	146.72-	N 147.16+
145.25-	146.76-@	147.18+@
145.33-	146.82-	147.20+
145.41-@	146.84-@	147.22+
145.43-	146.86-@	147.24+

145.49-   146.90-
145.15-@ N 146.68-   147.04+@ N

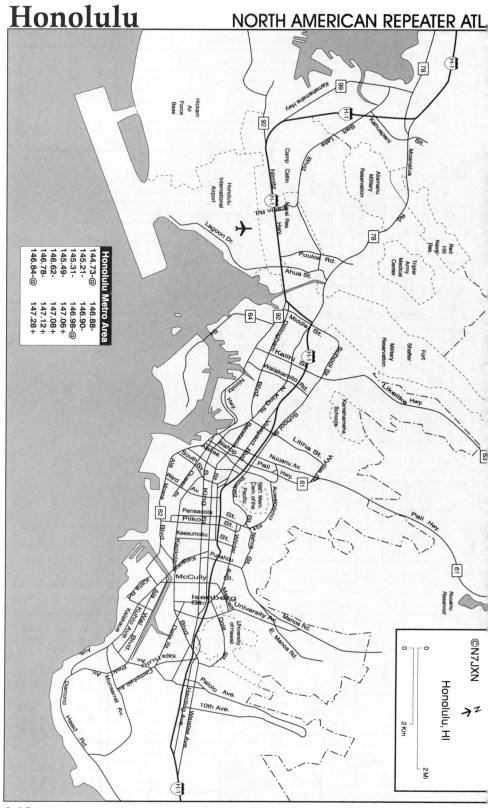

Honolulu Metro Area

144.73-@	146.88-
145.21-	146.90-
145.31-	146.98-@
145.49-	147.06+
146.62-	147.08+
146.78-	147.12+
146.84-@	147.28+

©N7JXN

Honolulu, HI

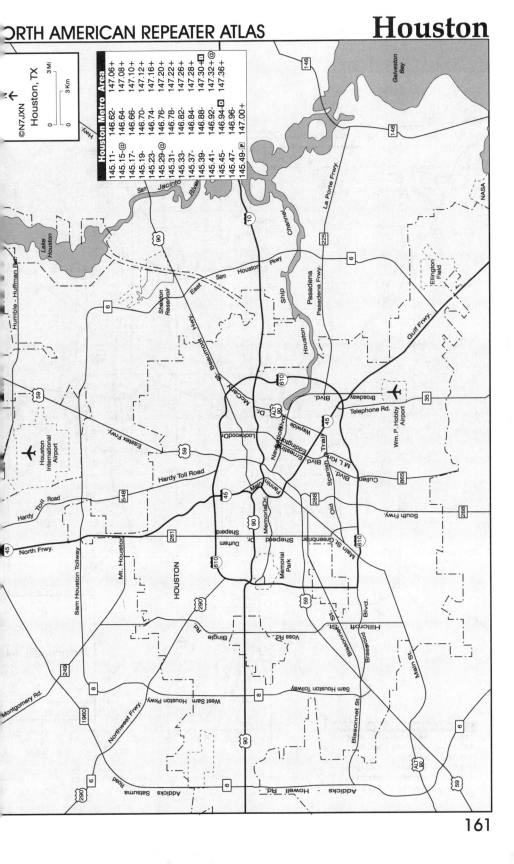

©N7JXN
Houston, TX

Houston Metro Area		
145.11-	146.62-	147.06+
145.15-@	146.64-	147.08+
145.17-	146.66-	147.10+
145.19-	146.70-	147.12+
145.23-	146.74-	147.16+
145.29-@	146.76-	147.20+
145.31-	146.78-	147.22+
145.33-	146.82-	147.26+
145.37-	146.84-	147.28+
145.39-	146.88-	147.30+ B
145.41-	146.92-	147.32+ @
145.45-	146.94- D	147.36+
145.47-	146.96-	
145.49- P	147.00+	

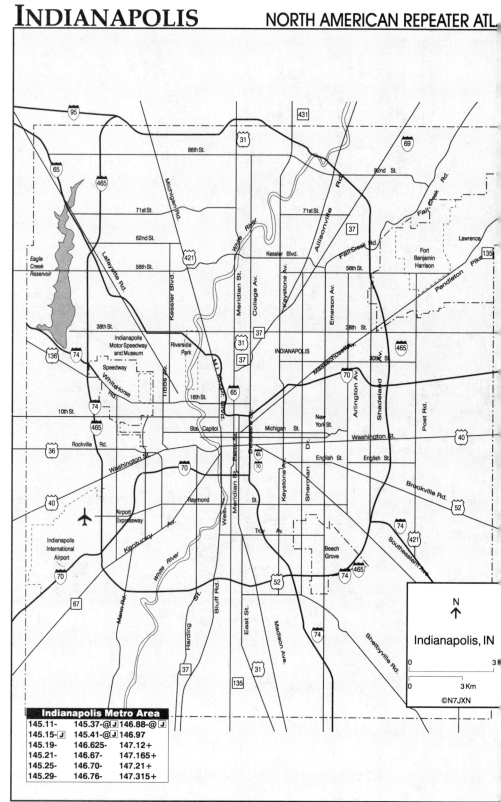

Indianapolis, IN

©N7JXN

Indianapolis Metro Area		
145.11-	145.37-@J	146.88-@J
145.15-J	145.41-@J	146.97
145.19-	146.625-	147.12+
145.21-	146.67-	147.165+
145.25-	146.70-	147.21+
145.29-	146.76-	147.315+

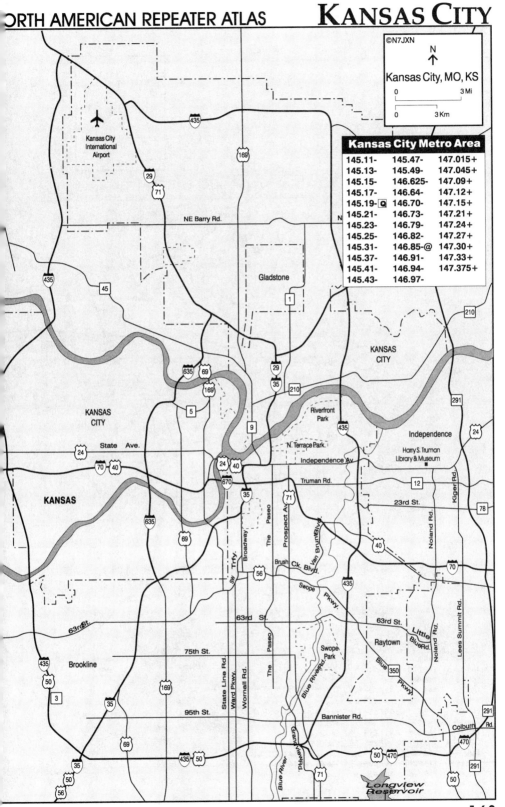

©N7JXN

N ↑

Kansas City, MO, KS

0   3 Mi

0   3 Km

Kansas City Metro Area

145.11-	145.47-	147.015+
145.13-	145.49-	147.045+
145.15-	146.625-	147.09+
145.17-	146.64-	147.12+
145.19-Q	146.70-	147.15+
145.21-	146.73-	147.21+
145.23-	146.79-	147.24+
145.25-	146.82-	147.27+
145.31-	146.85-@	147.30+
145.37-	146.91-	147.33+
145.41-	146.94-	147.375+
145.43-	146.97-	

Kansas City International Airport

Gladstone

NE Barry Rd.

KANSAS CITY

KANSAS CITY

Riverfront Park

State Ave.

N. Terrace Park

Independence Av

Independence

Harry S. Truman Library & Museum

Truman Rd.

KANSAS

23rd St.

Brush Ck. Blvd.

Van Brunt Blvd.

Swope Pkwy.

63rd St.

63rd St.

Raytown

Little Blue Rd.

75th St.

Swope Park

Brookline

95th St.

Bannister Rd.

Colburn Rd.

Longview Reservoir

State Line Rd.

Ward Pkwy.

Wornall Rd.

The Paseo

Blue River Rd.

Grandview Rd.

Blue River

Lees Summit Rd.

Noland Rd.

Kiger Rd.

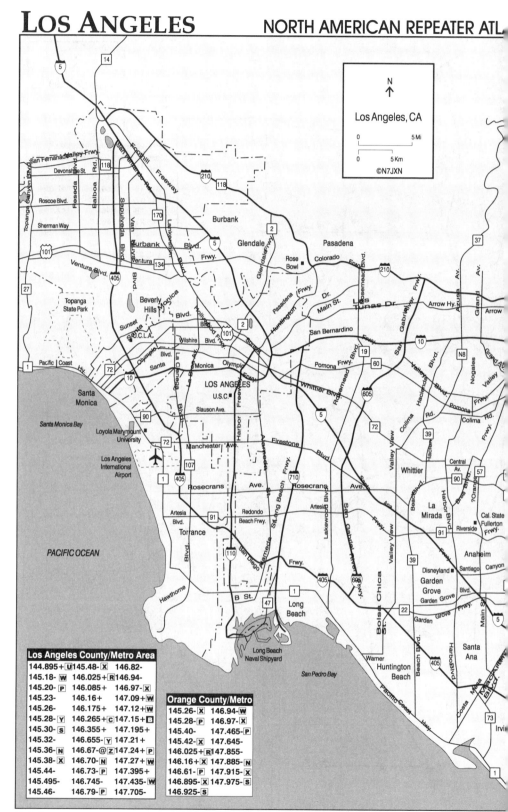

Los Angeles, CA

N

0   5 Mi

0   5 Km

©N7JXN

Los Angeles County/Metro Area		
144.895+ U	145.48- X	146.82-
145.18- W	146.025+ R	146.94-
145.20- P	146.085+	146.97- X
145.23-	146.16+	147.09+ W
145.26-	146.175+	147.12+ W
145.28- Y	146.265+ C	147.15+ B
145.30- S	146.355+	147.195+
145.32-	146.655- Y	147.21+
145.36- N	146.67+@ Z	147.24+ P
145.38- X	146.70- N	147.27+ W
145.44-	146.73- P	147.395+
145.495-	146.745-	147.435- W
145.46-	146.79- P	147.705-

Orange County/Metro	
145.26- X	146.94- W
145.28- P	146.97- X
145.40-	147.465- P
145.42- X	147.645-
146.025+ R	147.855-
146.16+ X	147.885- N
146.61- P	147.915- X
146.895- X	147.975- S
146.925- S	

Miami

Miami Metropolitan Area		
5.13-@	146.64-	147.12+
5.19-	146.73-	147.15+
5.21-	146.775-	147.195+
5.23-	146.805-	147.21+ R
5.31-	146.895-	147.27+
5.33-	146.925- L	147.30+
5.35-	146.94-@	147.33+
5.37-	147.00-	147.345+
5.39-	147.015+	147.36+ R
5.41-	147.045+@	147.375- R
5.47-	147.06+@	147.39+
6.625-@	147.09+	

N7JXN

N ↑

Miami/
Ft. Lauderdale, FL

0   3 Mi

0   3 Km

New Orleans

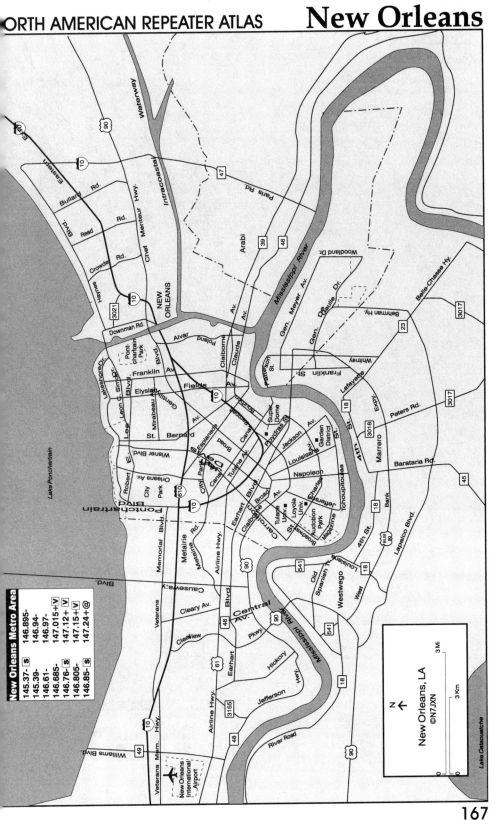

New Orleans Metro Area

145.37- [S]	146.895-
145.39-	146.94-
146.61-	146.97-
146.685- [S]	147.015+ [V]
146.76- [S]	147.12+ [V]
146.805-	147.15+ [V]
146.85- [S]	147.24+ @

New Orleans, LA
©N7JXN

N ←

3 Mi
3 Km

New Orleans International Airport

167

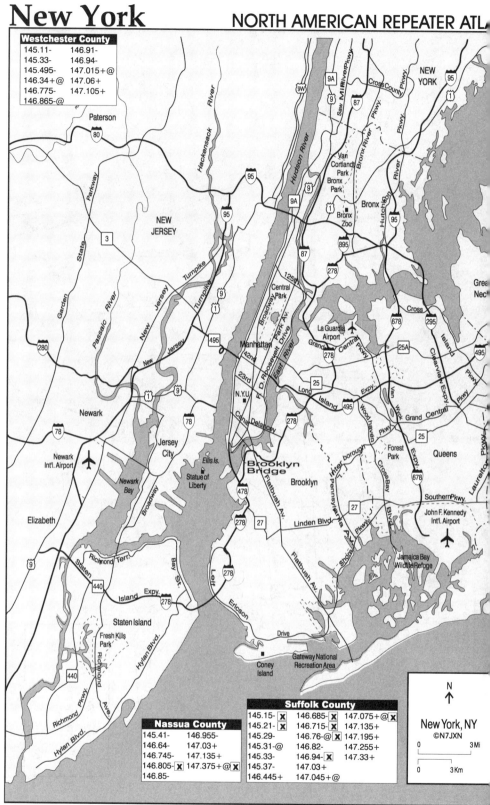

New York

Westchester County

145.11-	146.91-
145.33-	146.94-
145.495-	147.015+@
146.34+@	147.06+
146.775-	147.105+
146.865-@	

NEW
JERSEY

Paterson

Newark

Newark
Int'l. Airport

Newark
Bay

Elizabeth

Jersey
City

Ellis Is.

Statue of
Liberty

Brooklyn
Bridge

Brooklyn

Linden Blvd

Staten Island

Fresh Kills
Park

Coney
Island

Gateway National
Recreation Area

Van
Cortlandt
Park

Bronx
Park

Bronx
Zoo

Bronx

NEW
YORK

Central
Park

La Guardia
Airport

Manhattan

N.Y.U.

Long Island

Forest
Park

Queens

John F. Kennedy
Int'l. Airport

Jamaica Bay
Wildlife Refuge

Great
Neck

Cross

Nassua County

145.41-	146.955-
146.64-	147.03+
146.745-	147.135+
146.805- [X]	147.375+@ [X]
146.85-	

Suffolk County

145.15- [X]	146.685- [X]	147.075+@ [X]
145.21- [X]	146.715- [X]	147.135+
145.29-	146.76-@ [X]	147.195+
145.31-@	146.82-	147.255+
145.33-	146.94- [X]	147.33+
145.37-	147.03+	
146.445+	147.045+@	

N
↑

New York, NY
©N7JXN

0   3 Mi

0   3 Km

168

Phoenix

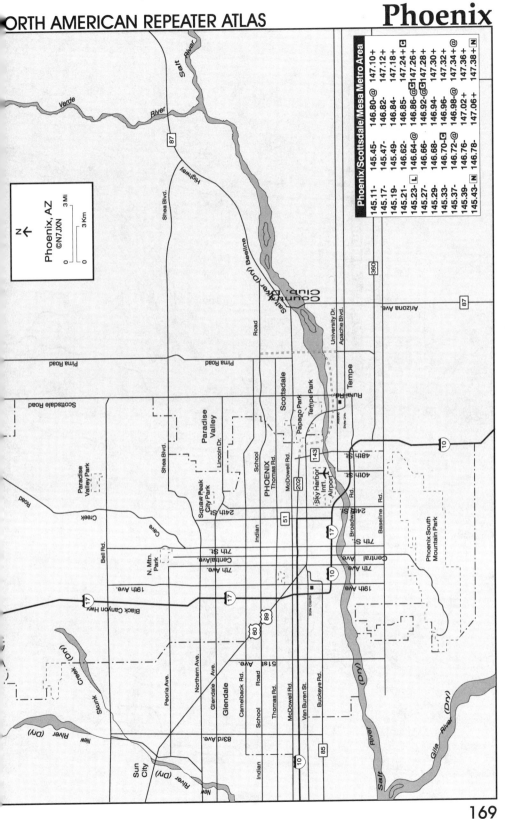

Phoenix/Scottsdale/Mesa Metro Area			
145.11-	145.45-	146.80-@	147.10+
145.17-	145.47-	146.82-	147.12+
145.19-	145.49-	146.84-	147.18+
145.21-	146.62-	146.85-	147.24+ [C]
145.23- [L]	146.64-@	146.86-@[C]	147.26+
145.27-	146.66-	146.92-@[C]	147.28+
145.29-	146.68-	146.94-	147.30+
145.33-	146.70-[C]	146.96-	147.32+
145.37-	146.72-@	146.98-@	147.34+@
145.39-	146.76-	147.02+	147.36+
145.43- [N]	146.78-	147.06+	147.38+ [N]

Phoenix, AZ
©N7JXN

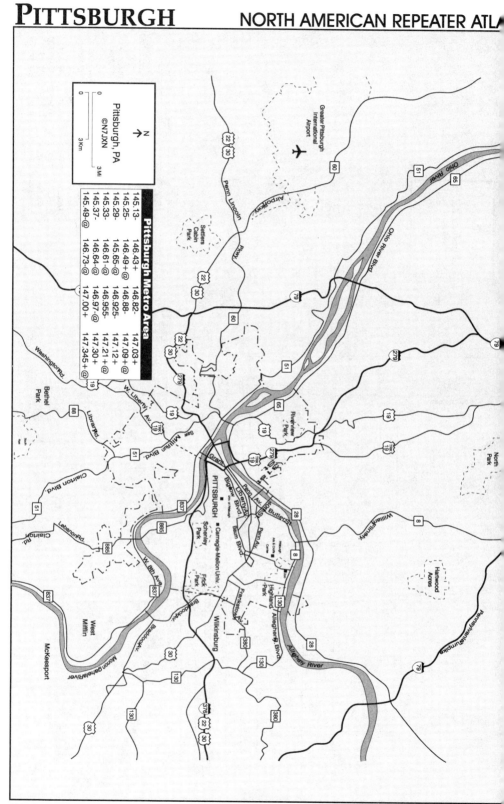

Pittsburgh Metro Area

145.13-	146.43+	147.03+
145.25-	146.49+	147.09+@
145.29-	146.65-@	146.88-	147.12+
145.33-	146.61-@	146.925-	147.21+@
145.37-	146.64-@	146.955-	147.30+@
145.49-@	146.73-@	146.97-@	147.345+@
		147.00+	

Pittsburgh, PA
@N7JXN

SAN DIEGO

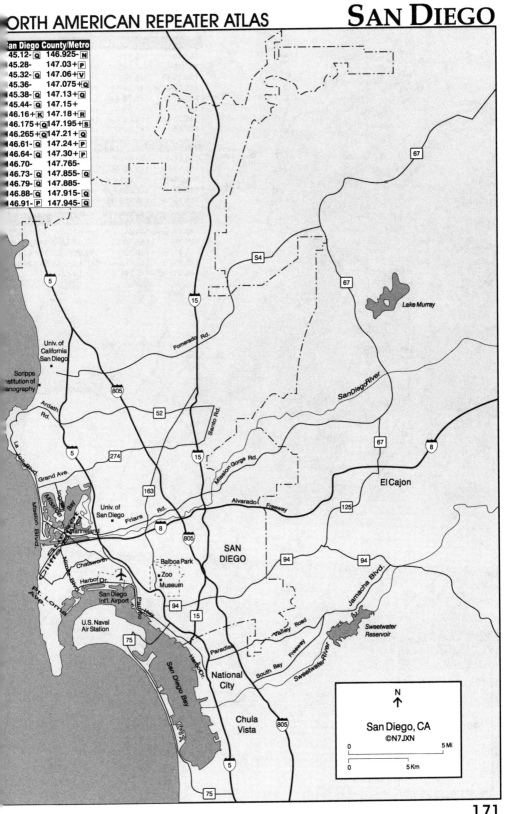

San Diego County/Metro	
45.12- Q	146.925- N
45.28-	147.03+ P
45.32- Q	147.06+ V
45.36-	147.075+ Q
45.38- Q	147.13+ Q
45.44- Q	147.15+
46.16+ K	147.18+ R
46.175+ Q	147.195+ S
46.265+ Q	147.21+ Q
46.61- Q	147.24+ P
46.64- Q	147.30+ P
46.70-	147.765-
46.73- Q	147.855- Q
46.79- Q	147.885-
46.88- Q	147.915- Q
46.91- P	147.945- Q

Lake Murray

Univ. of California San Diego

Scripps Institution of Oceanography

Ardath Rd.

Pomerado Rd.

San Diego River

La Jolla Blvd. Grand Ave.

Mission Blvd.

Ingraham St.

Marineland

Chatsworth

Harbor Dr.

Ft. Loma Ave.

Ninth St. Blvd.

Cliffs

U.S. Naval Air Station

San Diego Int'l. Airport

San Diego Bay

Santo Rd.

Mission Gorge Rd.

El Cajon

Univ. of San Diego

Friars Rd.

Balboa Park

Zoo Museum

Alvarado Freeway

SAN DIEGO

Jamacha Blvd.

Sweetwater Reservoir

Valley Road

South Bay Freeway

Sweetwater River

Paradise

National City

Harbor Dr.

Chula Vista

N
↑

San Diego, CA
©N7JXN

0   5 Mi

0   5 Km

171

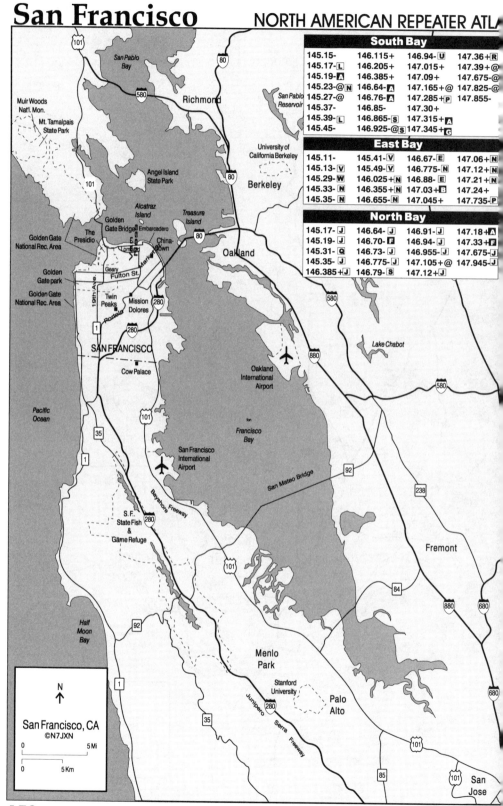

San Francisco

South Bay

145.15-	146.115+	146.94-U	147.36+R
145.17-L	146.205+	147.015+	147.39+@
145.19-A	146.385+	147.09+	147.675-@
145.23-@N	146.64-A	147.165+@	147.825-@
145.27-@	146.76-A	147.285+P	147.855-
145.37-	146.85-	147.30+	
145.39-L	146.865-S	147.315+A	
145.45-	146.925-@S	147.345+G	

East Bay

145.11-	145.41-V	146.67-E	147.06+N
145.13-V	145.49-V	146.775-N	147.12+N
145.29-W	146.025+N	146.88-E	147.21+N
145.33-N	146.355+N	147.03+B	147.24+
145.35-N	146.655-N	147.045+	147.735-P

North Bay

145.17-J	146.64-J	146.91-J	147.18+A
145.19-J	146.70-F	146.94-J	147.33+F
145.31-Q	146.73-J	146.955-J	147.675-J
145.35-J	146.775-J	147.105+@	147.945-J
146.385+J	146.79-S	147.12+J	

San Francisco, CA
©N7JXN

0   5 Mi

0   5 Km

Seattle

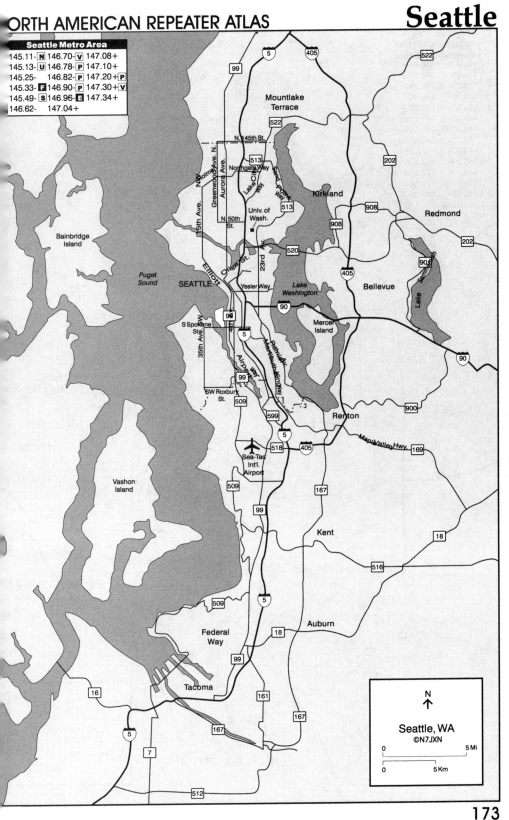

Mountlake
Terrace

N. 45th St.

Northgate Way

Univ. of
Wash.
N. 50th
St.

Kirkland

Redmond

Bainbridge
Island

Puget
Sound

SEATTLE

Yesler Way

Lake
Washington

Bellevue

Lake
Sammamish

Mercer
Island

S Spokane
St.

SW Roxbury
St.

Renton

Maple Valley Hwy.

Sea-Tac
Int'l.
Airport

Vashon
Island

Kent

Auburn

Federal
Way

Tacoma

N
↑

Seattle, WA
©N7JXN

0 _____ 5 Mi

0 _____ 5 Km

St. Louis

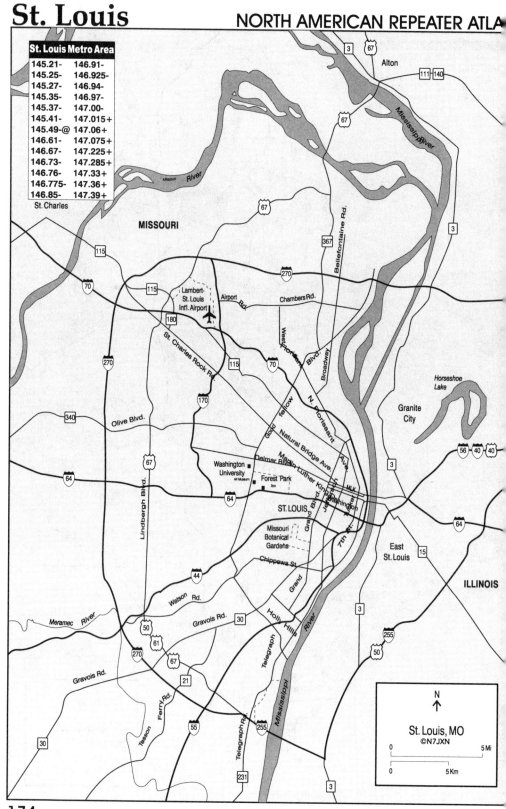

St. Louis Metro Area

145.21-	146.91-
145.25-	146.925-
145.27-	146.94-
145.35-	146.97-
145.37-	147.00-
145.41-	147.015+
145.49-@	147.06+
146.61-	147.075+
146.67-	147.225+
146.73-	147.285+
146.76-	147.33+
146.775-	147.36+
146.85-	147.39+

St. Charles

MISSOURI

Alton

Lambert-
St. Louis
Int'l. Airport

Airport Rd.

Chambers Rd.

West Florissant Blvd.

Broadway

Horseshoe
Lake

St. Charles Rock Rd.

N. Florissant

Olive Blvd.

Natural Bridge Ave.

Granite
City

Washington
University

Delmar Blvd.

Martin Luther King

Forest Park
Zoo

MLK

ST. LOUIS

Lindbergh Blvd.

Missouri
Botanical
Gardens

Washington

East
St. Louis

ILLINOIS

Chippewa St.

Watson Rd.

Gravois Rd.

Meramec River

Holly Hills

Grand

7th St.

Telegraph

Mississippi River

Gravois Rd.

Ferry Rd.

Tesson

Telegraph Rd.

N

↑

St. Louis, MO
©N7JXN

0   5 Mi

0   5 Km

174

WASHINGTON D.C.

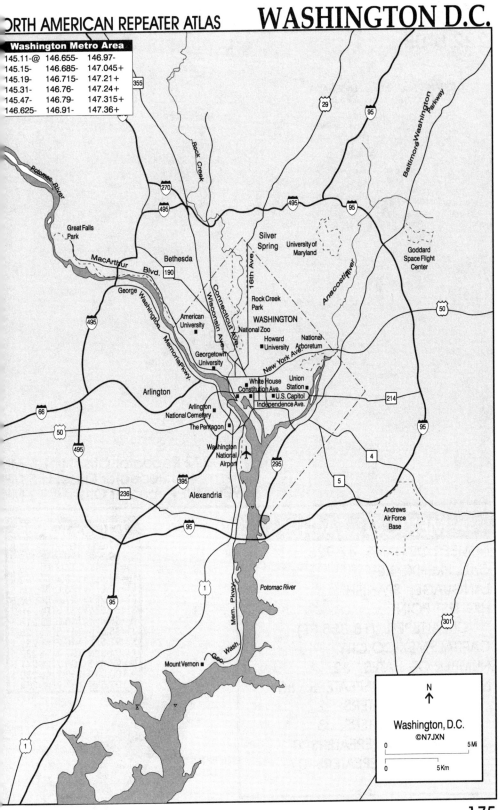

Mexico

222 & UP

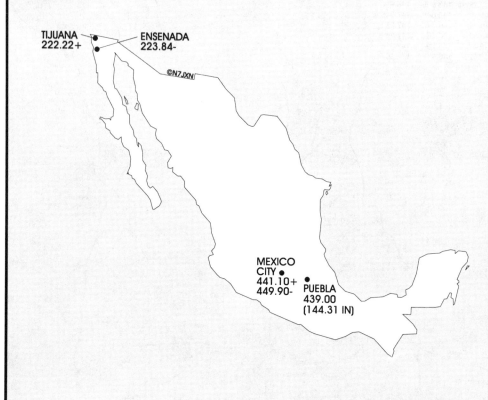

TIJUANA
222.22+

ENSENADA
223.84-

©N7JXN

MEXICO
CITY ●
441.10+
449.90- PUEBLA
439.00
(144.31 IN)

222 Repeater Offset is 1.6 MH
440 Repeater Offset is 5 MH
900 MHz Repeater Offset is 12 MH

MEXICO FACTS

NUMBER OF HAMS: 47,925
CALL PREFIX: XE
LANGUAGE: SPANISH
HIGHEST POINT:
    CITLALTEPETL (18,855 FT.)
CAPITAL: MEXICO CITY
NUMBER OF STATES: 32
NUMBER OF 2M REPEATERS: 80
    222 REPEATERS: 2
    440 REPEATERS: 3
    900 MHz REPEATERS: 0
    1.2 GHz REPEATERS: 0

CTCSS TONES

A=67.0	Q=107.2	E=173.8
B=69.3	R=110.9	F=179.9
C=71.9	S=114.8	G=186.2
D=74.4	T=118.8	H=192.8
E=77.0	U=123.0	J=203.5
F=79.7	V=127.3	K=206.5
G=82.5	W=131.8	L=210.7
H=85.4	X=136.5	M=218.1
J=88.5	Y=141.3	N=225.7
K=91.5	Z=146.2	P=229.1
L=94.8	A=151.4	Q=233.6
M=97.4	B=156.7	R=241.8
N=100.0	C=162.2	S=250.3
P=103.5	D=167.9	T=254.1

MEXICO

Mexico
2 METERS

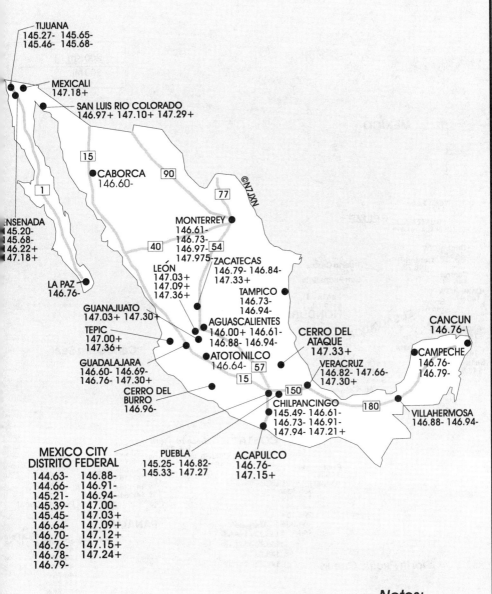

TIJUANA
145.27- 145.65-
145.46- 145.68-

MEXICALI
147.18+

SAN LUIS RIO COLORADO
146.97+ 147.10+ 147.29+

15

●**CABORCA** 90
146.60-

77

ENSENADA
145.20-
145.68-
146.22+
147.18+

1

MONTERREY ●
146.61-
146.73-
40 146.97- 54
147.975

LEÓN
147.03+
147.09+
147.36+

ZACATECAS
146.79- 146.84-
147.33+

LA PAZ ●
146.76-

GUANAJUATO
147.03+ 147.30+

TAMPICO
146.73-
146.94-

TEPIC
147.00+
147.36+

AGUASCALIENTES
146.00+ 146.61-
146.88- 146.94-

CANCUN
146.76-

**CERRO DEL
ATAQUE**
147.33+

ATOTONILCO
146.64- 57

GUADALAJARA
146.60- 146.69-
146.76- 147.30+

●**CAMPECHE**
146.76-
146.79-

VERACRUZ
146.82- 147.66-
147.30+

15

**CERRO DEL
BURRO**
146.96-

150

CHILPANCINGO
●145.49- 146.61-
146.73- 146.91-
147.94- 147.21+

180

VILLAHERMOSA
146.88- 146.94-

**MEXICO CITY
DISTRITO FEDERAL**

144.63-	146.88-
144.66-	146.91-
145.21-	146.94-
145.39-	147.00-
145.45-	147.03+
146.64-	147.09+
146.70-	147.12+
146.76-	147.15+
146.78-	147.24+
146.79-	

PUEBLA
145.25- 146.82-
145.33- 147.27

ACAPULCO
146.76-
147.15+

Notes:
+ indicates + offset
- indicates - offset
@ indicates Autopatch

for information on use of Autopatch
be sure to check with repeater owner.

**See UHF Map page
for CTCSS tone chart.**

2 Meter Repeater Offset is 600 KHz

Central America

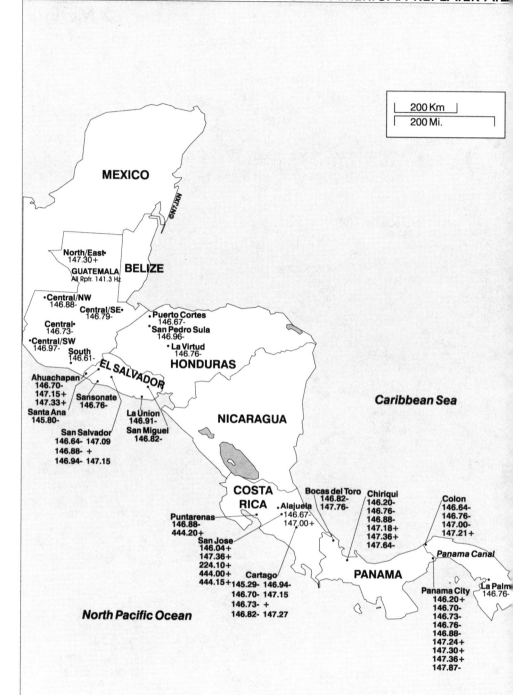

200 Km

200 Mi.

MEXICO

©N7JXN

North/East
147.30+

GUATEMALA **BELIZE**
All Rptr. 141.3 Hz

•**Central/NW**
146.88-
•**Central/SE**
146.79-

Central•
146.73-
•**Central/SW**
146.97-
South
•146.61-

• **Puerto Cortes**
146.67-
• **San Pedro Sula**
146.96-
• **La Virtud**
146.76-

HONDURAS

EL SALVADOR

Ahuachapan
146.70-
147.15+
147.33+   **Sansonate**
146.76-
Santa Ana
145.80-

La Union
146.91-
San Miguel
146.82-

NICARAGUA

Caribbean Sea

San Salvador
146.64- 147.09
146.88- +
146.94- 147.15

COSTA
RICA   •**Alajuela**
•146.67-
147.00+

Bocas del Toro
146.82-
147.76-

Chiriqui
146.20-
146.76-
146.88-
147.18+
147.36+
147.64-

Colon
146.64-
146.76-
147.00-
147.21+

Puntarenas
146.88-
444.20+

San Jose
146.04+
147.36+
224.10+
444.00+
444.15+

Cartago
145.29- 146.94-
146.70- 147.15
146.73- +
146.82- 147.27

Panama Canal

PANAMA

Panama City
146.20+
146.70-
146.73-
146.76-
146.88-
147.24+
147.30+
147.36+
147.87-

La Palm
146.76-

North Pacific Ocean

178

Caribbean Sea

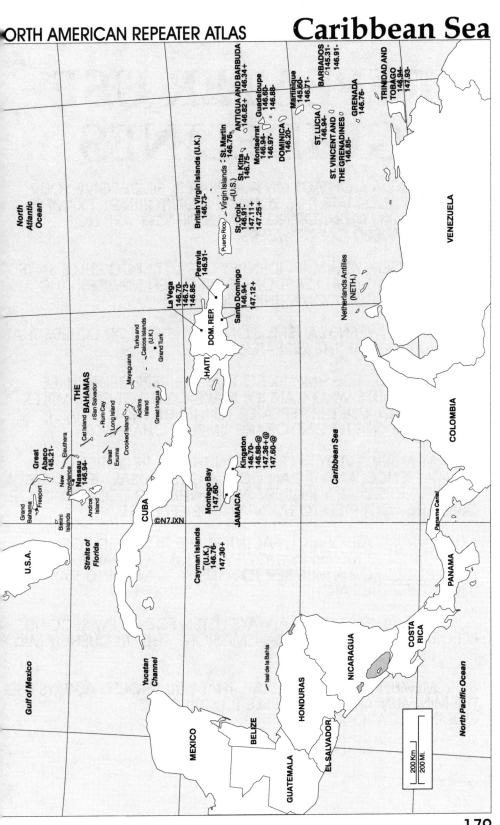

North Atlantic Ocean

North

ANTIGUA AND BARBUDA
146.82+ 146.34+

BARBADOS
145.31-
146.91-

TRINIDAD AND
TOBAGO
146.94-
147.93-

Guadeloupe
146.60-
146.88-

St. Martin
146.76-

Martinique
145.60-
146.71-

GRENADA
146.76-

Montserrat
146.94-
146.97-

ST. LUCIA
146.94-

Virgin Islands
St. Kitts
146.75-

DOMINICA
146.20-

ST. VINCENT AND
THE GRENADINES
146.85-

British Virgin Islands (U.K.)
146.73-

Puerto Rico
St. Croix (U.S.)
146.91+
147.11+
147.25+

VENEZUELA

Peravia
146.91-

La Vega
146.70-
146.73-
146.85-

Santo Domingo
146.94-
147.12+

DOM. REP.

Netherlands Antilles
(NETH.)

Turks and
Caicos Islands
(U.K.)
Grand Turk

HAITI

Mayaguana

THE
BAHAMAS

San Salvador

Cat Island
Rum Cay

Acklins
Island

Great Inagua

Long Island

COLOMBIA

Great
Exuma

Crooked Island

Eleuthera

Caribbean Sea

Kingston
146.70-
146.88-@
147.36-@
147.60-@

Great
Abaco
145.21-

New
Providence

Nassau
146.94-

Freeport

Grand
Bahama

Bimini
Islands

Montego Bay
147.60-

Andros
Island

©N7JXN

JAMAICA

CUBA

U.S.A.

Straits of
Florida

Cayman Islands
(U.K.)
146.76-
147.30+

PANAMA

Panama Canal

Yucatan
Channel

Gulf of Mexico

Isal de la Bahia

COSTA
RICA

NICARAGUA

North Pacific Ocean

HONDURAS

MEXICO

BELIZE

EL SALVADOR

GUATEMALA

200 Km.
200 Mi.

179

REPEATER USE GUIDELINES

1. TO MAKE A CONTACT ON A REPEATER, SIMPLY GIVE YOUR CALLSIGN AND STATE THAT YOU ARE MONITORING. EXAMPLE: "THIS IS N7JXN MONITORING." CALLS OF "CQ" ARE NOT GENERALLY USED ON REPEATERS.

2. REMEMBER, YOU MUST IDENTIFY LEGALLY. FCC RULES STATE THAT YOU MUST ID AT LEAST ONCE EVERY TEN MINUTES, AND AT THE END OF YOUR COMMUNICATIONS.

3. PAUSE BETWEEN TRANSMISSIONS TO LISTEN FOR OTHERS THAT MAY NEED TO USE THE REPEATER.

4. IF POSSIBLE, USE SIMPLEX SO THAT THE REPEATER WILL BE FREE FOR THOSE WHO CANNOT MAKE CONTACT ON SIMPLEX. IF NECESSARY, USE THE REPEATER TO INITIATE THE CONTACT, THEN MOVE OFF TO ONE OF THE SIMPLEX CHANNELS.

5. REMEMBER, EVERY REPEATER ON THE AIR REQUIRES MAINTAINENCE, AND IT CAN COST A GREAT DEAL. IF YOU USE A REPEATER REGULARLY INQUIRE AS TO WHETHER DONATIONS, OR DUES ARE ACCEPTED TO MAINTAIN THE REPEATER.

6. AS A RULE, AUTOPATCH FACILITIES ARE RESERVED FOR REPEATER CLUB MEMBERS, HOWEVER, IT IS GENERALLY ACCEPTABLE FOR A MEMBER TO ASSIST A TRAVELLING HAM IN USING THE AUTOPATCH.

7. AS ON OTHER BANDS, ALWAYS LISTEN FOR A FEW SECONDS BEFORE INITIATING YOUR TRANSMISSION. THE FREQUENCY MAY BE IN USE.

8. REMEMBER, FCC RULES STATE THAT YOU SHOULD ALWAYS USE THE MINIMUM OUTPUT POSSIBLE TO CONTINUE COMMUNICATIONS.

Frequency Coordinators

The ARRL is not a Frequency Coordinator, nor does the ARRL "certify" coordinators. Frequency Coordinators are volunteers normally appointed by a coordinating body. The ARRL *North American Repeater Atlas* reports only the fact of coordination or non-coordination as instructed by the coordinating body. Publication in the *North American Repeater Atlas* does not constitute nor imply endorsement or recognition of the authority of such coordinators, as coordinators derive their authority from the voluntary participation of the entire amateur community in the areas they serve.

In some cases the person or group listed only compiles the information for listings in the *North American Repeater Atlas*. In other cases the listed individual or group offers guidance but not coordination.

Frequency Coordinators keep extensive records of repeater input, output and control frequencies, including those not published in directories (at the owner's request). The coordinator will recommend frequencies for a proposed repeater in order to minimize interference with other repeaters and simplex operations. Therefore, anyone considering the installation of a repeater should check with the local frequency coordinator prior to such installation.

The following is a listing of groups or individuals for the United States and Canada who are active in Frequency Coordination and are acknowledged, by virtue of the recognition accorded them by the entire amateur community they serve, as the sole Frequency Coordinators in their respective jurisdictions.

ALABAMA - ARC
Dave Baughn, KX4I
3926 Woodland Hills Dr.
Tuscaloosa, AL 35405

ALASKA
(South-Central)
Mel Bowns, KL7GG
23708 The Clearing
Eagle River, AK 99577

(North/West/Interior)
Jerry Curry, KL7EDK
940 Vide Way
Fairbanks, AK 99712

(Panhandle)
Richard Caplan, KL7AK
PO Box 240646
Douglas, AK 99824

ARIZONA - ARCA
Dave Cowley, KD7DR
852 W Westchester Av.
Tempe, AZ 85283

Dick Woods, W7YDW
921 Miller Dr.
Tucson, AZ 85710

Dave Gorevin, N7DJZ
2310 East June St.
Mesa, AZ 85213-2912

Bill Jorden, K7KI
6861 Kenanna Pl.
Tucson, AZ 85704

Joe Oliver, WB7BNI
PO Box 80524
Phoenix, AZ 85060

Troy Hall, WA7ELN
PO Box 899
Oracle, AZ 85623

Michael Bucciarelli, N7CK
PO Box 607
San Manuel, AZ 85631

Ralph Turk, W7HSG
5232 W Calle Paint
Tucson, AZ 85741

ARKANSAS - MACC/ARC
Dan Puckett, K5FXB
PO Box 2458 U-A
Fayetteville, AR 72701

LaRoy McCann, N5OHO
208 Ada Dr.
Trumann, AR 72472

CALIFORNIA - 220SMA
James Fortney, K6IYK
PO Box 3419
Camarillo, CA 93011-3419

CALIFORNIA - MACC/NARCC
Frequency Cordinator
PO Box 60531
Sunnyvale, CA 94088
Web: http://www.narcc.org

Don Smith, W6NKF - President
1608 Rolling Hill Way
Martinez, CA 94553

Steve Stoehr, N6JXL
10705 E Butler
Sanger, CA 93657

Phil Hartz, WDØFFX
365 Grandview Dr.
Bishop, CA 93514

CALIFORNIA - SCRRBA
Secretary SCRRBA Coordinations
PO Box 5967
Pasadena, CA 91117
Web: http://www.scrrba.org

Joe Saddler, WA6PAZ
13909 Fidler
Bellflower, CA 90706

CALIFORNIA – TASMA
Larry Bryant, N6YLA
77 Hidden Valley
Monrovia, CA 91016

COLORADO - MACC/CCARC
Whitman Brown, WBØCJX
14418 W Ellsworth Pl.
Golden, CO 80401-5324

CONNECTICUT
(*No information Available at press time*)

DELAWARE
See Maryland - T-MARC

FLORIDA - FRC
Dana Rodakis, K4LK
6280 Fairfield Av. S
St Petersburg, FL 33707

Ray Kassis, N4LEM
1150 King St.
Cocoa, FL 32922

GEORGIA – SERA
Stu Sims, N4MXC - Director
112 Carol Dr.
Cochran, GA 31014
912-934-9236
Email: ssims@mail.bleckley.
public.lib.ga.us
Web: http://www.sera.org/

Bert Coker, N4BZJ - Vice Director
2102 Milican Ln.
Dalton, GA 30721
706-259-5625
Email: bcoker@ocsonline.com

HAWAII - HSRAC
Pat Corrigan, KH6DD
PO Box 67
Honolulu, HI 96810

IDAHO - SEICC
Rod Wilde, AB7OS
1061 E 1100 N
Shelly, ID 83274

Harold Short, WA7UHW
1100 E 1st Av.
Ellensburg, WA 98126-3517

Bud Dunn, KI7SI
779 S River Road.
St Anthony, ID 83445

IDAHO - SOUTHWEST
Larry Smith, W7ZRQ
8106 Bobran St.
Boise, ID 83709

ILLINOIS - MACC/IRA
Carl Bergstedt, K9VXW
PO Box 514
Naperville, IL 60566-0514
Web: http://www.enteract.com~ira

INDIANA - MACC/IRC
Indiana Coordination
1507 "H" Av.
New Castle, IN 47362

D.B.M - Bob Burns, N9KRS
PO Box 295
Brownsburg, IN 46112

Chuck Crist, WB9IHS (52)
6455 Madison Av.
Indianapolis, IN 46227

Andy Finick, N9FXT (29 902 +)
3006 98th St. West
Highland, IN 46322

Tim Crafton, K9TC
9501 W Wolf Mtn Rd.
Gosport, IN 47433

IOWA - MACC/IRC
Denny Crabb, WBØGGI
115 N 14th St.
Denison, IA 51442-1452
Web: http://www.rf.org/iarc

Tom Crabb, NØJLU
604 Locust St #612
Des Moines, IA 50309-3719

John Mauerer, NAØS
PO Box 310
Ames, IA 50010-0310

KANSAS - MACC/KARC
Slim Cummings, WAØEDA
PO Box 298
Pittsburg, KS 66762-0298
Web: http://www.qsl.net/karc

Ron Farthing, KØFFR
149 Emporia Ct.
Valley Center, KS 67147-3047

KENTUCKY - SERA
Jerry Shouse, N4EQT - Director
1050 Hickory Hill Dr.
Lawrenceburg, KY 40342
502-839-4041
email: jshouse@usa.net
Web: http://www.sera.org

LOUISIANA - LCARC
Roger Farbe, N5NXL
12665 Rounsaville Rd.
Baton Rouge, LA 70818

Tom Palko, WB5ASD
PO Box 8762
Alexandria, LA 71306-1762

David Breeding, KF5JC
17330 Sanders Rd.
Franklinton, LA 70438

MAINE
See NESMC

MARYLAND - T-MARC
Frequency Coordinations
PO Box 1022
Savage, MD 20763-1022

Owen Wormser, K6LEW - President
406 N Pitt St.
Alexandria, VA 22314-2316
Email: owormser@c3iusa.com
Web: http://www.t-marc.org

Bill Conaway, W8HNT
6074 Clerkenwell Ct.
Burke, VA 22015-3225

MASSACHUSETTS
See NESMC

MICHIGAN - Lower - MARC
Larry Tissue, N8QGE - President
851 Wheaton Rd.
Charlotte, MI 48813

Vince Vielhaber, KA8CSH
790 Glaspie Rd
Oxford, MI 48371

Pete Knappmann, N8NYQ
(All Bands)
PO Box 625
Troy, MI 48099-0625

**MICHIGAN - U/P - MACC/
UPARRA**
(For coordination information)
Noel Beardsley, K8NB
W 7021 CR 356
Stephenson, MI 49887

(For general inquiries)
Frequency Coordinations, UPARRA
PO Box 9
McMillan, MI 49853

MINNESOTA - MACC/MRC
Paul Emeott, KØLAV
3960 Schuneman Rd.
White Bear Lake, MN 55110

MISSISSIPPI - SERA
Steve Grantham, N5DWU - Direc
South
PO Box 127
Ellisville, MS 39437
601-763-3559
Email: sgranth@merlin.ebicom.
Web: http://www.sera.org

Joseph Wood, AJØX - Vice Direct
- Northwest
42 Clairmont Cir.
Laurel, MS 39440
601-426-3486
Email: jwood@c-gate.net

MISSOURI - MACC/MRC
Wayland 'Mac' McKenzie, K4CH
8000 S Barry Rd.
Columbia, MO 65201

Assistant Coordinator – St. Louis
Area
Jeff Young, KB3HF
6 Long Branch Ct.
St Peters, MO 63376
(314) 928-7348

Assistant Coordinator – Kansas Ci
Area
Dan Babilla, KAØOXH
8726 W 78th Cir.
Overland Park, KS 66204
(913) 381-1115

MONTANA - MACC
Ken Kopp, KØPP
Box 848
Anaconda, MT 59711-0848
Email: k0pp@mcimail.com
Phone: 406-797-3340

NEBRASKA - MACC
John Gebuhr, WBØCMC
2340 N 64th St.
Omaha, NE 68104

Billy McCollum, KEØXQ
1314 Deer Park Blvd.
Omaha, NE 68108

NESMC
Web: http://www.nesmc.org

NESMC - (MA - NH - ME - RI)
902-1240
Lewis Collins, W1GXT
10 Marshall St.
Wayland, MA 01778

NESMC - (MA - NH - ME - RI)
52
George Cleveland, WA1QGU
8 Bruno Dr.
Milford, MA 01757-2104

NESMC - (MA - NH - ME - RI)
29
Roger Perkins, W1OJ
Old Bay Rd.
Bolton, MA 01740

NESMC - (MA - NH - ME - RI)
220
Tom Greenwood, N1JQB
126 Haynes Rd.
Sudbury, MA 01776

NESMC - (MA - NH - ME - RI)
440
John Brunelle, KA1FYB
1 Paget Dr.
Hudson, NH 03051

NESMC - (MA - NH - ME - RI)
144
Bob Skinner, WA1YEG
68 Governor Dinsmore Rd.
Windham, NH 03087

NEVADA - MACC/CARCON
Frequency Coordinations
PO Box 7523
Reno, NV 89510-7523

Bob Davis, K7IY
1765 Dickerson Rd.
Reno, NV 89503

NEVADA - Southern - SNRC
Frequency Coordinations
PO Box 93803
Las Vegas, NV 89193-3803

Geoff Gomes, KB7BY
2750 Jim Hampton
Las Vegas, NV 89117

Lyle Bell, AA7AU
5475 Fire Island Dr.
Las Vegas, NV 89120

Wayne Schenk, K7WS
311 E Country Club
Henderson, NV 89015

Bob Woolum, WB6TNP
6916 N Creekside Ln.
Las Vegas, NV 89128

Chuck Young, KB7CG
5470 Palm Av.
Las Vegas, NV 89128

NEW HAMPSHIRE
See NESMC

NEW JERSEY
Southern – See Pennsylvania - ARCC
Northern – (*No information
available at press time*)

NEW MEXICO - NMFCC
Eddie Johnson, N5OBZ
1909 Somervill ST NE
Albuquerque, NM 871112-2859

NEW YORK - SLVRC
Peter De Wolfe, VE3YYY
RR 1
Braeside, ON K0A 1G0
Canada
Web: **http://www.igs.net/slvrc**

**NEW YORK - TSARC - (CT -
NNJ - NLI)**
(*No information available at press
time*)

NEW YORK - UNYREPCO
Frequency Coordinations
Ron Reagan, N2RWK
38 Clarke St.
Binghampton, NY 13905-3613
Email: **radiodad@aol.com**
Web: **http://spectra.net/~soltisrj/
unyrepco.htm**

Coordination Committee
John Storsberg, N2DCI
5440 Caughdenoy Rd.
Clay, NY 13041
315-699-2582

Corporate Office
Bob Soltis, WA2VCS
225 Dorothy St.
Endicott, NY 13760-1305
Email: **soltisrj@spectra.net**

NEW YORK - WNYSORC
Paul Toth, VE3GRW
4629 Queensway Gardens
Niagara Falls, ON L2E 6R2
Canada

NORTH CAROLINA - SERA
Danny Hampton, K4ITL - Director
5453 Rock Service Stn. Rd.
Raleigh, NC 27619
919-662-9797
Email: **dhampton@ipass.net**
Web: **http://www.sera.org**

Linville Couch, K4OLC - Vice
Director
1480 17th Street Dr. NE
Hickory, NC 28601
704-328-8267
Email: **k4olc@abts.net**

NORTH DAKOTA - MACC
Stanley Kittelson, WDØDAJ
261 10th St East
Dickinson, ND 58601

OHIO - MACC/OARC
Ken Bird, WB8SMK
244 N Parkway Rd.
Delaware, OH 43015

OKLAHOMA - MACC/ORSI
ORSI
Rt. 1, Box 78ZA
Chandler, OK 74834
Email: **hdeitz@ms.rose.cc.ok.us**

Hal Dietz, WB9VMY
PO Box 300123
Midwest City, OK 73034
Email: **hdeitz@ms.rose.cc.ok.us**

OREGON - MACC/ORRC
Frequency Coordinations
PO Box 4402
Portland, OR 97208-4402

Henry Burroughs, N7IFJ
6325 Joseph St. SE
Salem, OR 97301

George Pell, KB7PSM
27754 SW Strawberry Hill Dr.
Hillsboro, OR 97123

PENNSYLVANIA - ARCC
Coordinations, membership,
general info
PO Box 3006
Maple Glen, PA 19002-8006
Web: **http://www.arcc-inc.org**
Email: **info@arcc-inc.org**

Steve White, WA3IAO - President
2217 Palomino Dr.
Warrington, PA 18976
Email: **wa3iao@arcc-inc.org**

Jeff DePolo, WN3A – Data Base
Manager
216-C Clubhouse Rd.
King of Prussia, PA 19406
Email: **wn3a@arcc-inc.org**

PENNSYLVANIA - WPRC
*NOTE: All Coordination Requests
to this address only*:
Frequency Coordinations
10592 Perry Hwy 173
Wexford, PA 15090
Email: **wprc@bfdin.com**
Web: **http://wb3boi-
gw.physics.duq.edu/wprc/wprc.html**

Informal Inquiries to:
Joe McElhaney, KR3P
319 Mt Vernon Dr.
Apollo, PA 15613-8701
Email: **mch@nb.net**

PUERTO RICO - PR/VI VFC
Frequency Coordinations
PO Box 191917
San Juan, PR 00919-1917
Compuserve 76462,562

Guillermo Bonet, KP4BKY
PO Box 475
Mayaguez, PR 00681

RHODE ISLAND
See NESMC

SOUTH CAROLINA - SERA
Bill Jones, N4MNH - Director West
1609 Bur-Clare Rd.
Charlston, SC 29412-8148
803-795-0843
Email: **wejones@juno.com**
Web: **http://www.sera.org**

Vince Ott, WD4NUN - Vice Director
147 N Lakeshore Dr.
Goose Creek, SC 29445
803-553-6868
Email: **vcott@cchat.com**

SOUTH DAKOTA - MACC
Richard Neish, WØSIR
PO Box 100 - Brandt Lake A-58
Chester, SD 57016

TENNESSEE - SERA
Johnny Wofford, WA4ETE - Director
6781 Oakmoor Circle S
Bartlett, TN 38135
901-384-4349
Email: **woffer29@idt.net**
Web: **http://www.sera.org**

West Tennessee Coordinator
Andy Masters, NU5O
240 W White Rd.
Collierville, TN 38017
901-853-8671
Email: **rmusa@ibm.net**

Tim Berry, WB4GBI - Vice Director
214 Echodale Ln.
Knoxville, TN 37920-5042
423-579-3494
Email: **tim@novell.ur.utk.edu**

TEXAS - TVFS
Mark Cheavens, KC5EVE
Chairman FC Committee
16506 Dawncrest Way
Sugarland, TX 77478
713-277-4275
mcheaven@ix.netcom.com

Jim Reese, WD5IYT
Link Frequencies (440-902-1.2)
6002 Schuler
Houston, TX 77007
713-862-7101
jreese@a.crl.com

Paul Baumgardner, KB5BFJ
ZONE 1 - Northeast Texas - (29-52-220-902-1.2)
PO Box 181912
Arlington, TX 76096-1912
817-465-4942
pbaumg1@aol.com

Larry Pollock, N5XBM
ZONE 1 - Northeast Texas (144-62-440)
PO Box 181912
Arlington, TX 76096-1912
817-472-8649
n5xbm@cq.net

Howard Smith, KB5VAW
ZONE 2 - Southeast Texas (29-52-144-220)
PO Box 2734
Bryan, TX 77805
409-778-7153
1hrsmith@myriad.net

Paul Gilbert, KE5ZW
Database Manager - ZONE 2 (440-902-1.2)
1911 Pleasant St.
Huntsville, TX 77340
409-291-9532
vis_pfg@unx1.shsu.edu

Richard Norton, WB5FRO
ZONE 3 - South Texas (All Bands)
815 South Georgia
Weslaco, TX 78596
210-968-2447

Louis Bancook, WB5UUT
ZONE 4 - Central Texas (All Bands)
2200 Logan Dr.
Round Rock, TX 78664
512-255-3545
lgb@inetport.com

Fred Coonce, KC5BNS
ZONE 5 - West Texas (All Bands)
4805-B Dentcrest
Midland, TX 79707
915-699-1368
kc5bns@juno.com

UTAH - UVHFS
John Lloyd, K7JL
2078 Kramer Dr.
Sandy, UT 84092

VERMONT - VIRCC
Mitch Stern, W1SJ
PO Box 99
Essex, VT 05451

VIRGINIA - SERA
Don Williams, WA4K - Director West
412 Ridgeway Dr.
Bluefield, VA 24605-1630
540-326-3338
Email: **wa4k@amsat.org**
Web: **http://www.sera.org**

Douglas Sharp, K2AD - Vice Director
PO Box 10542
Lynchburg, VA 24506-0542
804-528-0870
Email: **doug.sharp@ericsson.com**

WASHINGTON - EASTERN - MACC/IACC
Doug Rider, KC7JC
E 11516 Mission Av.
Spokane, WA 99206

WASHINGTON - WESTERN - MACC/WWARA
Frequency Coordinations
PO Box 65492
Port Ludlow, WA 98365-0492
Web: **http://members.aol.com/wwara**

Mark McKibbin, WR7V
521 Verner Av.
Port Ludlow, WA 98365

WEST VIRGINIA - SERA
Dick Fowler, N8FMD - Director North
Route 3, Box 52
Clarksburg, WV 26301
304-623-9479
Email: **n8fmd@neumedia.net**
Web: **http://www.sera.org**

H. Alex Hedrick, Jr., N8FWL - Vice Director South
PO Box 417
Beckley, WV 25802
304-252-9765
Email: **n8fwl@inetone.net**

WISCONSIN - MACC/WAR
Dan Bolander, WB9TYT
6925 W Sheridan Av.
Milwaukee, WI 53218

Nels Harvey, WA9JOB
2104 W County Line Rd.
Mequon, WI 53092

WYOMING - MACC/WCARC
Don Breazile, N7MYR
4406 Greenhill Ct.
Cheyenne, WY 82001
Web: **http://www.breazile.com/ham**

CANADA

ALBERTA
Don Moman, VE6JY
Box 127
Lamont, AB T0B 2R0
Canada

BRITISH COLUMBIA
Ed Frazer, VE7EF
6695 Madrona Cres.
West Vancouver, BC V7W 2J9
Canada

CANADIAN AREAS
(Where no known coordinator exists)
Ken Oelke, VE6AFO
7136 Temple Dr. NE
Calgary, AB T1Y 4E7
Canada

MANITOBA
Thomas Blair, VE4TOM
121 Miramar Rd.
Winnipeg, MB R3R 1E4
Canada

MARITIMES
Ron MacKay, VE1AIC
PO Box 188
Cornwall, PEI C0A 1H0
Canada

ONTARIO - SLVRC
Peter De Wolfe, VE3YYY
RR 1
Braeside, ON K0A 1G0
Canada

ONTARIO - WNYSORC
Paul Toth, VE3GRW
4629 Queensway Gardens
Niagara Falls, ON L2E 6R2
Canada

QUEBEC - RAQI
Bruno Bouliane, VE2VK
440 DeCluny St.
Lavel, PQ H7N 5K6
Canada

SASKATCHEWAN
Ken Nyeste, VE5NR
123 Holland Rd.
Saskatoon, SK S7H 4Z5
Canada

Packet / Digital Listings are maintained in the North American Digital Systems Directory (NADSD) hosted by TAPR. See **http://www.tapr.org**.